THE
SYMBOLS
OF
SOVEREIGNTY

By the same author

When the Queen was Crowned

THE SYMBOLS OF SOVEREIGNTY

BRIAN BARKER OBE

Foreword by
J. P. Brooke-Little, MVO
Richmond Herald of Arms

ROWMAN AND LITTLEFIELD
Totowa, New Jersey

First published in the United States 1979
by Rowman and Littlefield, Totowa, N.J.

© Brian Barker

ISBN 0 8476 6192 X

Printed and bound in Great Britain

CONTENTS

FOREWORD

As a limb, albeit a metatarsal one, of the Queen's Household, and one of Her Majesty's Heralds of Arms, responsible, under the Earl Marshal of England, for heraldry and State ceremonies, I live in a world of symbolism; a professional protagonist of all that is here elucidated so accurately and lovingly by Brian Barker.

This book is no re-hash of what has been written before. It is essentially a new book which, for the first time, essays (and I believe succeeds brilliantly) to give an historical, physical and even emotional account of the symbols of authority and sovereignty in Great Britain. The author, appreciating that until 1707 there were two kingdoms in this island, each with its own traditions, ceremonies, symbols and regalia, has treated of both England and Scotland with equal diligence.

This alone would make the book unique, but what really gives it not merely a good value, but real quality, is the author's obvious sympathy with, and scholarly mastery of, his subject. I use the word scholarly cautiously, because it has connotations of aridity, stuffiness, pedantry and footnotemanship. Please rest assured that I describe Brian Barker's work as scholarly only because it is the result of careful and thorough research. It is a wonderfully readable book, which captures the history, beauty and importance of the symbols of sovereignty in a most compelling way.

It may be thought that symbolism and ceremony (which is, of course, immensely symbolic) have no relevance in the dynamic, realistic world in which we live. But, by any standards, such thinking is absurd. Ritual and symbolism are to be found everywhere and in everyone.

When we meet and depart, we go through the ceremony of shaking hands; in America it is illegal to make underpants based on the Stars and Stripes; jockeys wear symbolic colours; in professional football an almost prehistoric ritual is observed; when given a drink we say 'Cheers', 'Bottoms up', 'Good health' or utter some similar ritualistic phrase, depending on our social genesis. Ceremony and symbolic ritual are observed by Masons, Trades Unions, Churches, Local Authorities, Schools—need I continue? From the cradle to the grave our lives are encompassed and made liveable by ceremonial and symbolism, even if they masquerade as custom, totemism, manners, or whatever.

This book is totally relevant, because what governs the lives of the people, must also govern the life of the State. Great Britain is a monarchy, so the symbols of monarchical sovereignty are, or should be, part of the lives of the citizens, for the people are the State. We should know about these things and I cannot think of a more pleasurable way of doing so than by reading this book.

J. P. Brook-Little
Heyford House
November 1978

INTRODUCTION

Many of the symbols of sovereignty are part of our everyday lives—ubiquitous and unobserved. The coins in your pocket, for example, bear royal symbols which for centuries have often been impressed on British coins. The decimal half-penny bears a stylised version of the coronation crown which for hundreds of years has been known as St Edward's Crown; its circle holds the fleur-de-lis of yet another Edward's claim to the throne of France in 1338 and the cross symbolises the rule of Christ above all earthly kings, borne above the crowns of Christendom since the times of Charlemagne. This small coin is but one of very many examples of the way royal symbols have been incorporated in the coinage and the history they record.

The meanings of other symbols of sovereignty have become obscured by time, but royal names and emblems have for long proliferated on the signs of inns and taverns—the royal associations of the 'George', the 'Albert', the 'Hanover' and the 'Prince of Wales' are obvious. Others, less obvious, may once have had similar royal associations: the 'Black Bull' inn, for example, may not always have derived its name from a prodigy of a local farmyard but from the Black Bull which appeared on the royal arms of Edward IV after his victory over Henry VI in 1461; and the old cellars below the 'White Hart' may once have served to quench the thirsts of the royal retainers whose liveries bore the White Hart Badge of the young King Richard II and the 'Rising Sun' could also sometimes have been derived from the Sunburst Badge of this king.

Over the centuries the symbols of the royal past have multiplied on the gateways and walls of palaces, on the west fronts and tombs of cathedrals. The fervour which greeted the restoration of Charles II in 1660 is still commemorated in our parish churches by the royal arms which many of them display. During the present century royal symbols have been lavishly bestowed on thousands of bright Jubilee souvenirs.

The royal symbols are not merely traditional adornments. They still exercise their potent authority. The Acts of Parliament which impinge on so many aspects of our lives are still impressed with the Royal Seals as they have been since the reign of Edward III. Parliament is still called by Writs of Summons under the Great Seal of the Realm, although by a concession of the Crown Act 1877 it is now impressed on paper instead of parchment. The Privy Seal, another symbol of the royal authority, is still used to authenticate the numerous Orders in Council by which an increasing amount of legislation is now brought into effect. Ministers who are Secretaries of State, deriving their titles from the ancient offices of the Crown, still kiss hands and receive the seals of their offices and the judges on their benches still sit beneath the Royal Arms to remind them that the sovereign is the 'fount and source of justice'.

At the centre of this great diffusion of signs, emblems, shapes and ornaments are the three great symbols of the royal authority and presence—the crown, sceptres and swords with which each new sovereign is invested on accession to the throne. They are all endowed with ancient symbolism, but for over a thousand years the crown has been the transcendental symbol of majesty. Old chroniclers write with awe and reverence of the appearance of the king wearing his royal crown. This emotional attitude has persisted down the centuries. It was still there in the commentaries and reports of the Coronation of Queen Elizabeth II and there is also a strange undercurrent of the same emotion evident among the millions of people who are drawn by some irresistible attraction to the Jewel House in the Tower of London, irrespective of the country from which they have come.

The significance of symbolism goes right to the roots of human society. The Greek word for a symbol was derived from a term meaning the bringing-together—the name, sign, representative object or totem which united the members of a family, a tribe, or a city state. It was early recognised that veneration for their symbols played an important part in the preservation of a group or society and that a decline in the respect for their symbols was the prelude to decline and decay. Carlyle recognised the dependence of civilisation on symbolism in his *Sartor Resartus*: 'It is in and through symbols that man consciously or unconsciously lives, works and has his being.'

Philologists have pointed out that language itself is a form of symbolism and that writing began as the pictograph of an object associated with a sound. The growth of civilisation is based on an infinite multiplication of the symbols of speech, ideas, exchange, authentification, status, recognition and the respect for the symbols of authority, as well as for the reality of authority itself. Dr Ernest Jones has shown how conscious symbolism is used to enhance the value of what is symbolised and thus to strengthen the cohesive forces within a society. Psychologists like Freud and Jung, from different standpoints, have emphasised the part that subconscious motivation and instinctive behaviour have played in man's dependence on and veneration for the symbols of his family, tribe, overlord, king and state. History has confirmed the validity of these theories. To some extent this book, almost chapter by chapter, could serve to illustrate the fierce attachment of men to the symbols of their clan, their king, their nation.

The symbols and ceremonial objects of sovereignty are the most enduring of all men's emblems. The sceptre found in a Bronze Age barrow has its counterparts in the sceptres displayed in the Jewel House of the Tower of London and in the Crown Room of Edinburgh Castle. The ceremonial swords of the Celtic kings of Iron Age Britain have their successors in the swords which are still in the Royal Regalia, and the emblems on the Royal Arms had their origins in even more distant times and far away kingdoms.

This book has been a long time in growing. It is the result of both research and personal experience. I am fortunate to have served in a Ministry which involved me in the preparation for the ceremonies of State that are part of the long traditions of the United Kingdom. I owe much to my colleagues of these times—to Auriol Barker, the ceremonial officer with his deep knowledge of historical symbolism, and to B. H. St J. O'Neil, the Chief Inspector of Ancient Monuments who, on bleak excavation sites, showed me the early evidence in bone, bronze or iron of the importance of symbolism to man. I am indebted to Col E. A. Carkeet James, the then Resident Governor of the Tower of London, who introduced me not only to the splendours, but also to the historical associations of the Regalia in the Jewel House. I owe a further debt for my intensive indoctrination in the exacting require-ment of ceremony to the late Earl Marshal, the 16th Duke of Norfolk, and to the expert and informative guidance of the officers of the College of Arms. Not the least of my debts are to the meticulous records of coronation ceremonies in present and past centuries which were available to guide the precedents which we had to observe.

In the final stages of this book I have turned again to former col-leagues and to present officers of the Crown. I am grateful to J. P. Brooke-Little, Richmond Herald of Arms, who placed his wide knowledge of ceremony and historical scholarship at my disposal, read my text and made valuable suggestions. I am also grateful for the help I have received with information as well as guidance to illustrations, from past and present members of the Royal Household, to J. E. P. Titman and the staff of the Lord Chamberlain's Office, Miss P. Malley of the Office of the Clerk to the Crown, Graham Dyer, Curator of the Royal Mint, N. Beacham of the Property Services Agency and other officers of the Department of the Environment and J. L. Hocking of Her Majesty's Stationery Office. I had generous help from many sources in Scotland, including D. E. D. Robertson, the Queen's and Lord Treasurer's Remembrancer, D. Williamson, Keeper of the Registers of Scotland, Dr Imrie, Keeper of the Records, D. Fraser of the Scottish Information Office and other officers of the Scottish Office in Edinburgh and in London. Lord Home of the Hirsel provided a valuable clue to the early history of the Scottish Regalia and the early records of the Society of Antiquaries of Scotland were also important sources of information.

I have had indispensable help from several important library resources, including the British Library, the London Library, John Ryland's Library, Manchester, the Ashmolean Museum, Oxford, the National Library of Scotland, the Public Records Office and the Central Office of Information. In acknowledging all this help and co-operation I accept that the accuracy and the opinions are entirely my responsibility. Finally, I express my gratitude to my wife for her patient encouragement and quiet insistence on many necessary clarifications of the text.

I believe this is the first attempt to present in one book a history of the royal insignia of England and Scotland. I hope it will be of some interest to the historian as well as a guide for the far wider public who each year continue to show in Edinburgh and London their unceasing fascination with the Symbols of Sovereignty.

CHAPTER 1
RULERS OF THE DOWNLANDS

Symbols of authority appear in the earliest of human communities. It seems that almost as soon as two or more men came together one of them would take up a stone, a stick, or a deer antler in a gesture of authority.

The primitive man who, about 400,000 years ago, made the stone hand axe found at Caversham in the Thames Valley would have a superiority over other men still using the early palaeolithic pebble tools. From the practical exercise of a physical authority to the symbolising of it in signs and in ritual and ceremonial objects was part of the great leap into conceptual ideas by mankind. In Britain we find evidence of this development in the Upper Palaeolithic Period with the appearance of personal ornaments and ceremonial or status objects and the practice of magico-religious rites, including the careful burial of the dead.

Animal teeth and bones were worn as bangles and necklaces, and the face and body may also have been painted or tattooed to distinguish not only family units but also the status of an individual within his social grouping. Objects with a status significance have been found from this period. In Gough's Cave, Cheddar, for example, there were uncovered an ivory rod and two hand shaped antlers which the French archaeologists call *bâtons-de-commandement*. Other bones have been found with engravings like the horse head from Cresswell Crags, Derbyshire and the stylised human figure, possibly a masked male dancer, from the same site. That these symbols of status or of magico-religious authority were related to one individual is significantly shown by the fact that they were often buried with him in his grave. Men were holding the wands of authority in these islands 15,000 years ago.

Many millenia were to pass, however, before dead men could clearly demonstrate their temporal authority from their graves.

The first peoples to form farming communities in Britain crossed the Channel 4,000 years before the Romans landed on our shores. They brought their long-horned cattle and the practice of growing wheat and barley. They made their fields and their

A sceptre found in the barrow of a Wessex chieftain, c 2000 BC, in the Bush
Barrow, Wiltshire. The shaft is ornamented with bone, the head is polished stone.
The prototype of the royal sceptres

pastures along the chalk hills in a long arc from Wiltshire to
Dorset. They were led in this great migration by their chieftains
and these rulers have left the visible marks of their authority
on the hills of Southern England. Their tombs are symbols of their
power over their peoples in life as in death, and many men must
have laboured for many days to build their monuments of the
great long barrows laboriously raised with antler picks from the
chalk and rubble of the downs. These monuments of the ruling
caste were sometimes over 300 feet long and 100 feet wide. The
undistinguished dead found more casual resting places. You can
still see these symbols of Neolithic regality when you follow the
roads through Wiltshire to Salisbury Plain.

About 500 years after the Neolithic pastoral and farming folk
had established themselves on the downlands, another group of
settlers arrived from France or from the Iberian peninsula. They
were a tall dark-haired race whose religious beliefs inspired them
to devote their social energies to building huge stone chambers
for the burial of their priests, or their priest rulers. Their immense
chambered tombs had spread from maritime Spain and France
to along the west coast of Britain. Their concept of even greater
monuments for the grandiose dead reached the farming folk of
the Wessex downlands who were converted or conscripted to the
immense task of building the West Kennet chambered tomb, the
greatest monument of its type in Western Europe. Over 15,000
tons of sarsen stones were dragged from the hillsides to make the
passageway and burial chambers before the covering of chalk
rubble was piled above them. This megalithic tomb near Avebury
was raised at the same time as the step pyramids were being
constructed in Egypt. You can still enter the dark passageways
and look into the oppressive burial chambers of the first great
chieftains to hold their sway in Britain.

The remains of nearly 2,000 of these vast chambered tombs
have survived in the British Isles. They were mighty works for
men with puny tools. They called for a great community effort,
a unity of authority and the driving force of an intense religious

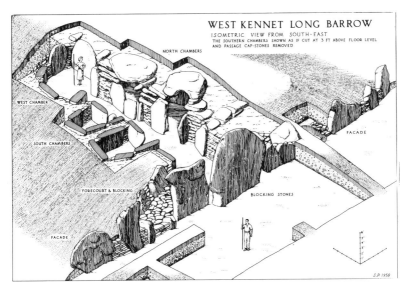

A reconstruction of West Kennet Long Barrow near Avebury, Wiltshire. Built about 3250 BC, it was possibly the tomb of a ruling family on the Downlands. During a thousand years only 46 people were interred. (*DoE*)

belief. They were also built by the many for the few. This is shown by the small numbers of internments there were over long periods of time and by the common physical characteristics among the bones of several generations—as at Lanhill in Wiltshire —which implies an hereditary order of succession. It seems, therefore, that the principle of a ruling family had been established at the beginning of settled communities in Britain.

The great innovation of the early people of Salisbury Plain was the use of the circle for sacred and ceremonial purposes. The great circular enclosures of their causeway camps are scattered along the downs, where their cattle were gathered for breeding and slaughter, and there was feasting before the winter came. They also built such remarkable structures as Woodhenge, a huge circular wooden building 200 ft in diameter with surrounding galleries from which the rites and ceremonies in the open centre could be seen. These incredibly industrious people began the first stage of Stonehenge in a way which suggests they had a knowledge of astronomy many centuries before the Greeks. There were certainly powerful rulers and intelligent men on the Wessex downlands nearly 5,000 years ago.

About 2400 BC another new group of peoples began to arrive in Britain from the Rhine delta. They were descended from the fusion of a race from Spain with the burly Battle-axe People of

Woodhenge: A reconstruction of one of the impressive works raised on Salisbury Plain by the early 'rulers of the Downlands' about 2200 BC. It was one of the few works raised in timber and had a diameter over 200ft. The centre was left open and could be viewed from surrounding galleries—the scene of early rituals. Recent excavations suggest it was used by the elite ruling group (*DoE*)

Central Europe. They were a warrior race bearing the new axes of copper and later of bronze. They seem to have moved quickly to occupy the strategic area of Salisbury Plain with its numerous shrines. We shall never know what happened when the small dark Neolithic people met the tall round-headed warriors from the Rhine. What is certain is that the new arrivals soon became the dominant race and that the round-bottomed pottery of the Neolithic folk was replaced by the high-necked or bell-shaped beakers of the so-called Beaker folk.

The Beaker warriors came to conquer, to trade and to build; they succeeded in all their objectives. They kept their trading connections with Europe as far as the Aegean and opened up new outlets with Ireland; and their traders also followed the ancient trackways to Wales and to Scotland. Trade brought the wealth which the warrior aristocracy used to increase their power and to add to their personal adornment.

It was to building that the Beaker lords turned the collective resources of their society, raising monuments to their beliefs which were without equal in Europe. Avebury, a massive complex of great standing stones and earthworks, is a colossal work covering nearly thirty acres. They began the rebuilding of

Stonehenge and brought huge stones of spotted dolerite from the Prescelly mountains in Pembrokeshire. These stones were part of an older shrine which they dismantled and with incredible labour by sea, river and land brought to Salisbury Plain.

The Prescelly mountains were also the source of the stone for some of the beautiful polished axes which were the symbols of the ruling caste, the traditional weapons of their ancestral Battle-axe people. The stone axe, the basis of their power, had acquired a cult significance for the warrior caste. They had carved its symbol on the standing stones of their predecessors in Brittany and on the great monoliths which they raised at Stonehenge. They took their axes with them to their round bowl barrow graves which are scattered in groups over the downlands. Their burials have yielded many beautiful ceremonial axes in green quartzite and red tourmalian as well as rare stones from Antrim, Brittany and central Europe.

The fine polished surfaces of these axes show that they had not been used but were cherished as the symbols of power. Their ceremonial use is confirmed by axes made of jadeite, a material which could not withstand an impact. They were the polished symbols of authority given to a chieftain on his accession, as the sword and the helmet would become in their turn. These axes are the prototypes of the royal regalia in Britain. Many of them have been found in graves with their shafts broken—the symbolic breaking of a ruler's power on his death. This practice has been followed down the centuries—the Celtic sword was broken, the wheels were taken from the chariot, the sea-king's ship was burned or buried, and the Great Seal, the potent symbol of the royal authority, is now defaced on the death of the sovereign.

By 1600 BC the chieftains of the downlands had become the rulers of the brilliant culture of Wessex. They were the merchant princes of their times, still raising great monuments and shrines on Salisbury Plain, but also employing goldsmiths from Ireland and smiths from Brittany. Their graves proclaim that a Wessex lord was a figure of splendour, with golden disc-like epaulettes and a golden plaque on his breast, while the scabbard and hilt of his long bronze dagger were plated with gold. Some of the Wessex barrows may yet give up a cloak of thin sheets of gold similar to that which was found in a grave of the period in Mold, Clwyd. This beautiful and fragile cloak could only have been worn on great ceremonial occasions. It was a robe of princely splendour.

The later lords of Wessex still carried their polished stone axes but a new symbol appears for the first time in their hands—the sceptre. The Bush Barrow at Normanton in Wiltshire has given us the earliest example of this piece of the regalia. It is an object of ceremonial use with an ornamented staff supporting a carved oval of shale. Other sceptres since found in Wessex barrows have stone heads embellished with gold and ornamented staves.

The Wessex lords have left us a supreme example of their absolute power: Silbury Hill, almost opposite the West Kennet Barrow, is the largest prehistoric mound in Europe; it covers $5\frac{1}{4}$ acres and contains about 14 million cubic feet of man-moved chalk rubble. This vast work could not have been a voluntary effort. Many hundreds of men had to be mobilised for the colossal task. Silbury Hill has not yet given up its secrets. Whether tomb or cenotaph, the man who, 3,600 years ago, could command its construction must have been the first great king on English soil and Silbury Hill is the place where England's royal history should begin.

CHAPTER 2
CELTS AND CHARIOTEERS

About 500 BC a new people with new weapons began to arrive in Britain. They were a tall, fair-haired race with blue eyes; they were excitable, warlike and imaginative; their new weapons were the sword and the war chariot. They began to raid the south and east coasts of Britain at the end of a long migration. The Greeks, who knew them as mercenaries and traders, called them *Keltoi*— the Celts.

These people had moved from their homelands in central Europe because of adverse changes in weather, the exhaustion of their farmlands, the expansion of their own population and the pressure of other peoples from the east. As they moved forward in warrior bands under their chieftains, their new weapons were as powerfully effective as the dive-bomber and the panzer, also from central Europe, were to be in a later millenium.

The Celts had learned the art of iron smelting from their contacts with the Eastern Mediterranean. The bronze weapon had been the work of a skilled craftsman with a knowledge of alloys and of the careful making of moulds. Copper and tin were scarce and iron ores plentiful. A man with a fire, bellows, the iron ores and a strong arm could become a smith able to produce a supply of weapons stronger and sharper than the soft leaf-flanged swords and daggers of the Late Bronze Age.

Iron made enduring bands for wheels and axles for chariots. The fierce, fast-riding peoples from the steppes of southern Russia had shown the Celts the speed and mobility which the horse could give to a chieftain warrior. Long before they left their homelands, the Celts were burying their chiefs with their chariots and their swords—the new weapons and new symbols of dominion.

They came in warrior bands to Britain and they were not welcomed. In the natural harbours of Lulworth and Hengistbury Head the Celts threw up fortifications in which the ditches were on the landward sides to protect their beach heads against attack from the interior. With their weapons and their warrior strength the Celts prevailed. They occupied the south of England and merged with the local people to found an aristocracy which was to last through the Roman period until the Saxons arrived a thousand years later.

It was to be a long time, however, before the tribal units were merged in the Celtic confederacies which the Romans first encountered. With a sharp sword in each tribesman's hand a small chieftain could maintain a rough independence. The signs of this independence can still be found in the traces of the early hill forts which appeared in scores along the escarpments of southern Ennland, each commanding its own hillside and river valley. Tribal wars and cattle raiding, as we can read from the folklore of the Celts in Ireland, were the main preoccupations of the Celtic peoples.

But warriors and their families must eat and a new plough with an iron tip made for improved cultivation. They lived in round farmhouses surrounded by a ditch and palisade, grew hard spelt wheat which they stored in pits, kept sheep and cattle, and withdrew into their forts when their tribal neighbours became too intent on reprisals. They were the first people of Britain to enter recorded history; about 330 BC, a Greek merchant, Pytheas of Marseilles, wrote of the 'Pretanic Islands', a name which in Roman times became 'Britannia'.

About the time the Greek merchant was keeping his trading records a new Celtic invasion reached the shores of Britain. There is evidence of the strengthening of the hill forts and other preparations for resistance. The newcomers had another new weapon, the sling, which enabled them to assault the defences beyond the reach of the throwing spear. When eventually they prevailed the hill forts which they occupied, like those at Maiden Castle in Dorset and the Trundle, near Goodwood, were greatly enlarged and strengthened with multiple ditches and ramparts against any further invasions by sling throwers. These Celtic people—called La Tène—by archaeologists—had brought to Britain another warrior aristocracy of a brilliance which the land had not known since the golden age of the Wessex lords nearly 2,000 years before.

Once again there was the aristocratic patronage of schools of artist-craftsmen which led to the flowering of a brilliant and insular decorative art. It was not mainly a representative art form. Its beautiful motifs were based primarily on the spiral and the circle. The Celtic artists, who, in Europe had once copied the flower patterns of Greece and Etruria, discarded the flowers and the foliage but kept the curving shapes of the floral cup, the oval petal and the flowing lines of the classical honeysuckle design. It was shape without the image. To bronze and gold they added the skilled craftsmanship of champlevé work, running thin sockets along their flowing designs, filling them with multi-colour enamelling, and firing the colours level with the surface.

Late Celtic shield of enamelled bronze for ceremonial use (*RTH*)

When they depicted a human face it was often as strange as the features seen in the hazy ferocity of battle, or had the sly ugliness of a face peering from a thicket. Their animals were grotesque.

Their art was applied to the brooches, neck chains and other personal ornaments of their chieftains as well as to the buckets, braziers, pottery, bowls and other utensils of his household. The finest expressions of their art were reserved, however, for the military equipment of the ruling class and for their insignia of rank and religious office—the sword scabbards and hilts, helmets, shields, their horse harness and their chariots.

There were two types of ceremonial sword. Votive swords of many designs and sizes have been recovered from the rivers and lakes where they were cast as offerings to the god or goddess of the place. The second type, the ceremonial sword, was the long two edged weapon in a bronze scabbard with rich enamelling or filigree work. These swords often had anthropoid hilts, a small figure on the pommel which represented the spirit within it, or which gave the sword its name. Many of these swords were unsuitable for use in battle. They were swords of rank, parade swords worn by a tribal ruler on his succession, or on occasions of ceremony. The same richness of decoration was also applied to his other weapons of ceremony, his helmet and his shield, which like his sword, were often placed in his grave. These ceremonial weapons, the insignia of rank, were still accompanying the rulers on British soil many centuries later. The ceremonial sword has survived as the sword of rank and a symbol of sovereignty down the centuries to the present day.

The most important symbol of rank in early Celtic Britain was undoubtedly the chariot. The Celtic chariot is nothing like the

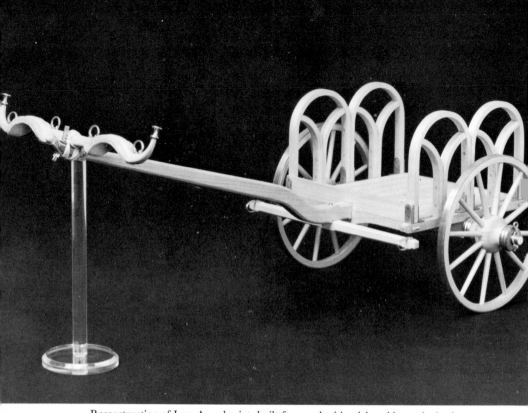

Reconstruction of Iron Age chariot, built for speed with wicker sides and wheels with shrunk on iron tyres (*National Museum of Wales*)

lumbering wain with scythes on its axles on which Boadicea stands at Westminster Bridge. Speed was the essential requirement of the chariot; they were made of light wooden frames with wickerwork sides, supported on wheels of from twelve to sixteen spokes cased in iron tyres. The wheels were about three feet in diameter. The chariots were drawn by two specially bred pony-sized horses, controlled by snaffle bits in large rein rings made of iron cased in bronze. The light war chariot could race at speed over almost any ground, swinging easily round any obstruction.

The chariot combined the advantages of cavalry and infantry with a complement of one warrior and the driver. The tactic was to drive swiftly over the battlefield, hurling javelins and creating panic with racing horses and thundering wheels. The warrior would race along the pole to hurl his weapons at full gallop. When attacking cavalry the warrior would dismount to fight as an infantryman, with the chariot waiting for a swift retreat. Centuries later the British chariots were to baffle the Romans until Caesar adopted the tactic of keeping his cavalry and infantry close together. The up-keep of the chariots was the responsibility of the chieftain, who recruited an elite company of charioteers around him.

In addition to the war chariots there were also the chariots of ceremony. Florus describes a chariot plated in silver. Highly decorated axle ends and yoke finials and elaborate horse harnesses have been found in the graves of the early Celtic chieftains. Some of the horse trappings were superb, including horse masks in bronze repoussé which could only have been used on ceremonial occasions. The chief, in his full regalia of shining helmet, variegated cloak held by its huge golden brooch, with ornate sword and shield and mounted on a chariot shining with bronze and silver and driving his masked horses, was undoubtedly a resplendent sight.

Long before Boadicea there were apparently woman rulers in Britain; in a grave in Yorkshire has been found a young woman buried with her chariot and other symbols of her temporal power.

The cult of the chariot found expression in the models which were made for votive offerings at shrines; these miniature chariots were sometimes drawn by the tribal and totemic emblems of the wild boar, the stag and the swan. The numerous shrines, where such votive offerings were made, show the wide influence of Celtic religious beliefs. The Celts saw another reality behind the surface of things, a pervading presence which was felt and acknowledged. They had a preoccupation with the natural environment which they personified in the spirits of woods, lakes and streams. They abstracted the qualities of things—the strength of the wild boar, the swiftness of the stag—and personified them in deities. These mystical undertones did not lead to a contemplative religion. Deities with savage qualities were propitiated with savage rites. There were, said the Roman poet Lucan, woods where the birds feared to perch and coverts where no animal would lie.

The Celts' devotion to their horses was reflected in the religious cult of Epona, the goddess and protectress of the horse. Epona was widely invoked by the tribes of Gaul and, when the Celts were recruited as Roman levies, she became the goddess of the Roman cavalry and had the distinction of being the only Celtic deity with a shrine in Rome.

The 'Divine Horse' had her shrines and ritual objects in Britain. A small bronze in the British Museum shows Epona holding a dish of corn over a horse's head. Small bronze horses as votive offerings to Epona have been found in many places, as well as on the crest of a Celtic helmet. The cult of Epona reached its widest diffusion with the arrival of the Belgic tribes in the late second and first centuries BC. The Belgae were of mixed Celtic and Teutonic origin and they had come to Britain as settlers and traders, but their great migration began with the Roman conquest of Gaul. With the coming of these refugees the light of recorded history is turned on Britain. We have the first real names of the peoples of these islands, the location of their principal towns and the configurations of the native tribal states: the Cantiaci of Kent and east Surrey, the Regnenses of Sussex, west Surrey and Hampshire, the Belgae of the rest of Hampshire, Wiltshire and north Somerset, the Dumnonii and the Durotriges of the South West; the Iceni of Norfolk, and the great confederation of the Catuvellauni from the East Midlands to the Thames who were able to confront Caesar with 4,000 chariots.

Epona still rode with the horsemen and their chariots and her image was impressed on the first coinage minted in Britain. The first coins to reach Britain were the gold staters of Philip of Macedonia, struck in the fourth century BC, which had been carried across Europe by slow migrations and the exchanges of trade. The staters carried the head of Apollo on the obverse and, appropriately for Britain, a charioteer on the reverse. Coins are the indices of history; they fill in the blank spaces in the records and also tell us what were the significant symbols of their times. They can be precise instructors. We know, for example, that there were six distinct and separate waves of Belgic immigrants from Europe. We can even follow the Ambiani from the Somme Valley after they landed in Kent, along the banks of the Thames beyond London until they turned north-west into Buckinghamshire and Hertfordshire. The casual loss and deposited hordes of their flat 'Bellovac' staters has enabled us to trace their footsteps on their journey towards the end of the second century BC. The worn pattern of their coins still bears the charioteer.

The first coins to be struck in Britain between 90 and 70 BC were gold staters in imitation of the faraway coins of Philip of Macedonia, with the head of Apollo and the charioteer. They were the forerunners of large groups of coins in bronze and silver which were struck by the tribal states of Britain. Although the boar, the bull and even a sphinx appear on some British coins, by far the most common symbol was the horse or the chariot—sometimes represented by a few stylised strokes, so commonly was this symbolism known and accepted. So far as we can possibly say that Celtic Britain had a national symbol before the Romans it was, undoubtedly, the horse and the chariot. Strangely, many centuries later it was another horseman who became the patron and the symbol of the English nation—the chivalrous figure of St George.

It is from a coin that we learn that Eppillus of the Atrebates, in

The White Horse of Uffington (*DoE*)

his territory of Berkshire and parts of Hampshire and Wiltshire, may have been the first Celtic chieftain to use the title of king in these islands. The inscription on his coin reads: *Epp* (Eppillus) *Rex* (king) *Calle* (Calleva Atrebatum, i.e. Silchester).

Long before Eppillus took the dignity of the Roman *Rex*, his Celtic predecessors had cut the symbol of the Celtic people in large dimensions and in a form which would remain as the witness of Celtic Britain, its gods and its beliefs to all future generations in these islands. So far as any man can tell, the great White Horse of Uffington was cut out of the chalk hillside on the Berkshire downs during the Celtic iron ages. Chesterton was close to the facts when he wrote:

> Before the gods that made the gods
> Had seen their sunrise pass,
> The White Horse of the White Horse Vale
> Was cut out of the grass.

Some opinions would, in fact, take the origin of the White Horse back to the first arrival of the Celts about 500 BC. They point to the nearby presence of an early Iron Age fort which could have been associated with the figure. The horse could, therefore, have preceded the figures on the coins by many centuries. It is, undoubtedly, however, a symbol from very ancient times long before it was recorded in a cartulary of Abingdon Abbey as *'juxta locum qui vulgo Mons Albi Equi nuncupatur'* ('near the place which is commonly called White Horse Hill'). It referred to the time when Aldhelm was the Abbot in 1072–84.

For many centuries the symbolism of the White Horse has placed a great emphasis on its 'scouring'—the clearing away of the growth of turf. This custom had been carried out at seven-year intervals and was associated with rites and revels which a clergyman in 1738 described as disorder and debauchery, and it could have been derived from ancient spring festivals of fertility. On Whit Monday, 1780, the *Reading Mercury* reported that 30,000 people were present at the scouring.

The White Horse, like other ancient monuments, came into the care of the then Ministry of Works and it has always treated the scouring with great seriousness. There is an old legend that Britain will cease to be independent when 'the White Horse no longer shines upon the grass'. During the last war there was some local agitation when the wartime shortage of local labour prevented the scouring and the Ministry secured the help of a company of infantry from the camp on the downlands.

The White Horse has been kept clean by many generations; the Romans had the work done and, when the Celts retreated to the west, the Saxons cut the turf away. A Norman lord must have accepted his responsibility, and a little later the duty was written into the charter of the local Lord of the Manor. The symbols of the peoples and kings of Britain have an enduring quality about them.

CHAPTER 3
THE TREASURE SHIP OF SUTTON HOO

In June 1939 a small group of men stood on a sandy heath at Sutton Hoo in Suffolk looking down into a hollow where a legend had come to life before their eyes. The great poem, Beowulf, must have suddenly become for them not the imaginary description of the burial of a mythical king, but the metrical blue-print of a reality. They knew that they were looking down at the ship burial of an early English king, interred in the manner the narrative had told.

> And there they brought the beloved body
> Of their ring-giving lord, and laid him near
> The mast. Next to that noble corpse
> They heaped up treasures, jewelled helmets,
> Hooked swords and coats of mail, armour
> Carried from the ends of the earth; no ship
> Had ever sailed so brightly fitted,
> No king sent forth more deeply mourned.

Below their feet was the outline of a great ship whose timbers had long ago decayed but the sand still held her exact shape with the compression of 1300 years. They could see her clinker-built construction, the planking secured by clench nails bent over the iron roves, the stout framing and the stem post joined to the keel with a scarf joint. The sand held the shape of a ghost ship over 80 ft long, with a maximum beam of 14 ft, which had been rowed by thirty-eight oarsmen with a steersman at the stern.

The centre of the boat held their attention. A burial chamber had been built there and the timbers had decayed bringing down the roof and the overburden of sand and turf. This had been removed to reveal an area which held a tangled mass of sand-encrusted objects. A small piece had come loose and brushing had disclosed a small gold buckle inlaid with jewels. They knew then they were on the threshold of a very important discovery.

Their feelings were described by O. G. S. Crawford in *Antiquity* a few months later. 'Each day of that exciting week yielded some first rate find, often of a type unknown before. As we worked along the keel we *knew* that under those mouldy looking lumps of decayed wood lay hidden things of priceless historic value. We anticipated the findings of a sword, shield, helmet and drinking

The Sutton Hoo burial ship uncovered in 1939 (*British Museum*)

horns and were not disappointed. Things we did not expect were found—the purse, silver bowls and tray, for instance, and later the axe and suit of chain mail. It was clear that more could be found when the final examination in the laboratories of the British Museum was completed.'

They had a long wait for that final examination. Three days after they had finished their work in 1939 war was declared, the finds were cleaned and treated, crated and sent for storage in a disused tunnel of the London Underground with other historic treasures of the Museum. The thoughts of the excavators of the Suffolk grave must have turned with impatience to what the future might reveal.

Those revelations were to exceed their expectations. Out of that ancient ship began to come, as it were, the resurrection of an Anglo-Saxon king with all his royal regalia. The grave goods were to give a new perspective to a king, his peoples and his times.

Who was this king? It was evident that he had been the ruler of the kingdom of the East Angles, one of the people from across the North Sea who had been invited to Britain by Vortigern, after the departure of the Romans, to repel the Picts. They had come as mercenaries, but had stayed as colonists and invaders to create the Anglo-Saxon kingdoms. The title of Bretwalda, or over king, had been one of vague authority, often briefly held by one of their kings.

The royal insignia from Sutton Hoo pointed to the burial being that of the Bretwalda of his time. There was another clue to his identity. A small collection of thirty-seven coins from Merovingian France had been found and those which could be dated gave the period of AD 624—630 for their assembly. The two facts came together—Raedwald had been the only king of the East Angles to become Bretwalda, and he died in 624–5.

The narrative poem *Beowulf*, written not much later, describes the regalia given to a king:

> Healfdanes son gave Beowulf a golden banner,
> A fitting flag to signal his victory,
> And gave him as well, a helmet
> And a coat of mail, and an ancient sword.

The men who had piled the treasure in the burial ship had included a more elaborate symbol of sovereignty than a banner, which has been accepted as the standard of the Bretwalda: a tall iron shaft with a bottom spike with two foot-treads to drive it into the ground. It was a unique object, similar to the Roman *signum*, the military standard which had also carried the figure of a wolf, horse, wild boar or eagle and a cross piece for a *vexillium*, or flag. The pattern of the Roman standard may well have been passed down the centuries.

The finding of a whetstone sceptre was further confirmation that Sutton Hoo was a royal burial. It was 2 ft long, weighed over 6 lb and had four fierce human faces carved at each end. It was surmounted by a small bronze stag, the totemic emblem of the Wuffings—Raedwald's family. The end knobs were surmounted by small saucers held in place by bronze strips. It could have been only for ceremonial use. The Keeper of Medieval Antiquities at the British Museum described it as a monstrous thing, 'a unique and savage thing and inexplicable, except perhaps as a symbol proper to the king himself'. Smaller whetstone sceptres have since been found for this period.

The expert report on the helmet described it as 'an object of burnished silver metal, set in a trellis work of gold, surmounted by a crest of massive silver and embellished with gilded ornaments, garnets and niello'. The eyebrows were decorated with silver wire and niello inlay and set below with garnets over gold foil, with a gilded boar's head at each end. The visor was decorated with silver, and the panels of the helmet were embossed with designs of armed warriors and god-like figures. When worn by the king it must have been an awe-inspiring symbol of majesty. It has been dated to a century before Raedwald's time, and the fact that it was buried in the ship is a tribute to his importance since Beowulf refers to the royal regalia usually being passed to the succeeding king.

Beowulf also speaks of the 'ancient sword' as the symbol of kingship. The sword of Raedwald had a hilt and pommel of gold worked with filigree and set with garnets in quatrefoils. The scabbard was set with jewelled bosses; two small gold pyramids with garnets were attached to the sword knot.

The shield had been magnificent, a great curved surface shining with gold, silver and bronze; around its raised rim were twelve dragons' heads. The great boss was also decorated with a dragon's head and the shapes of a dragon and a bird of prey were placed above and below the boss. The shield had been carefully repaired, proof of its ancestral significance.

These pieces of the regalia were outshone by the splendour of the king's body harness. Its jewellery has been described by Dr Bruce-Mitford as brimming with novel and daring ideas and displaying the highest level of craftsmanship—'excelling anything known in this medium from the rest of Europe in its era'.

This jewellery was enriched with over 4,000 garnets and worked in beautiful patterns of interlaced designs in superb cloisonné, millefiori and niello inlay.

The great gold buckle for the belt weighs nearly 15 oz and its surface had been covered with interlacing patterns of snakes with open mouths, birds' heads and biting beasts. Its beauty is matched by the shoulder clasps which are covered in garnets and enamel decorations with borders of animal processional themes. At either end of each clasp is the remarkable design of linked boars with tusks and crested backs.

The purse lid at the king's belt is the most gorgeous of all the jewellery, with its intricate patterns in garnets and gold of animal and human figures and complex geometric designs. Altogether there were twenty-six pieces of this superb and beautiful jewellery.

A tribute of other royal treasure was laid in the burial ship. Beowulf speaks of 'loud in the hall was the harp's rejoicing', and a fine harp had been recovered. There were household buckets which had held ale and cauldrons for seething meats. Two of the seven drinking horns had been made from the gigantic horns of the auroch; each held six quarts and could not have been put down without spilling until it was emptied. A great silver dish held the assay mark of the Byzantine Emperor Anastasius (AD 491–518) and there was a large bronze bowl from Alexandria in Egypt. All this treasure and household goods had been placed in the burial ship for a journey to the other world—its cargo was complete, except for the body of the king. The great ship and all its treasures were a memorial, a cenotaph, a tribute to a king who must have been lost at sea or buried elsewhere.

There are clues to this mystery. The struggle for the conversion of England had begun again with the arrival of St Augustine in 596. There had been a fluctuating ebb and flow between Christianity and the belief in the old gods and conversion was often followed by apostasy. Some tried to hold a balance between the old and the new. Bede tells that Raedwald had been converted to Christianity in Kent, but on his return home 'had turned back from the sincerity of the faith, and in the same temple had an altar to sacrifice to Christ and another small one to offer victims to devils . . . ' It could be, therefore, that Raedwald was given a Christian burial while his pagan followers had launched his spirit on its journey to the other world of the old heathen gods of his ancestors in the burial ship.

After Sutton Hoo the so-called Dark Ages from 410 to 870 have begun to look much brighter. A new impetus had been given to Anglo-Saxon scholarship and excavation. Jewellery similar to that of Sutton Hoo has been found. Older royal finds have been examined with a new interest, such as the ring of King Ethelwulf, father of Alfred the Great, and the inscribed ring of his daughter, Ethelwith. Two other great treasures of the Saxon house of Cedric are the Alfred Jewel and the Minister Lovell Jewel in the Ashmolean Museum at Oxford.

The Alfred Jewel was found in Somerset a few miles from Athelney where King Alfred in 878 launched his counter attack on the Danes, and later founded a monastery. The Jewel's association with the Saxon King is confirmed by the inscription on its gold filigree band: ALFRED MEC HEHT GEWYRCAN (Alfred had me made).

The design is of a man seated on an open stool, wearing a short-sleeved tunic and carrying against his shoulders two rods with floral heads. It is in cloisonné enamel on gold plate. The end of the jewel is shaped like the head of an animal holding an open tube which could have held an extension rod.

The Minster Lovell Jewel, found in Oxfordshire, is smaller but very similar to the Alfred Jewel, possibly from the same workshop and even from the same hand. It is also designed in cloisonné enamel with a green four-pointed star, with a white centre. This beautiful Saxon jewel also has a socket for fitting it to a rod.

These two Saxon jewels with their sockets have caused much speculation. The figure on the Alfred Jewel has been variously described as that of Christ, St Neot, or even the symbolic representation of Sight, one of the five senses. It has also been suggested that the sockets indicated that they were *astels*—pointers used to follow the text in a manuscript to avoid damaging the page with the fingers. A sharp jewel could surely do more damage, however, to a page than a finger. The more likely explanation is that they were both part of the Crown Jewels of King Alfred and once had their places at the top of his jewelled sceptres. This view would also seem justified by the opinion held by some experts that the figure on the Alfred Jewel is that of the king himself holding two foliated sceptres.

The jewels of Alfred, like those of Raedwald from Sutton Hoo, are the survivors of the royal splendour of the Anglo-Saxon kings. Asser, the biographer of Alfred, says that he had 'collected and procured from many races of men craftsmen in almost countless numbers'. Time and tomb robbers, Danes and Normans, and later vandals and fanatics have eroded and swept away the beautiful things they had once created. There was once in Anglo-Saxon England a magnificence, which, from century to century, was to remain part of the inheritance of the sovereigns of England.

CHAPTER 4
WESTMINSTER ABBEY— TREASURE HOUSE OF KINGS

The name of Edward the Confessor has a long association with the royal regalia of England. King Edward, the son of Ethelred the Unready, may have worn King Alfred's crown.

He was a strange man, an albino who saw visions. During the reign of Canute, while he was in exile in Normandy, he made a vow to go on pilgrimage to the tomb of St Peter in Rome if he should gain the English throne. Within the day a messenger arrived to say the Danes were gone and the Witan had elected him king.

When Edward told the Witan of his intention to go to Rome, the nobles protested, referring to the perils of the journey, 'the felon Romans who covet money as a leech sucks blood', and the dangers to the kingdom in his absence. Their views prevailed, and Edward sent an embassy to Rome to ask to be released from his vow. His petition was granted by Pope Leo IX provided he built a great Abbey to St Peter. When this news reached England, the abbot of a small monastery on the Island of Thorns hurried to tell the king that he had received a vision of St Peter saying that the new Abbey should be built on the site of his poor monastic foundation.

So speak the legends. What is certain, however, is that Edward devoted the remaining years of his life and the treasure of his kingdom to the building of the Abbey at Westminster. 'Destroying the old building,' he declared in its charter, 'I have created a new one on its foundations.'

The Saxon churches had been unpretentious buildings with wattle walls and wooden rafters. The new Abbey soared on rising pillars and on tall masonry from deep foundations. It had transepts with galleries, a central tower and two towers at the west end, with five great bells. It was the first cruciform church in England, symbolising the cross of Christ, and most splendid of its time; if King Henry III had not had his own visions, it might well have been standing today.

The monks were not forgotten; there were new cloisters, a chapter house, the refectory, the dormitory and a treasure chamber which was to have a long and historic association with the royal regalia.

There is a legend also about the making of that treasure

chamber. One night when King Edward lay on his bed, eyes closed in prayer, a scullion crept into the room and took a handful of treasure from the chest which the king kept under his bed. After an interval the thief crept back for another handful. Enough was enough. When the thief returned for the third time the king sat up in bed to warn him to escape before Hugolin, his chamberlain, returned. 'He will not even let you have one of my silver pennies,' said the king to the scullion. Hugolin was furious when he was told. He wanted to hang the thief. 'Let him be,' said the king, 'the thief hath more need of it than me. Treasure enough hath King Edward.' The chamberlain prevailed and the royal treasure was taken to a vaulted undercroft near the cloisters which had just been completed.

The legends still pursue the Confessor. One night he visited his treasure chamber and saw a black devil dancing in glee on the casks of money he had levied on his subjects to pay the Danes. The king decided to abolish the Danegeld for ever. The symbolism of that legend has come down the centuries. At the coronation of each sovereign there takes place the offering of the Glove. A soft leather glove is placed on the sovereign's right hand before the investiture with the Sceptre with the Cross. It was a perpetual reminder to each sovereign that, like Edward the Confessor, they should be gentle in the levying of taxes. Queen Elizabeth II was given the legendary reminder when a glove was placed on her hand in June 1953.

The dedication of the Abbey was the last act of Edward's life. 'At Midwinter,' says the *Anglo-Saxon Chronicle*, 'King Edward came to Westminster and had the minster there consecrated which he had himself built to the honour of God and St Peter.' He wore his crown for the last time on Christmas Day. He died on 5 January 1066 and was buried before the high altar of the new Abbey.

The legends followed Edward into his grave. Before his death he saw the Seven Sleepers of Ephesus turn from their right side to their left and had recognised the omen as foretelling seventy years of war, famine and pestilence. What is more certain is that a great comet appeared, the sign of impending calamities; this event is shown in the Bayeaux Tapestry, with the awestricken people pointing to the fearful migrant in the skies. The coming of the Normans and the death of Harold were to happen within the year.

The Sutton Hoo Burial: reconstruction of the magnificent helmet of the king (*BM*)

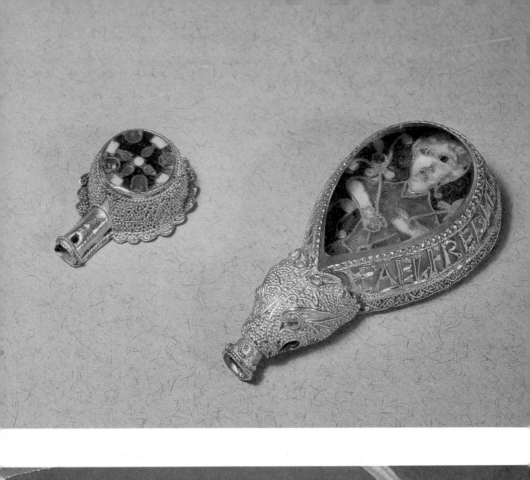

It has been claimed that Edward intended Westminster Abbey to be the coronation church of the English kings and there are copies of charters and a papal Bull to prove it. These documents are, however, still somewhat suspect. What is certain is that William the Conqueror set the precedent. The Byzantine-type crown designed by Guy of Amiens was set on his head amid uproar and violence.

William had insisted that he should be inaugurated with the rites of the Saxon kings. He took the oath the Saxon kings had sworn before the Witan to respect the laws of their predecessors, by promising to keep the 'laws and customs of the glorious King Edward'. Those words were set in the coronation service and were repeated by every crowned sovereign of England until the accession of James II in 1685.

The service was conducted jointly by a Saxon and a Norman prelate and the Abbey was filled with representatives of both peoples. The ancient form of election by the Witan required the people to proclaim loudly their acceptance of the king. When this question was put in the Saxon and then in the Norman tongues a babble of confusion was heard within the Abbey. The Norman cavalry, guarding all approaches to the Abbey, thought that their Duke was being attacked and drove their horses into the waiting crowds and began to storm into the Abbey with drawn swords. The congregation fled and William was left with the two prelates to complete the service, 'trembling as though in fear' for the first time in his life.

Since that fateful Christmas Day the Abbey has continued to be the coronation church of the English sovereigns. Only two kings of England in 900 years have not been crowned within its walls—Edward V who was born in the Abbey when his mother fled there for sanctuary, but was not allowed to return for his crowning—he was one of the two young princes murdered in the Tower. The other uncrowned king was Edward VIII who abdicated in 1936 before his coronation.

The Abbey and the legends of Edward the Confessor have become inextricably intertwined with the coronation service and the regalia of the English Crown. The name of King Edward is a

Opposite above: The Alfred Jewel and the Minster Lovell Jewel: the inscription on the Alfred Jewel (*right*) reads that it was made for King Alfred (871–90) and the Minster Lovell Jewel is attributed to the same source by the similarity of design and technique (*Ashmolean Museum*)
Opposite below: Head of the Sceptre with the Cross. The largest piece of the Cullinan Diamond, known as the First Star of Africa, of 530 carats, was set in the head of this Sceptre for the Coronation of King George V in 1911. It is thought to be the largest and most perfectly cut diamond in the world

recurrent theme in the tapestry of England's history. Eight kings of England have borne his name. At the coronation the crown is called 'St Edward's Crown', and the crown of the queen-consort is called after his wife, 'Queen Edith's Crown'. The royal sceptres have often been given his name and at each coronation St Edward's Staff is carried to guide the new sovereign's footsteps in his steps of righteousness. The jewel on top of the Imperial Crown is 'St Edward's Sapphire' and the vestments taken from his body after his canonisation in 1161 may have actually been worn by many kings before their investiture with the regalia. For 600 years the treasure chamber in the Abbey held the crowns, sceptres, vestments and the sacred vessels used at the coronations of the English kings and queens, although the monarchs were soon to seek a more secure repository for the crowns, swords and sceptures they used on other State occasions.

Relief from the chapel of St Edward the Confessor. The vision of the Seven Sleepers (*Dean and Chapter of Westminster*)

CHAPTER 5
THE ROBBERY OF THE PYX

King Edward had not been allowed to rest in peace before the altar of his Abbey Church. The severity of the Norman rule made men look back to the times of Edward as the golden age of England. The legends grew apace and the miracles attributed to him were widely recounted. The abbots of Westminster busily promoted his canonisation in Rome until the Prior, Osbert de Clare, was at last able to carry back in triumph to Westminster the Bull of Canonisation of Pope Alexander III. The abbots of Westminster and the kings of England had their own patron saint.

The dispute between Henry II and Archbishop Becket was still in the future when at midnight on 13 October 1163, the King and the Archbishop with a great procession of clergy and nobles entered the Abbey for the opening of the tomb of St Edward. The sapphire ring was taken from the dead king's finger to be placed with the royal regalia and the Abbot Lawrence gently plucked a hair from his beard to be kept as a sacred relic. The Abbey was filled with the glory of copes, the sounds of chanting and the rich smell of incense.

It was, however, the grandson of Henry II who exceeded all the other kings of England in his devotion to St Edward. Henry III decided to build a still more glorious Abbey in honour of the saintly king. There was also pride in his devotion. He wanted the new Abbey to outshine the high and lovely cathedrals of France. The work began in 1245 and, like Edward, he was to devote the rest of his life to the task.

Like the church of the Confessor, the new Abbey was also unique in one aspect. The two transepts were brought forward beyond the choir to form a wide space before the Sanctuary. This was to be the Place of the Crowning where all the future sovereigns of England would be recognised, acclaimed, consecrated and crowned in 'the gaze of all the nobles and the people'. It was in that wide space that we built the golden carpeted platform for the coronation of Queen Elizabeth II.

On 13 October 1269, a great concourse of high dignatories of state, nobles, prelates, abbots, foreign princes and citizens of London gathered in the Abbey for the translation of St Edward to his new shrine. Henry III had grown stout and old, with one un-blinking eye, and he was stooped with weariness from the long struggles of his reign. For the last time all his family were gathered around him, including his son Edward who was about to leave on pilgrimage to the Holy Land. Set amid the soaring columns, surrounded by every ecclesiastical splendour, was the chapel and shrine of St Edward. The shrine itself was the most splendid gold and jewelled shrine in Europe and one of its greatest works of art. It was plated with gold, encrusted with gems and enriched with beautiful enamelling. The altar frontal below it was of cloth of gold decorated with embroidery and bordered with jewels which had taken three skilled needlewomen four years to make. When the old king, with his sons, placed his shoulder to the coffin to carry it to the shrine he must have felt that he had indeed done well for his patron saint and kingly predecessor.

The Abbey now became the greatest ecclesiastical establishment in England. It was exempt from the jurisdiction of the See of London which surrounded it; even the Archbishop of Canterbury could not officiate within its walls without permission—as Archbishop Fisher was to find with wry amusement when he began to prepare for the coronation in 1953. Its Abbots were given the privilege of the mitre and the ring and, when Abbot Barking under Henry III became the chief Lord of the Exchequer and later Lord Treasurer of England, it was additional proof of how close had become the links between the Abbey and the Crown.

After the translation of St Edward, the Abbey itself must have become a house of gold and jewelled images and ecclesiastical ornaments. The golden shrine was surrounded by costly gifts in gold and silver from the devout and by the diplomatic embassies bringing relics, crucifixes and chalices. The Order of the Templars presented the King with the relic of the tooth of Athanasius, the stone which showed the footprints of the Saviour when he ascended to heaven, and most precious of all, a phial containing a few drops of the Holy Blood. As the great crowds of pilgrims thronged into the Abbey some of the richer testaments of devotion were moved to the security of the chamber in the undercroft.

In the last year of Henry III's reign an inventory of his jewels and regalia in the Tower included four crowns, an imperial cap and five garlands of gold. Henry III wore the lily crown on state occasions, a type worn by the emperors of the east and the west—a crown heavy with the symbolism of the lily shapes around the circlet, representing the golden lilies which God had commanded Moses to place on the Tabernacle, or the trefoil ornament which Constantine had placed on his imperial diadem over the largest gem to represent the Trinity, or even the lily flower regarded as the emblem of the Blessed Virgin. Henry's Great Seal shows him wearing a crown over a barred helmet and holding an orb with

The Pyx Chamber of Westminster Abbey, once a royal treasury of Edward I (*DoE*)

a long floreated stem. One of his crowns had been made for his expedition to Brittany in 1230 when the Abbot and the nobles had refused to let the Crown of St Edward leave the kingdom—a tradition which has been maintained. In 1255 Henry acquired an imperial crown for his son Edmund Crouchback whom the Pope, in his investiture struggle with the Holy Roman emperors, wished to make King of Sicily. Henry had to abandon this foreign adventure in the face of the opposition of his nobles, and the crown of Frederick II which he had redeemed from pawn for his son disappeared into the royal jewel house.

With the overflowing of the treasures and relics in the under-croft, Henry decided to establish a new treasury in the Tower of London to hold his state crowns and regalia while leaving the earlier crowns and regalia, including those of St Edward, in the Abbey. The Abbey also remained a royal treasury keeping monies collected by the Exchequer of Receipt and the monthly quotas of coins brought from the Mint for assay, as well as the ecclesiastical treasures. Those monies were kept in large iron chests known as pyxes, from which the room took its name of the Chamber of the Pyx.

His son, Edward I, once the Crown of St Edward had been placed on his consecrated head, abandoned the regular crown-wearing ceremonies which had been held on the great feastdays since Saxon times. He declared that 'crowns do rather onerate than honour princes'. His dominant ambition was to bring the crown of Scotland and the princely coronet of Wales into subjection to his own crown, declaring that he would 'exact full rights for the Crown of St Edward' of which he was the guardian.

However, there was a time when he might have lost St Edward's Crown. Matthew of Westminster, who kept the chronicles of the Abbey, recorded for April 1303 that 'a most audacious robber secretly entered the Treasury of the King of England'. Richard Podelicote was a travelling salesman in English wool, butter and cheese who peddled his wares in Holland. In 1298 he was arrested for debt in Flanders, fined and imprisoned. Eventually he escaped and returned to England to seek redress from the King's Court in Westminster. A charitable monk gave him a meal in the Abbey refectory where he was able to observe the valuable plate on the Abbot's and Prior's tables. Here was relief for his financial embarrassments. Entering the Abbey by night through a window in the Chapter House, he reached the refectory and carried away six silver cups and thirty silver spoons. He lived for a merry month of August on the proceeds, but by Christmas he was penniless. He had noticed near the Chapter House the wall of the undercroft wherein lay treasure which could not be so speedily spent. His planning was thorough, his patience inexhaustible and his accomplices carefully chosen. They were John Shenche, the Keeper of the Palace of Westminster, his deputy William, Adam Warfield, the sacrist of the Abbey, the monk Alexander of Pershore and John Albon who made the tools.

Richard Podelicote himself undertook the job of breaking in. He chose the east wall of the Treasury in an angle formed with the Chapter House and screened by an outside wall. He began work eight days before Christmas and he chiselled away at the wall, night after night, with long listening pauses, with the patience of a man who was confidently expecting his reward. He finally broke through to the Treasure chamber on the night of 24 April 1303 and found himself surrounded by all the gold and silver plate, jewels and coinage of his dreams.

He was a cool as well as a patient man and he returned for several nights, selecting and placing the treasure in bags and panniers, first concealing them in the thick crop of hemp which had grown up alongside the cloisters and which the worthy sacrist had stopped the Abbey gardener from cutting; from there the treasure was rapidly dispersed to other hiding places. Two large black panniers were rowed across the river by Alexander of Pershore and hidden opposite Mill Bank. Another consignment was buried under the precinct gate wall behind the church of

St Margaret, yet another bag was hidden in a ditch by the Mews of Charing and some were even placed inside the Abbey tombs. Podelicote, the mastermind, carried away thousands of pounds worth of spoons, saucers, brooches, rings, girdles, jewels and even a crown.

Something aroused the suspicion of the Abbot who had the Treasure House opened. Before the staring eyes of the monks lay the scattered treasures of England, the tumbled regalia of St Edward—even the ring which the king had worn at his coronation. The Abbot and the monks began to quake in terror of the impending wrath.

A messenger, terrified by the news he had to bear, reached King Edward at Linlithgow where he was occupied in his life-long pursuit of trying to subdue the Scots. When the king learned that a great deal of the treasure and coinage he had amassed to continue his wars had disappeared through a hole in the wall, his rage was terrible. He heard the news on 6 June and the writs which sped to his officers in London bear the same date. Day after day, saddle-sore messengers raced southwards with more writs, injunctions, commands and upbraidings. Judges and chamberlains as well as the monks cowered before the fury blowing from the north. The high standing of the Abbots of Westminster, the bonds with the Crown, even the sanctuary of the cloisters were gone. The Abbot and the forty-eight monks were abruptly transported to the Tower of London where they were to remain for two long years. Jurors were appointed to carry out enquiries in every district of London; proclamations demanded that anyone with any information should come forward; persons who had been seen near the Abbey without known cause were taken in for questioning. The search for the king's treasure was the greatest 'criminal investigation' which had taken place up to that time.

There was, and there still is, a strange blind spot in criminal minds which makes them exult at success but neglect to conceal their exuberance. William of the Palace began to hold high revels in his house by the Fleet, where he and his friends remained drinking for two days. On the third night 'they went armed towards Westminster and did not return until the daybreak'; they had collected more booty. They went forth on the next night and then 'went no more to Westminster'. They held open house by the Fleet and their carousing aroused curiosity and suspicion.

There had also been revelry in the Palace of Westminster where John Shenche and some of the monks were joined by several ladies of opportunity. One woman, found later with a costly ring in her possession, said that Adam the sacrist had given it to her 'so that she should become his friend'.

When the proclamations were issued the fingers of suspicion were quickly pointed in the right direction. Within a few days, Podelicote, the Keeper of the Palace and his deputy, the sacrist, the monk, Alexander of Pershore, and John Albon, the craftsman, were all behind the thick walls of the Tower.

Those who escaped the round-up hurried to get rid of their share of the plunder. A fisherman on the Thames found in his net a silver goblet. Passers-by discovered pieces of valuable plate hidden under hedges. A linen-draper, who had received a pannier of treasure, gave it to a shepherd boy to hide in the fields of Kentish Town. This wealth had become too hot to hold and it turned up in all sorts of places. The loss to the king was finally of small proportions.

Podelicote, who was found with his share of the valuables, boldly confessed and refused to implicate anyone else. He was hanged with five others, including the roistering William of the Palace.

Edward I returned from Scotland. Pleased with his triumphs over the Scots, he was inclined to be tolerant to his own subjects. The Abbot and the remaining monks were released from the Tower, but the Abbot could never again walk with the same dignity and sense of security through his own cloisters. There was also a strange foreshadowing of Colonel Blood's attempt to steal the regalia of Charles II, when Edward I pardoned John Shenche and actually restored him to the Keepership.

But for the monks, as well as for the Abbot, things could never again be the same in the cloisters. A double door with huge iron nails was fixed to the Chamber of the Pyx. On their way to their dormitory each night the monks of Westminster carefully averted their eyes from that door. Fixed into place by the huge iron nails was the flayed skin of a human being. The same terrible lining was fixed to the three doors of the revestry next to the Pyx Chamber. There were still pieces of skin under those nails when Dean Stanley examined the doors 600 years later. The message to the monks had been clear—'Better to store up treasure in Heaven than to meddle with the King's treasure on earth'.

CHAPTER 6
CROWNS IN PAWN

Over the centuries the jewels in the English crowns have come and gone like the sparkling of frost on a May morning. They have been lost, purloined, plundered, pledged and been flaunted by more than one king's mistress.

The English kings came to regard their crown jewels as investments to be pawned or sold to promote their wars, or provide their luxuries, or more worthily, like Henry III, to rebuild the Great Abbey of Westminster.

The kings came to have several treasure chambers, or Jewel Houses. There was an upper and lower Jewel House in the Tower of London, with state crowns and regalia in the upper chamber and plate, art treasures, gold and silver bars on the lower level. There were also 'secret' Jewel Houses in the palaces of Westminster, Windsor and elsewhere where the rings and other jewellery required for the daily use by the kings and the queen consorts were kept. In 1365, Edward III felt that this part of the royal possessions would be more secure in a specially built Jewel House which was erected as a tower within the Palace of Westminster under the care of the King's Privy Wardrobe. The Chamber of the Pyx still held the coinage for assay, ecclesiastical treasures and the coronation crowns and regalia. The Jewel House at Westminster, like the Chamber of the Pyx, has survived to the present day, but very few of the jewels which flowed through the Jewel Houses have remained in the royal collections.

A constant call on the royal treasure was the courtesy requirements of the kingship. A foreign noble or prince arriving at the court would expect not only to be sumptuously entertained but also to depart with a royal benefaction suited to his rank and state. The king's embassies to foreign courts had not only to reflect in their persons the king's magnificence but to bear the tokens of his munificence. A noble returning to court would expect to receive the appropriate royal recognition of his presence. The kings of England kept the goldsmiths and silversmiths busy producing the plate and ornaments of royal liberality. There were times when the treasure trickled out of the Jewel Houses like golden sand.

It was their wars, however, which imposed the greatest burdens on the whole resources of the realm as well as on the royal Jewel Houses. Edward III was the first king of England to pawn his

Crowns of the Kings of England, showing evolution from helmet type to arched crown (*RTH*)

crown. The men, arms and ships he required for his wars in France were beyond the resources of the medieval economy and the crown jewels became important assets in the financing of the Hundred Years War. In 1346, the glorious year of Crecy, one of the crowns of Edward III was pawned to Tidman de Limbergh, a Flemish banker, in return for a large loan. A year later the state papers show that there had been a piece of pawnbroking trickery when the king issued a writ ordering one Paul de Monte Florum to return the gold crowns which had been pledged for loans the king had not received. The king was now on the slippery slope of debt. He pledged his Great Royal Crown to the Bishop of Trier for 45,000 florins, another crown for 5,000 florins and a small crown for 4,000 florins. Three years later he appointed commissioners to find ways and means of recovering the Great Royal Crown he had pawned.

The rich loot from the fair provinces of France may have replenished the royal treasury for a time and added temporary adornments to a new crown. The treasure trickled away, however, on military expeditions as his successors pursued the wars in France, pawning their crowns and jewels to pay the costs.

Edward's son, Richard II, also placed the crown jewels in pawn. After the revolt against his efforts to raise money by the poll tax, he turned to the City of London in 1380 and pledged his Great Crown for a large loan. Two years later he parted with the crown of his grandfather to Matthew Cheyne, a Lombard banker, for another loan. In the end Richard went crownless and shiftless to his death.

During 'the scrambling and unquiet time', as Shakespeare described the reign of Henry IV, the Great Crown passed into the keeping of the Mayor and Commonalty of London as security for a loan of £4,000.

The great English victory at Agincourt in 1415 was financed by Henry V pawning his crown and his royal ornaments; even the crown by which his son Henry VI was crowned King of France seems to have been released from pawn for that purpose. In the desperate attempt to prop the declining fortunes of the war in France this king issued an urgent order to the officers of the Exchequer to sell or pawn all the crown jewels at once.

The resplendent Henry VIII also had his own moments of financial stress during the outbreak of the Pilgrimage of Grace when he ordered Thomas Cromwell to sell some of the treasures in the Jewel House; these may have included some of the gems from his crown. His daughter, the first Elizabeth, with her treasury full of Spanish gold and jewels, had made a new, beautiful but odd-shaped crown. She kept her crown jewels intact and indulged her passion for pearls of every size while keeping a thrifty eye on other expenditure. One of her officers wrote: 'She made no will, nor gave anything away: so that they which come after shall find a well furnished Jewel House.'

James I, after his deprived and impoverished youth as James VI of Scotland, gazed on the treasures of England with delight. At first he added to the treasures since he, also, had a passion for jewels and personal adornments. Within four years of his 'blessed coming to this Crowne' he had spent over £92,000 on plate and jewels—an enormous sum for that time.

In 1611 he dismissed his first Parliament and had to look elsewhere for money. His great pleasure was to go on royal progress around his realm with a large and sumptuous escort. Elizabeth had, more shrewdly, bankrupted her subjects by imposing on them the hospitality for herself and her court: James was bankrupting himself by the expenditure on his profligate entourage. He recovered some of the costs by the sale of some of the queen's jewels. This was followed by the sale of sets of gold and silver plate 'towards the Supply of our Occasions'. Finally, he turned a speculative gaze on the crown jewels.

With the caution of a Scot, James decided not to act until he was sure of the precedents and he invited Sir James Cotton to search the state papers for the precedents for the sale of the crown jewels. Sir James Cotton's research disclosed some of the occasions on which the kings of England had pledged their crowns. James never could make up his mind to part with his own crown, but there were, none the less, benefits for posterity. The great collection of state documents, chronicles, registers, charters and other records made by Sir James Cotton, now in the MSS collection of the British Library, have shed light on many aspects of English history.

When James's son, Charles I, began his protracted struggle with Parliament he did not delay for any precedents when his needs became desperate. He did move, however, with caution. Parliamentarians had now begun to say that the crown jewels were vested in the king only in his public and politic, and not in his private capacity. Sir Edward Coke, the great jurist, Speaker of the later Parliaments of Elizabeth, and Chief Justice of the King's Bench, held that 'the ancient jewels of the Crowne are heirlooms

James VI of Scotland, I of England. His love of dress and ceremony is reflected in this portrait dated 1610. He is wearing the Collar and George of the Order of the Garter. School of Marcus Gheeraerts the younger, now attributed to J. de Critz (*National Maritime Museum*)

and shall descend to the next successor'. Because of these doubts Charles had difficulty in selling the royal treasures in England where the purchaser might be challenged on the grounds that the valuables were the inalienable possessions of the Crown and might not pass even for a time into the possession of a subject. Charles simply circumvented the risk by exporting the royal treasures abroad. They included many of the great masterpieces of the goldsmiths' art, such as the famous 'Dream of Paris'; 'a great rich jewel of Goulde called the Mirror of Great Britain', and a mysterious stone which probably had belonged to his father called 'the stone of the lettre H of Scotland'. They were sold in Amsterdam for a fraction of their true values. When Charles I rode away from London for the last time he left behind an almost empty Jewel House, but the State Crown and the regalia in the Tower were intact. He also left for the future inheritance of his successors the great collection of paintings by the masters of his time.

Through all these pawnbroking affairs of the English kings, the Abbots of Westminster and their successors, the Dean and Chapter, had stubbornly held in tight ecclesiastical custody the coronation crowns, sceptres and regalia of the realm.

CHAPTER 7
THE DESTRUCTION OF THE REGALIA

The symbolism of the royal regalia was anathema to the Puritans. When Charles I, after his humiliating failure to arrest the Five Members, rode away from his capital on 10 February 1642, he left his palaces, the royal treasures and his crowns and sceptres in the hands of the Parliament.

Soon reports were reaching London that the king was peddling his crown jewels in Holland. The reports raised a great show of indignation. In June 1642 both Houses of Parliament declared that 'the king, seduced by wicked counsel, doth intend to levy war against his Parliament' and 'that the Jewels of the Crown (which by the law of the land ought not to be alienated) are either pawned or sold in Amsterdam'. The Order went on to declare all traffickers in the crown jewels to be enemies of the State.

Two letters were also read to members giving accounts of the attempts to pawn a great collar of rubies, some enormous diamonds and other royal treasures. The Order and the letters were printed and distributed to incense public opinion against the king. There were some elements of truth in the reports. The Queen had parted with Charles at Dover on the 23 February and sailed on *HMS Victory* for Holland, where she tried to raise money by selling her personal jewellery and possibly also certain gems of Queen Elizabeth which James I had declared should remain for ever the unalienable property of the Crown.

Parliament could not have had any real anxiety, however, about the royal regalia and plate in the Tower of London. Sir Henry Mildmay, the Keeper of the Jewel House, had 'defected to Parliament' while leaving most of the duties and all of the hazards of the post to his nephew, Carew Mildmay. He was of tougher fibre than his uncle.

Another year was to pass, full of the bitterness and struggle of the Civil War, before Parliament returned again to the subject of the crown jewels. This time the gaze of Pym and his associates was firmly focussed on the ancient regalia in the Abbey of Westminster. They had strong suspicions that the coronation crowns and sceptres were no longer where they should have been. It was widely believed that the Dean of Westminster, the eccentric royalist who had been appointed Archbishop of York, had taken regalia with him on his hasty departure for his northern see.

When the Sub-Dean and prebends of the Abbey, faithful to

their ancient trust, refused to open the door, with its six locks, of the Chamber of the Pyx, the full authority of Parliament was sought by a motion introduced on 2 June 1643, enjoining and requiring them to deliver up the keys of the Treasury where the regalia was kept. Even in that depleted House of Commons there was a reluctance to override the ancient rights of the Abbey, and the motion was lost by 37 votes to 58.

The pressures were applied and a new motion was introduced to the House. This time it provided for an inventory to be taken to remove the suspicions which had been aroused. This motion was passed by the slender margin of a solitary vote—by 42 votes to 41. It was resolved:

> That the Locks on the Doors where the Regalia are kept, in Westminster Abbey, shall be opened, not withstanding any former Order made, and Search made there: and an Inventory taken of what things are . . . and presented to the House: and new Locks set upon the Doors.

The order was enforced without conscience, respect or dignity by Henry Martin, the future regicide, and George Withers, a poet without sensitivity. Peter Heylyn, who after the Restoration became Sub-Dean and Treasurer of the Abbey, described the macabre scene when they forced open the great iron chest and piled on a table the crowns robes and sceptres, 'belonging anciently to King Edward the Confessor and used by all our kings at their inaugurations'. They made great fun with the crowns and the coronation robes of long dead English kings and queens. Martin dressed Withers in the royal robes and St Edward's Crown, 'who, thus crowned and royally arrayed, marched about the room with stately garb and afterwards with a Thousand Apish and Ridiculous Actions exposed these sacred ornaments to contempt and laughter'.

We shall never know which objects provided such amusement in the vaulted Chamber of the Pyx on that day. The crown of the Confessor had been among the treasures of the Abbey as well as his staff, his ring and the vestments taken from his body on its translation to its new shrine.

That old chest may also have held the regal ornaments of some of our Saxon kings. The coronation robes of Wiglaf, King of

Scottish Regalia: the Arms of Pope Julius II enamelled on the Scabbard of the Sword of State. The cartouche holds the oak tree and acorns of the Pope's family arms and above are the Crossed Keys of St Peter and the triple tiara crown of the Papacy. The Sword was presented by the Pope to James IV in 1507

Mercia in the ninth century, was one example of the many royal treasures which had been entrusted to the Abbey; that chest may have held the greatest of all the royal treasures—the crown of King Alfred the Great.

Parliament ordered all the regalia found in the Abbey to be transferred to the Jewel House in the Tower of London, where it was to remain while the Civil War continued.

Parliament and the commanders of its forces grew desperate for money to keep their forces in the field. An appeal for money and plate had produced a temporary relief by what Clarendon contemptuously called 'a multitude of seditious offerings'. By September 1644 the military leaders were warning of the state of their troops 'whose bare feet and hollow cheeks plead eloquently for pay and sustenance'. There were many desertions and some troops, contrary to the pictures of God-fearing Roundheads, were pillaging and terrorising the countryside. On 4 October a motion was passed by the House of Commons to melt down and convert into coinage all the remaining gilt and silver plate in the Tower. The House of Lords immediately raised objections, which showed their strong sense of traditional values, declaring that they could not consent to the passing of the ordinance for disposing of the King's Plate 'for that Plate is ancient Plate: The Fashion of it and the Badges upon it, more worth than the Plate itself: And the Particular Affection set upon that Plate could make it of ill consequence if it be disposed of: though Necessity be the Motive.' They were significant but unheeded words. The Commons sent 13,000 ounces of the plate in the Tower to the melting pots. The plea that an object could be worth more than its materials and that long historic associations have their intangible valuations was also ignored when the Puritans again turned their attentions 'to those detestable emblems of kings, their crowns, sceptres and heathenish ornaments'.

When, on 30 January 1649, they had executed King Charles they turned to dispose of his crown. They appointed trustees and contractors who were to receive the regalia and 'cause the same to be TOTALLY BROKEN and that they melt down all the gold and silver and sell all the jewels to the best advantage of the Commonwealth.'

The trustees had unexpected difficulties in getting their hands on the royal treasures since their orders were returned marked

Queen Elizabeth I: the earrings may be the pearls now in the Imperial State Crown (*National Portrait Gallery*)

'not obeyed'. It was a brief, futile but heroic act of resistance by
the Clerk of the Jewel House, Carew Mildmay, while his uncle,
Sir Henry, was again conveniently absent. He was swiftly committed to the Fleet prison.

An inventory was published of all the regalia in the Tower,
including that taken from Westminster Abbey, together 'with an
appraisement of their value. During the 300 years since that inventory was made generations of historians, antiquarians and other
experts have tried to resolve all the enigmas which it contains.

Their attention in particular has been directed to the item in
the inventory which refers to 'King Alfred's Crowne of goulde
wyerworke sett with slight stones and two little bells. 79½ Ounces
at 3 li per Ounce . . . £248'. Had this indeed been the crown of
King Alfred the Great? There is some evidence which points to
that possibility.

Robert of Gloucester in 1250, describing the meeting between
Alfred and Pope Leo IV, wrote: 'The Pope blessed him and the
king's crown of this land, which is in this land yet'. Later still Sir
Richard Spelman, the antiquary, in his life of Alfred written in
the seventeenth century, wrote: 'In the arched room in the
cloisters of Westminster Abbey where the ancient Regalia of this
Kingdom are kept, upon a box which is the cabinet of the antients
crown, there is (I am informed) an inscription to this purpose:
*Haec est principalior corona cum qua coronabantur reges Aelfredus et
Edwardus* . . .'. He described the crown as of 'very ancient work
with flowers adorned with stones of somewhat plain setting'.

This reference and description could correspond to the inventory's 'Crowne of goulde wyerworke sett with slight stones'
since its purpose was to record metal and gem values and they
would not waste time on describing such artistic embellishments
as the shaping of the 'wyerworke' to floral decorations.

The description fits what we know of the crowns of the Saxon
kings. Their crowns were copied from the styles of the Byzantine
emperors who wore the *stemma*, a simple circle of gold with a
double row of pearls between which were set a row of precious
stones. The 'little bells' could approximate to the string of pearls
or other ornaments, the *castaseistae*, which were also suspended
from the Byzantine crown.

The illustrations of the crowns on the Anglo-Saxon coins, when
compared with the *stemma* of the emperors, show the close degree
of approximation. There is, therefore, a strong possibility that the
Crown of Alfred the Great was among the regalia in the Abbey,
that it was worn by his successors including Edward the Confessor
and that because of the great reverence for the Confessor it was

buried with him in his tomb in Westminster Abbey. When the
tomb was opened by Henry II it was assumed that the crown had
belonged to him; it was added to the regalia and has been used
in the name of St Edward's Crown as the coronation crown of
England. It could, therefore, have been a priceless legacy from
our Saxon past. It was valued at £248.

Other inventories had been made of the regalia over the
centuries, principally in 1203, 1357, 1532 and 1605. Comparison
of the inventory of 1649 with the old records provides some clues
to the identification of the other items.

The 'Queen's Crown of massy gold', enriched with twenty
sapphires and twenty-two rubies was almost certainly the crown
from the Jewel House which had been made for the coronation of
Henrietta Maria, the consort of Charles I. It was valued at £338.
By contrast, we have what is described as 'Queen Edith's Crowne
formerly thought to be of massy gould but upon trial found to be
of silver gilt enriched with Garnetts foule pearle Sapphires and
some odd stones' valued at a mere £16. Queen Edith was the wife
of the Confessor and her name had been given to the coronation
crown of the consorts of the English kings. The description is that
of a queen's crown before the Tudors began to lavish gems and
gold on their regal emblems. An early queen of England had worn
it on her day of splendour or it would not have been among the
regalia in the Abbey.

The 'small crowne found in an iron chest' has been identified
as the crown worn by the young King, Edward VI, at his coronation on 20 February 1547. The 'staff of black and white ivory
with the dove' is the traditional form of the sceptre given to a
queen consort at her coronation. The absence of elaborate
decoration and its trivial value of £4 suggests that it was of some
antiquity. 'The large staff with a dove on top' was evidently the
long rod known as St Edward's Staff; in the Bayeaux Tapestry
St Edward is shown with a long staff shod with a ferrule. This
staff was carried by the sovereigns, or was borne before them, as
they passed down the centre aisle of the Abbey to their coronation.

The most trivial valuations were placed on the robes found in
the old chest in the Abbey. 'One livor cullered silke robe' was
described as 'very old and worth nothing'. These 'worthless'
robes were the coronation vestments of the early kings of England
and may indeed have included those of the Confessor.

There was a sad and neglected item in this part of the inventory—'one old combe of horne, worth nothing'. It was
undoubtedly the comb used to arrange the king's hair after the

oil of the anointing. This insignificant object could only have kept its place among the regalia by reason of its sacred and historical associations—which suggests that it could have been the comb which had smoothed the hair of the Confessor after his coronation. Charles I, when he sat down in the Chair of Estate at his coronation, may have felt some foreboding of its fate when 'he called for the comb that he might see it'.

The trustees and contractors made careful preparations for the sale of the disposable items other than the gold and silver which was consigned to the melting pots of the Mint. The jewels, the glass, crystals, ivory and other objects were put on display to buyers in the hall of Somerset House. The trustees insisted that 'there must be some days for the buyers to look upon them'.

The more I enquire into the arrangements for this sale, contrary to what some of the Keepers of the Jewel House and others have written, including myself, I am now convinced that the public sale was honestly and properly conducted. There may have been some unauthorised dealing by Mildmay and others, but this does not seem to have happened under the trustees. The valuations appear trivial until we recall that they were sober assessments of the materials, taking no account of any sentiment or historical associations. One speculator, Phillip Lavender, put in a bid of £307 for the sapphires from the Imperial Crown, the offering price, but on closer inspection he must have thought the jewels inferior and he paid a forfeit of £76 to be released from his bid.

The destruction and the sale of the regalia remains, however, an act of vandalism of historic proportions. The sale value of the ancient regalia in the custody of the Abbey was £612.17.8d. For this trivial sum we have lost the crowns and sceptres, the royal ornaments, robes and treasures of the English and possibly also our Saxon kings.

Fortunately, not everything was lost. The public sale provided the opportunity for royalist sympathisers to purchase jewels and other pieces of the regalia. The inventory referred to 'a silver spoon gilt'. This was purchased by a Mr Kinnersley for sixteen shillings at a weight of 3 ounces; this is exactly the weight of the Anointing Spoon which reappeared in 1661 and was used at the coronation of Queen Elizabeth II. The Black Prince's Ruby, Queen Elizabeth's Earrings and St Edward's Sapphire also appeared after the restoration of Charles II and again took their place in the new Imperial Crown.

There is indeed the prospect that more than the jewels and the spoon may have survived. General Sitwell, when he was Keeper of the Jewel House, made exhaustive enquiries into the fate of

'King Alfred's Crown'. It had been recorded as 'delivered to the Mint' but he could find no evidence that it had reached the melting pots. The 1649 inventory gave this crown a weight of 79½ ounces. When the new regalia was prepared for the coronation of Charles II, the Crown of St Edward was shown first on the list of the costs incurred, but there was not any charge in the column opposite the entry, merely a flourish of the pen. On the other hand the cost of the new Imperial Crown was shown as nearly £8,000. The old crown in the inventory weighed 79½ ounces, the new crown of St Edward weighed 82½ ounces and significantly no charge was made for it. Was the new St Edward's Crown made from the frame of the much older one? It may be that behind the present crown of St Edward is the shadow of the 'wyerworke' frame of the diadem of that far-off king 'who came from Athelney to wear the English crown'.

There is speculation that the crown was saved for the head of the Lord Protector himself. Soon after the execution of Charles I the pamphleteers were referring to 'a coffin for the King and a crown for Cromwell'. The idea was often pressed upon him by the army officers. Edmund Waller put the suggestion boldly in rhyme after the seizure of the Spanish treasure fleet.

> Let the rich ore forewith be melted down
> And the state fixed by making him a crown
> With ermine clad and purple, let him hold
> A royal sceptre, made of Spanish gold.

In February 1657 a Humble Address of Parliament urged Cromwell to assume the monarchy, the Speaker commending to him the 'Title and Office of a King in this nation: as that a King first settled Christianity in this island: that it hath been long received and approved by our ancestors, who by long experience found it to be consistent with their liberties, most agreeable to their constitution and to the temper of the people.' One member urged him to accept because 'the law knows no Protector but above all loves a monarchy'—strange words from those who eight years before had thought they were sending both the monarch and the monarchy into oblivion.

Cromwell declined the crown, but was installed as Lord Protector in royal state with most of the symbols of sovereignty except the actual crown. For the first time the Coronation Chair was taken out of the Abbey to the ceremony in Westminster Hall where the kings had once been raised to their royal dignity. The Garter King of Arms and the Heralds went before him, the great

Sword of State, symbol of the royal authority, was borne on high, he was clad in the royal purple and given the royal sceptre. Eventually after his death even the crown itself appeared at the formal lying in State in Somerset House. As was the case with all Royal lyings in state, Cromwell was represented by his effigy in royal garb and the royal crown was placed on a golden chair beside it so that 'all the people could see'.

There was one man close to the Lord Protector, who would have his own secret motives for preserving an ancient crown. The Keeper of the Wardrobe during the period of the Commonwealth bore the significant name of Kinnersley—which was also the name of the man who bought the Spoon and possibly some of the other jewels. After the Restoration of Charles II he emerged as a papist and royalist.

When Charles II came into his own again, a committee was formed to direct the remaking of the regalia for his coronation. They had, wrote the then Garter King of Arms, to 'settle the form

Effigy of Cromwell at his lying-in-state in 1658. The Royal Crown is on the chair behind his head (*RTH*)

and fashion of each particular; and of which do now retain the old names and fashion, altho' they have been newly made'. A new Keeper of the Jewel House, Sir Gilbert Talbot, was ordered to provide: 'Two Imperial Crowns set with precious stones, one with which the King was to be crowned, to be called St Edward's Crown and the other to be put on after his Coronation'. The other traditional items of a king's inauguration included the Orb, the Sceptre with the Cross, the Sceptre with the Dove, St Edward's Staff, a Ring with a Ruby, a pair of Golden Spurs, two ingots of Gold for the Oblation and the Spoon and an Ampulla for the Oil.

The Ampulla, a small survivor, is the small eagle-shaped vessel which holds the oil for the Anointing which is dripped from its beak on to the Spoon. It had not been kept with the regalia in the Chamber of the Pyx, but had been with the ecclesiastical plate of the Abbey and so escaped destruction. Sir Robert Vyner, the king's goldsmith who provided the new royal ornaments, added new gold work on its base and wings, but the neck and body were already ancient in the days of Charles II. This Ampulla was possibly the 'egle' which was used at the coronation of Henry IV in 1399. It was resting on the altar in Westminster Abbey on the morning when Elizabeth II came to her own Coronation.

CHAPTER 8
'IT WAS FOR A CROWN'

Not long after their restoration the regalia were again in peril. In May 1671 Colonel Blood made his notorious attempt to steal the Crown Jewels.

The career of this desperate adventurer runs ahead of the wildest inventions. His courage was beyond question and his loyalty to his associates as fanatical as his unrelenting pursuit of his enemies. He moved dangerously through the obscure and often violent aftermath of the Civil War.

He was born in Ireland in 1618 and, as a young man, joined the Parliamentary forces in that country. He was noticed, promoted, made a Justice of the Peace and given an estate for his services to the Commonwealth. The Restoration brought ruin and the loss of his estate. He joined the ranks of embittered and desperate men.

Blood planned an insurrection. He aimed to capture Dublin Castle and hold the Lord Lieutenant, the Duke of Ormonde, until the forfeited lands were restored. It is an indication of the extent of desperation around Dublin that over a hundred men were soon enlisted for this audacious attempt—one of them, Philip Arden, took an early reward by betraying the plot to the Duke of Ormonde. Blood also had his own agent who warned him that the plot had been revealed. This fact did not deter Blood; once he had set his hand to an enterprise he never turned back. He brought forward the attempt from 10 March 1663 to five days earlier.

The plan was simple: several of them would enter the castle as petitioners while eighty would wait outside posing as workmen busy around the Castle. A pretended baker would stumble in front of the entrance guards spilling his loaves on the ground. The guards would be seized as they helped to pick up the bread. Ormonde acted, however, before the yeast could rise: the conspirators were rounded up. Blood was one of the few who escaped.

Blood's brother-in-law, Lackie, was among those captured and executed. Blood made a gallant but unsuccessful attempt to save his relative. The ruling passion of Blood's life became vengance on the Duke of Ormonde.

A large reward was offered for Blood's capture, but he took pleasure in avoiding his pursuers until he crossed to Holland where he joined other discontented exiles. It is said that this time he 'obtained the countenance of Admiral de Ruyter', and may have been enlisted into the undercover world of the secret agent; in that guise he returned to England where he joined the ranks of the Fifth Monarchy men.

The Fifth Monarchy were fanatics working ceaselessly to ensure 'the overthrow of the Kingdom of Rome and its replacement by the Kingdom of Christ'. They held that any means were justified which would hasten the Millennium. They had agitated for the execution of Charles I and became later so troublesome that many of them were imprisoned by Cromwell. At the Restoration they had disappeared into secret coteries to emerge with apocolyptic prophecies of the coming Millennium. They were suspected of plotting against the life of the king and a vigilant watch was kept on them. Blood may have had only one purpose in associating with these strange fanatics—to act as the double agent of the British and possibly of the Dutch government which was interested in fomenting discontent in England. He rose rapidly in their coteries to preside at the court-martials which sentenced their 'traitors'.

We next hear of him in Scotland, where he had joined the ranks of the Covenanters. Scotland was a land disturbed by religious discontents and the rejoicing at the King's restoration had turned to bitterness and anger. The Act Recissory had annulled all legislation passed since 1633, the episcopal system had been brought back, and no minister of religion who had not been collated by a bishop could retain his living. Thousands of dispossessed ministers went out on to the moors and hillsides to hold their 'conventicles'. The Privy Council of Scotland recruited a large number of secret informers, including the 'King's curates' who had been placed in the forfeited livings. In November 1666 the Galloway covenantors rose, marched on Edinburgh and were routed in a hopeless action at Rullion Green. Blood left Scotland immediately afterwards.

His next exploit was to rescue his friend, Captain Mason, who was being sent to the York assizes with an escort of eight troopers. Blood with three companions ambushed the escort at Doncaster, killed seven of the troopers and carried away his friend. He had been badly wounded, however, and had to lie hidden until he recovered, with yet another reward of five hundred pounds on his head. He recuperated at Rumford in Kent in the role of a medical practitioner retired by his wounds from military service.

While he was in Kent he had news of his old enemy, the Duke of Ormonde, and the old hatred stirred again. He never lacked followers, and five companions joined him in his second attempt to capture the Duke.

Once again Blood was acting on inside information. In November 1670 the young Prince of Orange on a State visit was entertained at a banquet in the City of London at which the Duke of Ormonde would be a guest. Afterwards the Duke returned by coach to his residence at Clarendon House. London was then a precarious place for citizens after midnight and the Duke had six walking footmen in attendance on his coach. In some mysterious way the footmen were diverted from their duties; Blood and his companions leaped out of the darkness and dragged the Duke from the coach, while a pistol was held at the coachman's head. The Duke was then forcibly mounted on a horse and buckled by straps to its rider. Blood, seeing him secured, rode off to prepare the gallows at Tyburn where it was his intention to hang the Duke as a common felon. In the meantime, two of the footmen hastily came up and one of them promptly jumped on the horse and pulled the Duke and his assailant, still buckled together, to the ground. Before the attackers fled they fired a shot at the Duke which missed its mark in the dark. Once again, Blood went into hiding with this time a price of one thousand pounds on his head.

Was this episode a frustrated act of vengeance? Revenge was a motive, but in the complex life of Blood nothing was straightforward. There seemed to have been strange links between Blood and Buckingham. An enemy of Blood, the government spy, William Levings, had been poisoned in York prison at a time when Buckingham resided in the city as the Lord Lieutenant of Yorkshire. Shortly afterwards Buckingham was arrested on a charge of corresponding with sectaries and dissidents, a charge strangely reminiscent of Blood's own association with the Fifth Monarchy men. With the knowledge that Buckingham was a bitter enemy of the Duke of Ormonde, the inference grows strong indeed. Certainly Ormonde's own son, Lord Ossory, believed in their complicity. He confronted Buckingham who had been restored to favour at court, saying: 'My Lord, I know well you are at the bottom of this late attempt of Blood's upon my father'.

Within the year Blood was back in London preparing for the most daring attempt on the Crown Jewels which has ever been undertaken.

The new Jewel House had been built in the Martin Tower at the north-east corner of the Inner Ward of the Tower of London. Sir Gilbert Talbot, Keeper of the Jewel House had placed an old servant, Talbot Edwards, then 77 years old, in charge of the regalia. Edwards did not get any wages; Sir Gilbert later said that the king, to spare his own Treasury, had agreed that Edwards 'doth tacitly shew the regalia to strangers, which furnisheth him with so plentiful a livelihood'. The regalia was displayed in cupboards along one side of the room and visitors were even allowed to handle the crown and sceptres.

In April 1671, a benevolent clergyman and his wife knocked on the door of the Martin Tower and asked to see the Crown Jewels of England. Talbot Edwards was eager to oblige. Unfortunately, the clergyman's wife became indisposed and was invited to recover in Edwards' lodging above the Jewel House. The grateful clergyman returned the next day with four pairs of white gloves for Mrs Edwards.

The path of cordiality was garnished with further presents and flattery. The clergyman dined with the Edwards family, 'taking upon himself to say grace, performed with great seeming devotion, he concluded it with a prayer for the King, the queen and the royal family'. The king's jewels he obviously felt were past praying for. The clergyman mentioned that he had a nephew with an income of £300 a year, of about the same age as Edwards' pretty young daughter. The prospects of a marriage suddenly blossomed and it was arranged that uncle and nephew would return at 7 o'clock on 9 May.

Blood arrived with three companions, Thomas Hunt, Parrot and Hallowell. Hunt, posing as the nephew, was asked to wait at the door until the young lady could properly receive him. Blood suggested his relatives would like the favour of seeing the Crown Jewels. Inside the room all pretence vanished; Edwards was seized, a wooden plug was thrust into his mouth and an 'iron hook was fastened to his nose so that no sound might pass from that quarter'. The old man struggled until he was stabbed in the stomach and beaten over the head with a mallet.

Parrot stuffed the orb down his breeches, Hallowell began to file through the sceptre to shorten it and Blood battered the crown with a mallet to hide it inconspicuously under his cloak. Their plans were abruptly shattered by the unexpected arrival of the Edwards' son, on leave from the English army in Flanders. Hunt at the door had to let him enter before rushing to warn the others. Blood thrust the battered crown under his cloak and fled with his companions. The old man got rid of his gag and shouted 'Treason!' 'Murder! The Crown is stolen'. His son rushed out shouting the alarm. The Yeoman Warder at the gate tried to stop them with his halberd until Blood fired his pistol. Then they were out of the Tower running along Tower Wharf to St Katharine's Gate where their horses were tethered. As they reached for the saddles they were overtaken; Parrot was seized by two Yeomen; Blood struggled with a Captain Beckman, dropping the crown, the agile Hunt reached his saddle but rode into a projecting cart pole and only Hallowell escaped. Blood declared arrogantly as he was led away: 'It was for a crown', a remark which was later to be given many interpretations.

What happened next must strain credulity. Blood was brought before Sir Gilbert Talbot, Keeper of the Jewel House, and other officers of the Tower. Blood refused to answer any questions, boldly demanding to be taken to the King—a strange demand for a captured felon and unlikely to be granted in the ordinary run of events. But this was not an ordinary event. The improbable occurred. On 12 May, on the personal order of Charles II, Blood was taken to Whitehall and questioned by the king, the Duke of York and other officers of the household. No records of these interviews have been found. Rumour alone has supplied the deficiency. Blood, it was said, had boldly confessed to his years of crime and his attempts on the Duke of Ormonde, but he had refused to implicate any of his associates. He had even confessed that he had planned to shoot the king when bathing at Battersea but had abandoned the attempt 'in awe of majesty'. He was ready to pay the price for his crimes; his great anxiety was, however, that his scores of associates might avenge his death.

Charles II, unlike his grandfather, James I, was nobody's fool and his personal courage was beyond dispute; he would not be impressed by plausibility or overawed by threats to his life. Was Charles, a connoiseur of human failings, so cynically amused by this villain that he decided to spare him? Did he decide to accept Blood's offer to serve the Crown and get a valuable contact with the plots and plans of the dissident and dissaffected? Was the sinister figure of Buckingham at his elbow, conniving, explaining, exculpating? We can only guess at the explanation.

I think improbable the imputation, made then and since often repeated, that Charles had been involved in the theft of his own Crown Jewels. Charles was cynical and dissolute but not dishonourable. The proceeds of the Crown Jewels would not have amounted to much in the royal pocket after they were shared with unscrupulous villains. The new regalia had cost £12,184, but nearly £20,000 had been spent on plate to be kept in the Jewel House; most of this plate, a more realisable asset, was still there and could have been sold by the king. Furthermore, at the time, Charles had the prospect of a vast increase in his income under the secret Treaty of Dover with Louis of France, which promised him £200,000 a year for the support of the English fleet. Charles must have feared disaffection since the treaty promised him the support of 6,000 French troops in the event of an insurrection in

The Crown Jewels c 1870 (*RTH*)

England. In Colonel Blood he had a bold villain, already known to the king's officers in England and in Scotland as a reliable undercover agent with a nose to smell out disaffection. That the king spared him to use him is the most likely explanation.

In the event Blood and his associates were pardoned. Blood was given the generous pension of £500 a year and his forfeited estates in Ireland were restored. When this became known the whispers of rumour became a roar of speculation.

Blood was often seen at court in the king's presence chamber. His career presents its final enigma in 1680. Blood quarrelled with Buckingham whom he accused of a 'notorious crime' which was never specified in the proceedings taken in the King's Bench for damages of £10,000 by the slandered Duke. Blood was released on bail and returned to his house in Bowling Alley, Westminster. The years of reckless bravado and hard living had taken their toll. We are told that he fell into a lethargy and passed away on 24 August 1680, 'not fearing death'. He took many enigmas to his grave.

The King's generosity did not extend to the humble old man who had been desperately wounded in the struggle to save the Crown Jewels. After long and desperate pleadings Talbot Edwards was awarded £200, but had to wait so long for the money that he had to pledge the future payment for half the promised amount. The raffish Earl of Rochester wrote this sardonic comment on these events:

> Blood that wears treason in his face,
> Villain complete in parson's gown,
> How much he is at Court in grace,
> For stealing Ormonde and the Crown.
> Since loyalty does no good
> Let's steal the King and outdo Blood.

Afterwards the security of the Tower was tightened by the posting of a company of foot guards who, on rotation, still provide the armed guards today. The public display of the Crown Jewels was also stopped for about thirty years. When the public was again admitted things eventually became as bad as ever. William Hutton in 1785 wrote an account of entering a hole like a condemned cell lit by three tapers and escorted by a yeoman warder. A woman with a voice like a fairground showman proclaimed that the Crown Jewels were worth £6 million pounds. Hutton was glad to leave.

The Jewel House came under the supervision of the Lord Chamberlain but the Treasury persistently refused to spend any money, even for cleaning the jewels, except before a coronation. After the lavish coronation of George IV, and especially after the coronation of Victoria, papers like *The Times* published engaging pictures of the young queen wearing her crown and there was a great surge of interest in the Jewel House. The Treasury now saw a return for expenditure and the accommodation and display were greatly improved.

The Treasury almost wasted their money. On the night of 30 October 1841 the Crown Jewels were again in peril when a great fire destroyed the Armoury and threatened to engulf the White Tower and St Peter's Chapel. The wind then veered sweeping the flames towards the Martin Tower. The keys of the jewel cage were locked up in the Lord Chamberlain's office so crowbars were brought and the bars forced apart until Superintendent Pierce was able to squeeze inside and hand out the regalia and other treasures. They were carried across Tower Green to the Governor's house and *Punch* later carpingly complained that the 'Crown and Regalia were jolted with much injurious activity'. The courageous policeman, like Talbot Edwards, was overlooked by the authorities.

In 1869, the Crown Jewels were moved to new accommodation in the Wakefield Tower. Their display was improved, as were the security arrangements, which were upgraded from time to time with the growth of technical resources. In 1937, the Keeper, General Sir George Younghusband, remarked that anyone trying to emulate Blood would be guillotined or electrocuted!

During the First World War the German daylight raids made the Tower a prime target and, after four near misses, the Regalia and the other treasures were removed to the deeper security of Windsor Castle. The same precautions were taken for their security during the Second World War when the Tower was in the centre of a heavily bombed area of London.

After the war, Britain and the world became footfree again and a large number of those feet were finding their way into the ever growing queue outside the Jewel House. Within the foreseeable future over a million people each year would come to see the Crown Jewels. The ministry with responsibility for the care of historic buildings began to make plans for a new Jewel House in consultation with the Palace and the Lord Chamberlain's Office. In 1967, the Crown Jewels were moved to the best accommodation which has yet been provided for them, in the Tower of London. The most priceless and historic collection of jewels in the world can be viewed from only a few feet away, yet they are in one of the safest places in the world.

CHAPTER 9
THE JEWELS IN THE CROWNS

The great jewels of the world have often been the loadstones of violence and tragedy. The jewels in the English crowns have attracted their own strange and eventful histories.

THE BLACK PRINCE'S RUBY

This is a Balas ruby, the old name for a red spinel when stones were mainly classified by their colours. The word 'balas' was possibly derived from Balacia, the old capital of Badakstan in Afghanistan whence these stones were exported to Europe during the Middle Ages.

The stone has the appearance of being of Eastern origin; the size of a small hen's egg, it had been pierced at one end so that it could be worn as a pendant or on an Eastern turban. It has an ancient gold setting on its back which the Crown jewellers have left in place in case the stone should break up.

This red spinel was obtained by the Black Prince from Don Pedro of Castile during a bloodstained episode in the life of the proudly arrogant son of Edward III.

Don Pedro had been driven out of his kingdom of Castile by his half-brother, Don Henry, in 1362. Don Pedro was ugly, perverted and cruel to the point of insanity. He killed without regard even to the consequences for his own fortunes. He had murdered his wife, Blanche of Bourbon, sister of the Queen of France, within a year of the marriage, and on the smallest pretexts had assassinated his own friends and supporters. Even the Spaniards, experts with the swift dagger, called him Pedro the Cruel. This bloodthirsty refugee from Castile appealed to the Black Prince for assistance to regain his throne.

Don Pedro arrived full of lavish promises at the Prince's headquarters at Bordeaux: the costs of the expedition would be repaid, but for the present he was, it seems, without any means at all. The Black Prince himself melted down his gold and silver plate, recruited Gascons and freebooters and awaited the arrival of his brother, John of Gaunt, with reinforcements from England. In February 1366 the Black Prince with an army of ten thousand men began to cross the Pyrenees through the historic pass of Roncesvalles. At Nejèra, a village on the Logrono-Burgos road, the Anglo-Gascon forces of the Black Prince and the army of Don Henry of Castile met for their encounter. It was another famous victory for the Black Prince, based once again on the fire power of the English archers. Don Pedro rode among the prisoners with a drawn sword looking for his half-brother Henry, who had fled the field. When he failed to find him he began to cut the throats of the more important prisoners until stopped by the Black Prince who was horrified by this violation of the canons of chivalry.

After a triumphant entry into Burgos the Black Prince asked Don Pedro to pay his debts. The Castilian became effusively evasive. After all the fighting, he said, there was not any money left in Castile. Before the High Altar in the Cathedral of Burgos Don Pedro swore on the Bible that all his debts would be paid. He gave the Black Prince in earnest of his good intentions a basket of jewellery, which the Prince distributed among his principal followers. He kept for himself only one jewel—a large balas ruby.

It was the only payment the Black Prince ever received from Don Pedro. He marched back over the Pyrenees with empty pockets and the start of the illness which was to bring him to an early death. In Castile the reign of terror of Don Pedro brought its own retribution. Don Henry returned with a new army and by trickery slew his brother with his own dagger.

The Black Prince had but a few years to take his pleasure in his ruby; it is said that after the death of Don Pedro he wore it frequently in his cap. It next appeared in the Parliamentary Rolls as the ruby in 'the golden crown for bascinet'—the crown which Henry V wore over his helmet on the field of Agincourt. During that fierce engagement the sword of the Duc D'Alencon damaged Henry's crown and almost struck the ruby from its setting.

The stone was set in the crown which Richard III lost at the Battle of Bosworth and which was plucked from a bush by the Earl of Derby to place on the head of Henry of Richmond. In the crown of his son, Henry VIII, we are told that the 'great ruby' was set in its front.

From the list of the jewels of the regalia sold by order of the Commonwealth Parliament it is very possible that the balas ruby was the big Rock Ruby sold for £15, which was purchased by a royalist to be restored to the crown of Charles II. It has appeared in the crown of every monarch since that time. It is still in the position of honour in the front of the Imperial State Crown of Queen Elizabeth II.

Throughout history rich and powerful men have felt the desire to possess the brilliant and precious jewels of their times; and great gems are soon in great hands. The Koh-i-Noor, the great diamond in the Queen Mother's crown, is not only the most famous diamond in the world, it is the epitome of the ambitions, greed and the violence which have been focussed on the great gems whose history is known to us.

The history of the Koh-i-Noor is a long one. It was found by the Godaveri river and held as a sacred treasure by the rajahs of Malwa in India—in 1304 it was reported to have been in their possession 'time out of mind'.

When the Moguls invaded Malwa they seized the great gem as tribute. It came into the hands of the Sultan Baber, the founder of the Mogul Empire in India, who was a descendent of Tamerlane and one of the earliest diary keepers on record. In his diary for February 1526 he mentions a famous diamond so valuable that 'it would pay half the expenses of the world'. This diamond passed into the keeping of his successors, Akbar, Jehanger and Shah Jehan.

Shah Jehan is reputed to have given the stone to his beautiful queen, Mumtaz Mahal, to whose memory he built the incomparable Taj Mahal. From this came the legend that the great gem was the harbinger of death and misfortune to any man who possessed it. The Koh-i-Noor was held to be a woman's diamond 'for ever'. It is certainly a strange fact that the men who afterwards wore it suffered misfortunes, torture and death.

The great diamond was reputed to be of 1,000 carats and, before he gave it to his wife, Shah Jehan decided to recut it to improve it brilliance. The Venetian Ortensia Borgia attempted the delicate task, discovered a flaw and in the cutting greatly reduced its size. The Shah was furious; the Venetian was fined all his other gems and was fortunate to escape with his life.

In 1665 another diamond merchant, Jean Baptiste Tavernier, came to India in search of precious stones. He saw the last of the great Mogul emperors, Aurunzebe, son of Shah Jehan, who called himself the Grasper of the Universe and wore on his hand an iron claw as a disembowelling weapon. This formidable emperor was gracious to Tavernier and agreed to show him his diamonds, many of which had come from the fabulous mines of Golconda in Hyderabad.

Tavernier said he had never seen such magnificence. Aurunzebe sat on one of seven jewel encrusted thrones while four eunuchs

The recutting of the Koh-i-Noor. The Duke of Wellington examining the stone
after it had been set in the 'dop' of the grinding wheel (*DoE*)

brought in two trays lacquered with gold leaf. All but the emperor stood to attention while Mir Jemla, the court jeweller,
counted each stone three times and wrote each one down in an
inventory. The jewels were then placed one by one in Tavernier's
hand. Among them was a diamond called the Great Mogul which
he was told had been recut from a much larger stone by a Venetian
jeweller; its form, he said, was like an egg cut in half.

In 1739, thirty years after Aurunzebe's death, Nadir Shah of
Persia invaded India and took possession of the fabulous palaces of
the Moguls and the rich stores in their treasure houses. The great
diamond was not to be found, however, among those treasures.

For eighty-five days Nadir Shah looted every palace in Delhi in
his search for the diamond. Then a woman from the Mogul harem
whispered the secret to one of his bodyguard: the jewel, she said,
was hidden in a fold of the turban of the captured emperor,
Mohammed Shah. In the East, as in the West, the person of a
ruler was sacred and the Mogul emperor had not been executed by
his conqueror. The Shah took advantage of another Oriental
tradition and invited the Mogul emperor to a banquet. During
the meal the Persian suggested that they should exchange turbans
which was customary on occasions of ceremony. While speaking
he deftly effected the exchange. The unfortunate Mohammed

was incapable of protest. Back in his palace the Shah unwound the turban until the diamond fell into his hand. 'Koh-i-Noor' he exclaimed as he looked upon it with delight. 'Koh-i-Noor—Mountain of Light!'

He did not live long to enjoy its splendour; soon after he returned to Persia he was assassinated. His son, Shah Rukh, was deposed. He refused to reveal its hiding place, although he was tortured and blinded by the pouring of boiling pitch over his head. He was eventually restored to the Peacock Throne and so the second legend of the Koh-i-Noor was born—that it was the ultimate symbol of Eastern sovereignty; whoever held the stone ruled the world.

Amed Shah, founder of the Durani dynasty of Afghanistan, secured the diamond and took it back to his mountain kingdom. His grandson, Shah Zeman, was deposed, tortured and his eyes pierced with a lance by his brother Shah Shuja to get possession of the stone. The British envoy to Afghanistan saw this Shah wearing the great diamond in 1809. This Shah, in his turn, was deposed and fled with the diamond to the court of Ranjit Singh, the Lion of the Punjab, who eventually obtained possession of the Koh-i-Noor.

After the death of Ranjit Singh in 1839 the subsequent possessors of the diamond suddenly died or were swiftly murdered until there was no one with sufficient authority to restrain the Sikh army from launching an attack on the British across the Sutlej river. This led to the end of the Sikh Empire, the annexation of the Punjab and to the discovery of the Koh-i-Noor in the Treasury at Lahore.

There is a story that the diamond was handed to Sir John Lawrence, the administrator of the Punjab, who put it in his waist-coat pocket. At a Council meeting of the East India Company it was decided to give the diamond to Queen Victoria. Reminded of its possession the horrified Sir John hurried home to find that his Indian servant had sent his waistcoat to the laundry. He threw up his hands in despair. 'Did you not empty the pockets?' he cried. 'Yes, sahib,' the servant replied. 'There was only a large piece of glass in one of them. I put it in that drawer.'

The diamond was brought to England and presented to Queen Victoria. The expectations aroused by its name, 'Mountain of Light', were not realised. The stone was dull and when it was put on display in a gilded cage at the Great Exhibition of 1851 there was general disappointment. The Queen decided to have the stone recut to improve it brilliance.

Mr Voorsanger of the great Coster firm of Amsterdam was

brought over to do the work. A steam engine of 4 hp was set up in the Crown jewellers' workshops. Prince Albert set the stone in the dop, or holder, and the Duke of Wellington started up the wheel. For thirty-eight days of twelve hours the patient Voorsanger bent over the wheel. The Koh-i-Noor lost 81 carats in weight—reduced from 187 to 106 carats—but gained very little in brilliance. Voorsanger was able to do no better than the Venetian had done nearly three hundred years before. The Koh-i-Noor has been described as a sleepy diamond. It still remains, however, a most splendid object, unique among the great and ancient gems of the world.

Queen Victoria wore the diamond as a brooch without super-stition—was she not a woman and the ruler of a quarter of the world! It has never been set in the Imperial State Crown, or been worn by any of the succeeding kings. Edward VII had it set in the crown of his consort, Queen Alexandra, and George V in his turn had it mounted in the crown of Queen Mary. Finally it was mounted in the crown of Queen Elizabeth, the consort of George VI, and has remained in her crown as the Queen Mother. After all its associations with death, torture and depositions, the Koh-i-Noor, the ancient stone of the great Mogul Emperors, shines with a peaceful radiance among the brilliant splendour of the Regalia in the Tower of London.

THE CULLINAN DIAMONDS

The Cullinan diamonds in the royal regalia have a much shorter and happier history. The Cullinan was found in 1905 in the Premier mine of De Beers in the vast diamond belt near Kimberley in South Africa. The manager of the mine, Frederick Walls, prised what he thought was a piece of rock crystal out of the side of a gallery. It was not only genuine but gigantic—a diamond of 3,106 carats, the largest ever known. It had a natural cleavage which suggested that it had once been part of an even greater diamond. The missing part has never been found. The De Beers Company named the stone after their President, Sir Thomas Cullinan, and two years later sold it to the Transvaal Government for the token price of £150,000 when they knew that it was intended to be presented to King Edward VII on his sixty-sixth birthday.

The stone was meant to be a gift of reconciliation after the bitterness and suffering of the Boer War, with the expressed hope that the great diamond might become the brightest jewel in the British Crown. A stone was supposedly despatched to London with great publicity under the protection of burly guards, but the real stone was sent off by ordinary parcel post.

King Edward VII was delighted with the gift but perplexed by the problems of cutting the huge stone into sizes suitable for the regalia. This task was entrusted to the famous firm of Asscher of Amsterdam, whose principal, J. Asscher, decided to undertake the delicate and complicated task himself. In February 1908, after months of study and making drawings of the possible lines of cleavage, the Dutchman laid his fine steel blade against the diamond and made his first stroke. The blade broke but the stone was intact. He picked up a new blade and made his second stroke; the stone cleaved exactly as he had planned and Mr Asscher fell to the floor in a dead faint.

For months the work of dividing and sub-dividing went on. Two of the major gems are today the largest diamonds in the world. The first is the Great Star of Africa, sometimes still called the Cullinan, of 530 carats and polished to seventy-four facets, it was set in the head of the Royal Sceptre. The Second Star of Africa, a square-cut brilliant of sixty-six facets, weighs 317 carats and was set in the Imperial State Crown under the Black Prince's Ruby. The smaller Third and Fourth Stars of Africa were later set in Queen Mary's Crown, one on the band and the other on the cross patée. They are all gems of incomparable splendour which strike the light rays from their facets. When the Sceptre was placed in the hand of Queen Elizabeth II at her Coronation, I saw the movement of the Great Star of Africa in its head sending swift and delicate shafts of light across the Queen's face.

THE STUART SAPPHIRE

The sapphire was once the gem of ecclesiastical authority worn in mitres and set in cardinal's rings. The Stuart Sapphire now in the Imperial State Crown may once have shone in the mitre of George Neville, the Archbishop of York during the reign of Edward IV. The Archbishop had been a supporter of the deposed Henry VI and among the property he forfeited was the fine sapphire in his mitre.

There was a 'great sapphire' among the royal jewels in the succeeding reigns, possibly the sapphire which was set in the new crown of Henry VII and was inherited by his son, Henry VIII, who had it placed in the front of the magnificent jewel-encrusted crown described in an inventory of 1532. The young King Edward VI, his successor, had the small crown with a great sapphire made for his coronation, which was sold under the Commonwealth for £60.

Like other gems purchased by secret royalists, the sapphire reappeared at the Restoration and was mounted in the State Crown of Charles II. The crowns displayed in the Tower were often set with coloured glass substitutes and the real sapphire was, therefore, ready to James II's hand when he left on his hasty flight to France. It was not discovered when the sailors searched him for valuables during the voyage and he carried it in his pocket during his years of exile. He passed it to his son, the Pretender, and it came into the possession of his grandson, Cardinal York, the last of the Stuarts, who died in July 1807.

The Cardinal, grateful for the pension awarded him by the Hanoverian king, bequeathed his royal treasures to the English Royal House. This sapphire was not, however, among them for it had been sold after the French Revolution to a Venetian merchant, Arenburg, who was told that the stone had belonged to the Stuart kings of England. It was purchased from him by an emissary of the Prince Regent, Angiolo Bonelli, who brought it back to England.

The Prince Regent gave the sapphire to his daughter, Princess Charlotte; after her tragic death in childbirth, the King asked her husband to return the stone since it belonged to the Crown Jewels. Its next appearance was not in that guise. Greville in his *Memoirs* for June 1821 stated that King George IV had dined at Devonshire House when Lady Conyngham was wearing a head dress which sparkled with the great Stuart Sapphire.

The jewel, retrieved by William IV after his accession, was mounted in the new Imperial Crown of Queen Victoria, below the Black Prince's Ruby. It was later moved to the back of the Crown and was replaced by the Second Star of Africa, where it remains to the present day.

QUEEN ELIZABETH'S EARRINGS

The first Queen Elizabeth possessed what can be called a plethora of pearls. It was a taste which she may have inherited from her father, Henry VIII, whose Great Crown was encrusted with 168 pearls. Her State Crown was also garnished with the same lucent gems, which she collected all her life. There is not a portrait of her without a profuse scattering of pearls in her hair, and on her neck and her garments.

It is impossible therefore to identify the pearls which, by long tradition are described as Queen Elizabeth's Earrings, now attached to the intersection of the arches of the Imperial State Crown.

There are several possibilities. The four pearls may have been taken from her father's crown, or they were the seven drop pearls which she is known to have acquired, or they may have been among the jewels which Mary, later Queen of Scots, secured after her marriage to the Dauphin of France. The last is, in fact, a strong possibility.

Catherine de Medici, on her marriage to Henry II of France, received a wedding present of seven great pearls from Pope Clement VII. In her turn she gave these pearls to Mary as a wedding present on her marriage to the Dauphin. Mary returned to Scotland after the death of her husband and brought her jewels with her.

Later when she was a prisoner in Lochleven Castle she entrusted her jewels to her treacherous half brother, the Earl of Moray, who had no scruples about selling them to her rival, Queen Elizabeth of England, for 12,000 crowns. This transaction is said to have included 'pearls of matchless beauty'. Queen Elizabeth wore many of the jewels of the unfortunate Queen of Scots and the four drop pearls may have been selected from the seven Medici pearls.

When James I inherited the royal treasures a record was made of 'a fayre Flower with three great ballaces in the myddest a great pointed diamond with three great pearles fixed, with a fayre great perle pendante called the Brethern'.

These pearls, in their turn, may have been given by James I to his daughter Elizabeth on her marriage in 1612 to Frederick the Elector Palatine, and later the King of Bohemia. There is a portrait of her wearing four pearl earrings which match those now in the Crown. Elizabeth of Bohemia returned to England with Charles II and died shortly afterwards. In this way the four pearls may have returned to the royal regalia and were set in the State Crown of Charles II. Today they occupy their place in the intersections of the arches of the Imperial Crown of another Elizabeth the Queen.

CHAPTER 10
THE LEGENDS OF THE REGALIA

The royal regalia are the bearers of many tales. They have come out of the distant past heavy with symbolism and surrounded by legends.

The crowns of Christian Europe shine with mystic lights—they symbolised Christ's Crown of Thorns, bear the trefoil of the Trinity, and were attributed to the conversion of Constantine or the Christian Empire of Charlemagne. The orb surmounted by the Cross still symbolises the rule of Christ over the world and the sceptres betoken the rule of law and justice.

THE SWORDS

The swords came into the regalia of kings in Britain long before any of them wore crowns. The Hallstatt warriors of the early Iron Age carried the sword into these islands and it replaced the axe as the symbol of dominion. The sword of the Celtic chieftains went with them to their graves and among them must have been many great swords which had performed legendary deeds.

We lost the legends of the Celtic chieftains and of their swords when the Romans stamped out the bardic memories of the Celtic priesthood. In Ireland, however, the bards survived to pass on the heroic legends of their sword bearing chieftains. Their account of the beginning of Irish history starts with Éoghan leading the Tuatha de Danann into Erin with a sword of the gods which made his followers invincible when it was unsheathed.

The legends of the swords also ring through the Scandinavian saga and eddas which represent the residue of the early folk history of those northern people. Volund the Smith of the *Verse Edda*, the maker of fabulous swords, had his counterpart in Britain in Wayland the Smith, from whose anvil came the swords of unsurpassable keenness.

In the Dark Ages we catch a gleam of the mystic sword of King Arthur, the legendary Excalibur, taken from the stone only by the hand of the undoubted king. Its blade was said to bear the inscription: 'Ich am y'hole Excalibure, unto a king fair tresore'. Among its attributes it could 'kerve steel, yren and al-thing'. It passed as mysteriously as it came as the boat bore away the stricken king to his resting place in Avalon.

The *Karla magna sagea* relates that the Emperor Charlemagne

gave his great sword the name *Joyeuse* because of the precious
relic it contained. In return for his help against the infidels, a king
of the Greeks gave Charlemagne the point of the Holy Lance
which had pierced the Saviour's side on Calvary; the Emperor had
this relic encased in the pommel of the sword. The French kings
made an early claim to have inherited this legendary sword and
a sword called *Joyeuse* was used at the coronation of the kings of
France. It is now in the Louvre, but regrettably modern methods
of examination do not support such claims to its antiquity.

The legends of Charlemagne and his paladins also impinged at
an early period on the regalia of the Saxon kings. It is said that
one of his paladins, Ogier the Dane, received from Charlemagne
a fine sword called *Curtein*. In a fierce contest with his adversary
and kinsman Renowde the paladin smote him so hard on the
helmet that the point of the sword was broken off. As Ogier
raised the sword again for the final stroke he heard a voice from
Heaven bidding him show mercy to his stricken foe; he heard
and obeyed.

Ogier is said to have married the daughter of Angert, or
Edgar, King of the Saxons and his sword eventually came into
the possession of the English royal house and became part of the
royal regalia.

Whatever may be the substance behind the legend it is true
that a sword called *Curtana* has appeared at the coronations of

Relief from the Chapel of St Edward the Confessor: the ring being returned to
the pilgrims (*Dean and Chapter of Westminster*)

English kings and queens for many centuries. Its symbolism still follows the legends. It is called the Sword of Mercy, and like the sword of Ogier the point has been broken off to show that power should be tempered by mercy.

Other swords renowned in fable were allegedly among the royal regalia. There was the Sword of Constantine given to King Athelstan by Hugh the Great when he sought the hand of the king's sister in 926; William of Malmesbury, who died in 1143, claimed that the name of Constantine appeared on its blade in letters of gold and that 'on the pommel might be seen an iron spike, one of the four which were prepared for the Crucifixion of Our Lord'. By other accounts the Treasury of England once held the sword of Tristan which King John received from the Emperor Otto and later lost in the Wash. As late as the reign of Henry VIII one of the great swords of Wayland the Smith was also counted among the royal treasures.

These fabled swords have gone from the royal regalia but the sword called *Curtana* with its blunted point has continued to be used at the cornations of our kings and queens. The present sword is certainly not that of Ogier the Dane. Three swords with scabbards of cloth-of-gold were sold at the breaking up of the regalia in 1649 and no trace of them has ever been found. The present sword appeared for the coronation of Charles II on his restoration and it is a fine double-edged blade marked with the 'running wolf' of Passau or Solingen with the point broken off. The legendary sword has gone but the ancient symbolism still remains. The *Curtana*, the Sword of Mercy, was borne at the Coronation of the young Queen Elizabeth in June 1953.

ST EDWARD'S RING

A beautiful legend of the royal regalia concerns St Edward's Ring. The account was written by Ailred, Abbot of Rievaulx, who died in 1166. It was printed by William Caxton, the first English printer, in *The Golden Legende*. One day as King Edward came to inspect the progress of the work on the great abbey at Westminster he met an aged beggar who humbly asked him for alms. Kings do not carry coins on their person, so Edward took the beautiful sapphire ring from his finger and gave it to the beggar with his blessing.

The sequel came from the Holy Land. Two English pilgrims on their way to the Holy Sephulchre had lost their way in a wilderness in Syria as darkness was falling. Suddenly they beheld a bright light coming towards them and saw an old man with white

hair and flowing beard escorted by two youths carrying lighted
tapers. He learned that the two pilgrims were English and expressed great joy at meeting them. He took them to an inn where
food and lodging and every comfort were provided for them.
The next morning the old man revealed his identity; he was John
the Evangelist and he had befriended them because of their king
and his charity to the poor. He gave the pilgrims a ring which he
told them he had received from King Edward and he wished them
to return it to the king's own hand. They were to tell the king that
within six months he would be with the Evangelist in Paradise.

The pilgrims hurried back to England with the ring and the
message. Edward recognised the ring he had given the beggar.
He prepared for death and six months later was buried in his
newly consecrated Abbey with the sapphire ring on his finger.

When Henry II obtained from Pope Alexander III the Bull of
Canonisation for the Confessor, the tomb was opened at a midnight service in Westminster Abbey on 13 October 1163. Abbot
Lawrence took the sapphire ring from the king's finger and kept
it with his crown, his vestments and his staff to be part of the
regalia of the English kings. The sapphire ring of St Edward
became the coronation ring, the 'wedding ring of England'.
Edward II had such belief in the legend that at his coronation in
1308 he offered as his second oblation a gold figure of St Edward
with his ring and the beggar reaching out his hand to receive it.
An inventory of his treasury shows that it contained a ring with
a great sapphire which 'is without price'.

The use of a sapphire in the Coronation Ring has persisted down
the centuries. The ring which was placed on the finger of Queen
Elizabeth II at her Coronation had a sapphire background with
a cross of rubies, originally made for William IV and since used at
the crowning of every sovereign except Queen Victoria.

When the Crown Jewels were broken up and sold during the
Commonwealth the sapphire from St Edward's ring was
purchased at the auction in Somerset House by a royalist
sympathiser who returned it to Charles II on his restoration; it
is now the big sapphire in the Cross patée on top of the Imperial
State Crown. If this tradition is correct then this sapphire is
one of the oldest jewels in the English crown.

THE AMPULLA

The little golden eagle holding the oil for the Anointing is a
survivor from the old regalia and the legend attributes a celestial
origin to this anointing vessel.

The anointing of Edward the Confessor on his Coronation (*Cambridge University Library*)

When Thomas à Becket was driven into exile by Henry II he spent his time in the Church of St Columbe at Sens praying that the king of England and his heirs might be more faithful followers of the Church. During a midnight vigil, the Virgin Mary appeared holding an eagle of gold which she gave to him saying that it held the oil with which the future kings of England were to be anointed. Henry II could not receive this boon because of his grave crimes against the Church. The Archbishop should give the sacred vessel to a monk of St Cyprians at Poitiers. The eaglet with the holy oil lay hidden for nearly two hundred years until the dream of a hermit led to its discovery. It was brought to Henry, Duke of Lancaster, who gave it to his nephew, Edward the Black Prince, the heir to throne, who placed it in the Tower of London.

It was overlooked at the coronation of the unworthy Richard II in 1377 but, when Henry of Bolingbroke deposed Richard II and became Henry IV, the celestial oil was found in time to be used at his coronation. There were sceptical people who thought that the legend and the oil were revived to bolster his dubious claims to the throne.

A letter from Pope John XXII, however, contains a broadly similar account of the origin of the Ampulla, and there is a record that the Black Prince deposited two vials of sacred oil in the Tower in 1345. A faint breath of life exists in almost every legend.

The oil in the Ampulla continued to be used until the coronation of James I when the sacred unguent was exhausted. It became somewhat pungent for Queen Elizabeth I who complained that the 'grease smelt ill' at her coronation. Charles I had a new unguent prepared which had forty ingredients, and there was no complaint about the unction made for James II. He was so pleased with its fragrance that he rewarded the apothecary with a huge fee of £200. A famous firm of apothecaries prepared from the old formula a new supply of oil for the coronation of Queen Elizabeth II: it was consecrated in St Edward's Chapel in Westminster Abbey on the morning of her Coronation, on 2 June 1953.

The kings of France, not to be thought less hallowed than the kings of England, also claimed a celestial origin for the oil used at their anointing. By their account the chrism used at their coronations had been brought down from Heaven by a dove in a vial for the consecration of Clovis in 496. This sacred vial, the *Sainte Ampoule*, was shattered at the Revolution, but a disguised priest scooped up a fragment on his finger; this was preserved for the anointing of Louis XVIII and Charles X on the temporary restoration of the Bourbon monarchy.

ST EDWARD'S CROWN

Special attributes were once conferred on the stones in the English crown. In 1586 Sir John Ferne published an account of the symbolism attached to the twelve stones in the crown of Queen Elizabeth I. The former Keeper of the Jewel House, Major-General H. D. W. Sitwell, has pointed out that if the crown really did contain those stones it could have been worn by Edward the Confessor.

This is the account which Sir John Ferne has left us in his *Glory of Generosity* of the 'twelve stones of precious esteem in the triumphant Crown of our Sovereign Lady':

Sardius   The first stone showing in colour like unto red gold and is placed on top of the diadem. It admonisheth the wearer that although respect be shown to the Throne above all men yet if he look to his terrestrial nature and creation he shall perceive that he is but earth and son of Adam which was red earth.

Topaz   The second stone, the colour of all stones whereby Kings are warned to exercise all virtues.

Smaragd   Commonly called Emerald. It represents justice in the King.

Chryolyth   It exhorteth the King to shine in wisdom and prudence.

Chalcedony   It instructs the Sovereign that he exerciseth the cardinal virtues of fortitude and courage of mind.

Hyacinth   The colour of the sun's beams is intended to shine in the King in divine and celestial virtues.

Jaspar   This stone showing a grass green colour admonisheth the King not be careful for the provision of his own diet, but to study the sustenation of his people . . . so that they may live without famine or complaining in the streets.

Chrysoprase   The gold in this stone admonisheth the King to wisdom and the green warneth him that he should aspire to the everlasting joys of Heaven.

Beryl   This stone is palely coloured and persuadeth to heavenly contemplation. For presentation to his people the King ought to be wan and lean rather than through epicurism, like Heliogabus, fatted as a monster.

Sapphire   The colour of blue light which should instruct to continence and cleanliness of body.

Amyethyst   This stone is decked with purple and violet and rose. The purple putteth the King in mind of the duty which cometh with the wearing of his purple robe. The violet that the herb though low sendeth forth sweet and fragrant smells to remind the King to yield the sweet odours of a commendable life, and the colour of rose sheweth the great and ardent love he should bear for all his people in whose defence he should be ready to spend his blood.

Sardonyx   This stone consists as it were of two rich gems, the Sardyx and Onyx, is black at the bottom, red in the middle and white above, whereby the King is instructed to humbleness, charity and sincerity.

Queen Elizabeth would certainly have read Sir John's *Glory of Generosity*. It was possibly a method of conveying certain admonitions to the autocratic Queen which none of her courtiers had the courage to deliver in person!

THE FALLEN JEWEL

There is a legend which has its origins in modern times. At the coronations of our kings and queens even slight mischances have given rise to grim forebodings—often inspired by hindsight. The young Richard II was carried fainting from the Abbey after the long fast of his coronation service, thus foretelling his falling away from the crown and his eventual death. Charles I is said to have stumbled on entering the Abbey, thereby displaying the insecurity of his hold on his Throne. The jewel which fell from the crown of George III is said to have presaged the loss of the American colonies.

A similar mishap occurred immediately after Edward VIII had acceded to the Crown on the death of his father, King George V, in 1936. The new King walked with his brothers behind the draped guncarriage bearing the coffin of his father from Kings Cross to the Lying-in-State in Westminster Hall. He must have felt that the incident was significant since he recorded it fully in his autobiography, *A King's Story*.

> 'I especially remember a curious incident that happened on the way and was seen by very few', wrote the Duke of Windsor. 'The Imperial Crown, heavily encrusted with precious stones, had been removed from its glass case in the Tower of London and secured to the lid of the coffin over the folds of the Royal Standard. In spite of the rubber-tyred wheels, the jolting of the heavy vehicle must have caused the Maltese Cross on top of the Crown—set with a square sapphire, eight medium sized diamonds and one hundred and ninety two smaller diamonds—to fall. For suddenly, out of the corner of my eye, I caught a flash of light dancing along the pavement.
>
> 'My natural instinct was to bend down and retrieve the jewels, lest the equivalent of a king's ransom be lost for ever. Then a sense of dignity restrained me and I resolutely marched on. Fortunately, the Company Sergeant-Major bringing up the rear of the two files of Grenadiers flanking the guncarriage had also seen the accident. Quick as a flash, with scarcely a

The Ampulla and the Anointing Spoon, the oldest pieces in the present regalia. The Ampulla is of late fourteenth century style and the Spoon is attributed to the twelfth century with elements of Byzantine workmanship. They were renovated and ornamented anew for the Coronation of Charles II

missed step, he bent down, scooped up the cross with his hand, and dropped it into his pocket. It was one of the most quick-witted acts I have ever witnessed. It seemed a strange thing to happen: and although not superstitious, I wondered whether it was a bad omen.'

Before that year was out, on the morning of 12 December 1936, HMS *Fury* slid silently and unescorted out of Portsmouth Harbour, carrying away the man who had ceased to be king.

Sixteen years later I was on duty in Westminster Hall for the Lying-in-State of his brother, King George VI. On a night of bitter cold and driving sleet the Duke of Windsor came in by the private entrance in Palace Yard to stand in the archway opposite the catafalque where the King lay beneath the Imperial Crown, the Orb and the Sceptre placed on the draped folds of the Royal Standard. His face was grey and deeply lined as he looked at the catafalque, the glittering gems of the Crown, the immobile guards and the two long slowly passing lines of mourning people. As he turned to go he must have remembered the earlier incident. 'You must make sure that this time the cross stays in place!' he said.

The Four Sceptres. *Left to right:* the Queen's Ivory Rod and the Queen's Sceptre with the Cross are used only at the Coronation of a Queen Consort. The two other sceptres, used only for the investiture of a King or Queen Regnant, are the Sceptre with the Dove (also described as the Rod of Equity and Mercy), and the Sceptre with the Cross, both made for Charles II

CHAPTER 11

THE GREAT SOLEMNITY

The coming to the throne of a new king or queen has been a significant date not only in the history of the nation but also in its people's lives. It gives a sense of continuity which stretches the temporal limits of our own lives into the succession of the future, and at the same time deepens the sense of our own past and unites us to whatever greatness there may have been. It is an occassion which touches certain deep and not easily definable emotions; it creates, what has too often been the illusion, that we are moving into a new epoch of progress; just as many people felt in 1953 that they had reached the beginning of the 'New Elizabethan Age'.

We have not been unique in these feelings. History resounds with the excitement and even the exultation of many peoples at the coming of their new chieftain, king or emperor: the forward surge of the Roman legions to raise their emperor on the shield; the Saxon thanes and ealdormen rushing forward to raise Athelstan to the royal stone of Kingston-on-Thames; the fierce clashing of the spears on shields around the Hill of Scone, the enraptured London citizens who greeted the first Elizabeth as she rode from the Tower to her coronation, and the great roar of welcome in 1953 from the vast crowds who had waited through the coldest June night of the century for the coming of the second Queen Elizabeth.

These displays of a universal emotion, like the ceremonies of the royal inauguration, go far back into the obscuring mists of time. The traditions and pageantry of the past seem to crowd together when a sovereign comes to be crowned. In Britain the coronation rites have carried forward the symbolism and the ceremony of more than a thousand years. The acts which are performed, the words which are spoken, the crown which is placed on the sovereign's head and the regalia which are put into the royal hands are all loaded with the sacred or the secular symbolism of the distant past.

So it was in 1953. Queen Elizabeth II was anointed and crowned with the solemn rites and ceremonies which had been drawn from the remote past of the British peoples. As Columba

Westminster Abbey prepared for the Coronation of Queen Elizabeth II. King Edward's Chair is in the centre and beyond it, on the steps, the Throne Chair

long ago had reached out his hand in benediction to Aidan on the
Isle of Iona, so the Archbishop of Canterbury blessed and dedicated the young Queen to her sovereignty. Enshrined within that
Christian service were the relics and customs of a remote and
pagan past. At the heart of the Abbey, beneath the Chair on
which the Queen was crowned, was the old Stone of Scone, that
solitary waif from those prehistoric times when kings were 'made'
on the royal stone.

The Queen was given a sceptre which had its descent from the
polished stone axes which the Beaker and Wessex lords had borne
on the southern downlands more than 4,000 years ago. She was
crowned with a diadem which had evolved from the beautiful
ceremonial helmets that were once the regal symbols of the
warrior rulers in Britain for over a thousand years.

The ritual of the Queen's Coronation also carried within it
acts and words which were once performed at the crowning of the
Norman and Plantagenet kings—the peers in the Abbey in 1953
knelt to speak the feudal words of homage, the prelates gave their
solemn vows of fealty, and the bishops and peers formally 'raised'
the Queen to the Throne, as kings have been lifted to their royal
seats from time immemorial.

Those standing around the Throne derived their titles from the
offices of the men who had served in the households of Saxon kings,
had their places in the courts of the Yorkist kings and had sat in
the Council of the first Queen Elizabeth. There was the Lord
High Steward—the steadward of the Saxon kings, and his
companion of the same times, the bowerthane, now the Lord
Great Chamberlain. There was the Constable of England, first
given that title and the staff of office by William the Conqueror;
the Lord Chancellor whose office came with Edward the Confessor,
and the hereditary Earl Marshal, the Duke of Norfolk, master of
the ceremony, whose ancestors had prepared the coronations of
many kings and queens. In the Abbey on that June morning
were many other ancient titles of State and holders of gilded
staffs of office which, like my own, would be held only from sunrise
to sunset on that particular day.

I had watched the transformation of the Abbey, and attended
the almost daily rehearsals in May while the Earl Marshal and the
Garter King of Arms patiently and meticulously drilled the peers
and other participants in their roles. These were the preparations
for a complicated pageantry of State until the moment when the
Queen, a young woman wearing a diadem and a magnificent
gown covered with thousands of seed pearls, had stepped through
he arch of the Choir Screen. The fanfare of the trumpets, the

surge of the choir were suddenly stilled and the clear voices of the Westminster schoolboys rang out 'Vivat Regina! Vivat Regina! Vivat Regina Elizabetha! Vivat! Vivat!' It was a moment of compelling impact when the ceremony moved from a pageantry to a rite of participation in which everyone was involved. The symbolism of the Recognition increased that sense of involvement. 'Sirs,' said the Archbishop, 'I here present to you Queen Elizabeth your undoubted Queen, wherefore all of you who are come this day to do your homage. Are you willing to do the same?'

It was the moment of the 'Election' with its symbolism derived from the primitive democracy of choosing their chieftains, which Tacitus has described, among the tribes who later came from Europe to Britain; this was perpetuated in the rights of the Saxon Witan to declare the king and which, despite the claims of autocratic kings, has always been inherent in the nature of the monarchy in Britain.

The coronation service has become the centre where all the royal symbolism of Britain has been gathered once in the lifetime of each sovereign. The symbolism of the crown, the swords and the sceptre has been enacted anew for each new sovereign. The symbolism of the royal robes, the tabards of the heralds, the robes of chivalry and the emblems of royalty—the coats of arms, the banners, the roses of York or Lancaster, the leopards of England, the tressured lion of Scotland have been woven on tapestries and displayed as badges, shaped in gold and silver ornaments, as each new king and queen came to their crowning. It was from here that all the symbolism of sovereignty of each new reign had flowed out to be chiselled on the stonework of palaces and cathedrals, to be displayed on coats of arms and Royal Seals, as well as on the new coinage of the realm and in a hundred other emblems and forms which became part of the patterns of everyday life.

The thread of the symbolism and allegory unfolded in the splendid liturgy of the coronation service, illuminated by words written centuries ago by men like St Dunstan and the Abbot Lawrence who could express that inherent symbolism with the rhythm and majesty of the Psalms.

The taking of the Oath, the presentation of the Bible and the Anointing were filled with a symbolism which had come down from the early ages of the Christian faith. From Saxon times the kings had sworn to govern according to the laws and customs of their peoples and to rule justly. The Bible was itself the source from which this ceremony had derived much of its form and inspiration and the central act, the Anointing, was the continuation of the rite by which the kings of Israel had been cleansed with oil and dedicated to the service of God and their people. For the Church the Anointing and not the crowning had always been the central act of the ceremony, which for centuries had been described as the 'hallowing' of the King.

After the Anointing the slow and formal vesting of the Queen was begun. The robes which were placed upon the Queen were not the familiar robes of the royal estate. For centuries only a few people close to the scene had ever seen those garments. They were worn only for a few hours in the lifetime of each sovereign. In 1953 when for the first time in history millions of people saw the Queen wearing these regal robes on colour films and TV, there was a universal feeling of perplexity and surprise. She had become remote from the traditional figures of royalty. The splendid garments which they were putting upon the Queen belonged to a very different tradition of royal splendour and carried a royal symbolism older even than that of the English state. They were the robes of the Emperors of Byzantium.

The first of these royal vestures was the Colobium Sindonis—a 'muslin undergarment'. It was made of white linen cambric, sleeveless and opened at the side so that it slipped easily over the Queen's beautiful Hartnell gown. The ancient world knew this garment as the *tunica*, or *talaris* worn by all classes of society. The Emperors of Byzantium wore it at their coronations as the symbol of deriving their authority from the people.

The Queen was invested with a garment of great splendour—the Supertunica—a long coat of cloth-of-gold with wide sleeves and lined with rose-coloured silk. This beautiful tunic, derived from the ceremonial dress of the Roman Consuls—the *tunica palmata*— which later became the imperial *sakkos* of the Byzantine Emperors. Vested in this imperial splendour, the sovereign could now receive the symbols of the royal estate.

The secular pieces of the royal regalia were now taken one by one from the High Altar and given to the Archbishop of Canter-bury, who was himself one of the long line of his predecessors who had stood before King Edward's Chair for the Investiture. They were delivered singly to the Queen with words which expressed their ancient symbolism and historic meanings.

The Lord Chamberlain knelt to present the Golden Spurs to the Queen who touched them in symbolic acceptance. The spurs had first appeared at the coronation of Richard I when they had been put on the king's heels by two earls, and now after 800 years, two peers, by hereditary claim, had carried the spurs to the coronation of Queen Elizabeth II. They were the symbols of the high chivalry of the Middle Ages and the badge of knighthood, which were presented to the sovereign both as a military leader and the fount of honour and chivalry.

The ceremony of the Swords is more elaborate and of a far older historic significance. A sword had once been the first weapon with which a ruler had been invested and the last to be laid in his grave. The sword became part of the mythology of Britain like the mystical sword of King Arthur and the four golden swords which were said to have been borne before him at his coronation by the sub-kings of Albania, Cornwall, Dametia and Vendotia. The carrying of the sword became an act of feudal homage.

The sword bearer of the king held a position of great honour and as early as the coronation of Stephen in 1135 other swords were introduced to share the honours and mitigate the rivalries. Three swords in golden scabbards were carried at the coronation of Richard I, and this number was later increased to four, with a fifth sword added by George IV for use at the Offering of the Sword.

The names still borne by two of the swords reflect the fierce controversies of the Middle Ages between the Pope and the Emperors, the Popes claiming the right to invest the ruler with his temporal authority. From this dispute came the Doctrine of the Two Swords—with the first sword the symbol of temporal power and the second sword representing the spiritual authority of the Church. The Popes claimed the right to invest the Emperor and other rulers with both swords by the hands of the prelates of the Church.

Two of the swords in the English regalia borne at the coronation of Queen Elizabeth II and displayed in the Jewel House are still known, therefore, as the Sword of Justice to the Spirituality and the Sword of Justice to the Temporality, although these names had long ago come to have less controversial meanings in this country.

The next sword, the *Curtana*, the Sword of Mercy, has been described on page 78.

The heavy Sword of State, a large broadsword in a crimson scabbard, is a symbol of the royal authority. It also signifies the 'royal presence' and it is carried before the sovereign on occasions of State like the Opening of Parliament.

These swords are not presented to the sovereign, but their bearers stand on each side of the Chair of Estate during most of the ceremony.

Finally, there is the Sword of the Offering. This is one of the most beautiful and valuable swords in the world. It was made for the coronation of George IV, with a scabbard set with diamonds, sapphires and emeralds forming the emblems of the Tudor Rose, the Thistle and the Shamrock. At this stage in the ceremony, this light sword was exchanged for the heavy Sword of State and given to the Archbishop, who moved towards the Queen accompanied by other prelates as though the whole weight of the Church was behind the giving of that Sword:

'Receive this kingly sword, brought now from the Altar of God, and delivered to you by the hands of us the Bishops and servants of God, though unworthy. With this Sword do justice, stop the growth of iniquity, protect the Church of God, help and defend widows and orphans, restore the things that are gone to decay, maintain the things that are restored, punish and reform what is amiss, and confirm what is in good order.'

A king would be girded with the sword but a regnant queen has it placed in her hands. She then returned the Sword to the Dean of Westminster standing on the Altar steps, from whom it was redeemed for a hundred shillings. The sword was drawn from its scabbard and carried upright by its bearer for the rest of the ceremony.

The Queen was then invested with the armills, or bracelets. From ancient Egypt to India the bracelet has been regarded as a sacred as well as a royal emblem. It became associated with the most solemn form of oath taking—for example, it was on the *baugr*, or bracelet that the Danes swore to keep the peace with Alfred. The bracelets have appeared at the English coronations since the reign of Henry I, when they were presented to him with the continuing symbolism of oath-keeping as the 'bracelets of sincerity'. The words still held their ancient symbolism in 1953 when the Archbishop said to the Queen: 'Receive the bracelets of sincerity and wisdom . . . for symbols and pledges of that bond which unites you with your people.'

The Queen now rose from King Edward's Chair to be invested with the Stole Royal, a long richly embroidered and jewelled scarf, which included in its beautiful designs the emblems of the four Evangelists and of St Peter on the background of the floral emblems of Great Britain and the Commonwealth. The rulers of Christendom had been invested with the stole from very early times. It was among the vestments of Edward the Confessor. The stole had also been part of the imperial robes of the Emperors of Byzantium, the *loros*.

The next garment was of incomparable splendour. It was the Robe Royal of Cloth of Gold, its golden textures covered with designs of silver coronets, fleurs-de-lis, thistles, shamrocks and the

The Great Solemnity: the Archbishop of Canterbury raises St Edward's Crown above the head of Queen Elizabeth II

symbols of the Commonwealth. Very prominent in its design were the shapes of the imperial eagles. In the Middle Ages this robe had been described as 'square and worked all over with golden eagles.' Its four corners signify that 'the four corners of the world are subject to the power of God and that no man can reign on earth who has not received his authority from Him'.

Similar robes had appeared on the 'day of joy and glory' when the Eastern Emperors came in their magnificence to the Church of St Sophia to be invested with the Imperial Mantle; this was the *Chlamys*, blessed by the Patriarch and put on the Emperor by the Royal Chamberlain. In Britain the eagles have appeared on the robe since Saxon times, symbolising that Britain was an independent empire. In 925 Athelstan, the grandson of Alfred the Great, had been styled 'Emperor of the Kings and Peoples of Britain', and Edgar in 973, had actually taken the Greek imperial title of 'Basileus'.

How it came about that Elizabeth II, like the long line of her predecessors, was garbed in the dazzling splendours of Byzantium, we do not know. A modern historian of the coronation rites, Edward Ratcliff, Ely Professor of Divinity at Cambridge, has speculated:

By the tenth century we find in England a Coronation Order that exhibits parallels with the Byzantine tradition of such a kind that it is difficult not to think them the results of imitation. Respect for the institutions of the Empire was universal, and their influence far reaching, and the Byzantine imperial title was known and used in England.

The coronation robes which have been used by the sovereigns since Queen Victoria can be seen in the Jewel House in the Tower.

Robed in imperial splendour, the Queen next received the Orb and the Ring. The Coronation Ring had its place among the regalia at least from the reign of Henry I. The use of a ring by kings and priests extended from east to west; it was described by St Gregory in 590 as 'the distinction of honour and a symbol of faith'. In England it was placed on the fourth finger of the right hand of the sovereign at the Coronation—the finger which from ancient times had been regarded as the 'wedding finger', from which it derived its name of the 'Wedding Ring of England'. The first Elizabeth, when she was urged to marry, displayed her ring saying that 'England was her husband and all Englishmen her children'.

For the coronation of Queen Victoria the Ring had been made to fit her little finger, but the aged Archbishop of Canterbury forced the Ring on to the traditional fourth finger, causing her acute pain. In her case there was certainly some truth in the old adage about the Ring that: 'The closer the fit the longer the reign'.

The Orb is also a symbol of great antiquity. Strangely, the round globe of the Orb originated with the Greek philosophers of the sixth century BC who used a crystal globe as the prototype of the universe, which they conceived to be a sphere with the earth at the central core. Much later this cosmic sphere was adopted by the Romans as the emblem of their world dominion, with the Emperor as the *Dominus Totius Orbis*—Lord of the whole globe. The Emperor Constantine, on his conversion, placed a cross above the globe as the symbol of Christ's dominion over the earth; the Orb retains this form in the English regalia.

In England the first representation of the Orb is on the first seal of Edward the Confessor where he is shown with the Orb with a Cross in his left hand. Harold is shown in the Bayeux tapestry holding an Orb before the Battle of Hastings.

In the Middle Ages the coronation service required the king to hold the Orb at the same time as the Two Sceptres. This awkward feat was avoided by elevating the Cross on a long staff to unite the Orb and the Sceptre with the Cross in one piece of the regalia. This long-stemmed Orb was shown on coins and seals until 1432 when the Cross was again placed directly on the Orb, which made it a much easier object to hold during the long royal ceremonies:

By the accession of Edward IV in 1461 the Orb was finally separated from the sceptres. The imagery of Constantine is still reflected in the words with which the Orb is given to the sovereign. 'Receive this Orb set under the Cross, and remember that the whole world is subject to the Power and Empire of Christ our Redeemer.'

The Sceptre probably had its origins in the shepherd's staff, or crook, the natural emblem of authority among nomadic or pastoral peoples. The tomb paintings and bas-reliefs show the kings of Egypt, Assyria, Persia and Parthia with crook-like sceptres in their hands. Homer wrote of the *Skeptron* as the attribute of Grecian kings and recounted how it descended from father to son. The Judges in Israel also carried a long wooden staff as the emblem of honour, and the rod of the priests had a sacred significance. In the Middle Ages the English sceptres were sometimes called the Rod of Aaron and their ends were decorated in foliate shapes to represent its miraculous blossoming. This symbolic association with the judges and priesthood of Israel has given one of the sceptres the symbolism of the judicial authority vested in the king.

In Celtic times the ceremonial sword was the symbol of power, but the sceptre returned with the coming of the Angles and the Saxons, to share the honours of the regalia. I have described the sceptre found in the ship burial of the Anglian King Raedwald and the two sceptres that are shown on the Jewel of King Alfred. The sceptre appeared again on the coins of Ethelred the Unready and was repeated on the coins of Canute the Dane, to reappear again on the silver penny of Edward the Confessor in the form of a sceptre surmounted with a dove. A sceptre in this form has been placed in the hands of the English kings and queens almost continuously until the present time. The two meanings of the sceptres are embraced in the words with which they are delivered to the sovereign.

The Sceptre with the Cross is given to the sovereign with the words which expressed the symbolism which has remained unchanged through the long succession of the English sovereigns, with the Archbishop saying: 'Receive the Royal Sceptre, the ensign of kingly power and justice.'

The second sceptre is still known as the Rod with the Dove and it is placed in the sovereign's left hand with the symbolic words which have also come down from distant times: 'Receive the Rod of equity and mercy. Be so merciful that you be not too remiss: so execute justice that you forget not mercy. Punish the wicked, protect and cherish the just, and lead your people in the way wherein they should go.'

CHAPTER 12
ROYAL ARMS AND EMBLEMS

The Romans brought the dragon to Britain. About 101 AD the Emperor Trajan in his campaign against the Dacians captured a standard showing a dragon struck down by a horseman—the possible basis for the legend of St George and the Dragon. He took the dragon as his imperial emblem and it was displayed on the standard of the Roman legions all over the Empire, including the Roman province of Britain.

When the Romans left the Britons themselves raised the dragon symbol of imperial authority against the Anglo-Saxon invaders. From that confused period there is the legend that Uther, the father of Arthur, saw two golden dragons in the sky and took them as omens that he would become king. He had two dragons made; one he dedicated to the Church at Westminster and the other he placed on his standard. His title, Pendragon, the 'dragon-headed', suggests that he used the dragon as a crest for his battle helmet.

The golden dragon of Wessex enters history about 495 with the arrival of the West Saxons in Britain. They may have brought the dragon emblem with them from their homeland, or, like Trajan, adopted it from the defeated Britons. The dragon standard was borne by the House of Cerdic to many battlefields and when King Alfred fought against the Danes.

The dragon of Wessex was raised for the last time by a Saxon king at the Battle of Hastings when the house-carls of Harold made a carpet of their dead around the ancient emblem of the House of Cerdic. The Norman kings are reputed to have for a time followed the examples of the other conquerors and used the dragon of the defeated Saxons on their standards.

The dragon made another famous entry on the stage of history when Henry VII marched behind the red dragon of Cadwalader —emblem of his Tudor ancestors—to gain the English crown at the Battle of Bosworth. Henry VII afterwards offered in St Paul's Cathedral his victorious banner with the fiery red dragon on a field of white and green silk. At the same time he placed the dragon name in the College of Arms with his appointment of the Rouge Dragon Pursuivant in honour of his Welsh descent. Thereafter Henry VII placed the red dragon with a golden lion among the supporters of his royal arms. His successor Henry VIII sometimes used a red dragon with a black bull as the supporters of the royal arms, but his son, Edward VI, reverted to the combination of golden lion and the Tudor dragon.

The dragon made another heraldic entry on the Great Seal of Cromwell's time when in 1655 the Welsh dragon replaced the Scottish unicorn as a tribute to Cromwell's Welsh descent. The lion supporter wore a royal crown and over the shield was set a golden helmet of sovereignty, surmounted by another royal crown and the lion crest of the Plantagenets—an odd excess of crowns for one who had 'defaced and destroyed' the crowns of previous English kings and had executed a king for good measure.

The red dragon—*ddraig goch*—still flies on banners at Welsh festivities, but the arms of the Principality are those of the old Princes of Gwynedd, including Llewellyn ap Griffith who was slain at Builth and his brother David, the last prince of their line, executed at Salisbury. The shield is quartered red and gold, with four passant lions regardant in the gold quarters and *vice-versa*.

The most beautiful representation of the dragon appears on the badge which hangs from the splendid collar of the Order of the Garter, the premier order of English chivalry, founded by Edward III in 1348. This pendant badge, superbly enamelled, represents St George slaying the dragon.

The Prince of Wales bears the Royal Arms with the royal crest and lion and unicorn supporters. His badge as heir apparent of three ostrich plumes and the red dragon of Wales are placed below his shield with the motto ICH DIEN. Patriotic Welshmen claim that this is not the German for 'I serve' but the old Welsh words *Eich Dyn*—'Your Man'—uttered by Edward I at Caernarvon when he presented his infant son as a native-born Prince of Wales.

The red dragon takes its proud and solitary place on the present Royal Badge of Wales, ensigned with the Royal Crown and surrounded by the motto Y DDRAIG GOCH DDRY CYCHWYN which, I am assured by Welshmen, loses much of its force and significance in the official English translation 'the red dragon gives impetus'.

THE WHITE HORSE

The White Horse came to England with the Celtic invasions of the second century BC and left its imprint on the coins and upon the hillsides.

The White Horse returned again to England in the desperate years which followd the Roman departure. About 450 AD the British king Vortigern appealed to two Jutish leaders, Hengest and Horsa, for assistance against the Picts and Irish. The Jutes were rewarded for their help with the gift of the Isle of Thanet, separated from Kent by a broad estuary. At a great feast to celebrate their victory, Vortigern was handed the wassail cup by Rowena, the beautiful daughter of Hengest; he was captivated by her and ceded the rest of Kent to her father in return for her hand. Vortigern was deposed by his indignant subjects but with the help of the Jutes was reinstated. A peace conference was summoned at Stonehenge. In the midst of the discussion Hengest suddenly called to his followers: '*Nimath eowr eseaxas*'—'Take your swords'— and the English chiefs were instantly slain. Vortigern alone was spared, for whose ransom was paid the three provinces of Essex, Sussex and Middlesex. The arms of Middlesex and Essex today contain three notched swords, or *seaxes*. There is an old tradition that the East Saxons derived their names from this weapon.

Modern philologists insist that the names Hengest and Horsa are synonymous, both meaning 'horse'—the Friesians called him Hengest and the Anglians, Horsa. The names represent one leader whose symbol was a white horse.

After many centuries the White Horse came back into the Royal Arms on the accession of George I of Hanover in 1714. The Elector of Hanover had fourteen quarterings on his arms, including lions, a stag, an eagle and 'two bears'. He abandoned this menagerie and replaced the arms of Hanover in the fourth quarter of the Royal Arms by the two golden lions on red for Brunswick, the blue lion and red hearts of Luneberg and a white horse running in a red field for Westphalia. In 1726 when George attached two heralds to the new-founded order of the Bath, he named one of them 'Coursier'—steed or charger.

With the accession of Queen Victoria the White Horse went from the Royal Arms since, by Salic law, a woman could not succeed to the throne of Hanover. But the White Horse came back again to stand sentinel outside Westminster Abbey on 2 June 1953 when the young Queen Elizabeth II came to her Coronation. The White Horse of Hanover was one of the famous Queen's Beasts which were placed below the great window of the Abbey Annexe in 1953.

THE LION OF ENGLAND

The lion has guarded the thrones and tombs of kings and appeared on their symbols over the millenia. The royal crouching lions of Assyria and the lion body of the Sphinx stand at the beginning of man's recognition of sovereignty.

So far as the English records go the lions appear to have come

Royal Arms: *above left* the 'leopards' as first used by Richard I; *above right* Edward III quartered the Arms of France on his Arms when he claimed the Crown of France (when France changed the number of fleurs-de-lis to three, Henry IV adopted the same quartering to maintain the claim to the Crown of France); *below left* England and France quartering the Lion of Scotland and the Harp of Ireland on the Arms of Charles I (the form of quartering introduced by James I); *below right* the Royal Arms today, as used by Queen Victoria and all subsequent sovereigns in many ornate variations (*HMSO*)

somewhat obscurely into the royal armory. Henry I may have used the lion as his badge from the chronicler's description of him as the 'Lion of Justice'. It may also be significant that it was in his reign that the lion was first seen in England, in the king's menagerie at Woodstock. Furthermore, when this king knighted his son-in-law, Geoffrey of Anjou, the father of Henry II, the king gave him a shield charged with golden lions. Henry I may also have added a second lion to his arms when he married Adila, daughter of the Count of Louvain, whose arms held a lion.

Henry II would, therefore, have inherited two golden lions from his grandfather and he added a third when he married Eleanor of Aquitaine. Since the time of Henry II the three golden lions on the red field have been on the Royal Arms of England.

Richard I fixed both the number and the attitudes of lions, described as *passant guardant*. In this position the lion is presented as walking with the off fore leg and the off hind leg advanced and the 'face' looking towards the viewer. It is a *lion rampant* which appears in the Scottish quartering of the Royal Arms, with the lion standing erect, with the fore legs in the air and the off hind leg raised.

The lion makes its first appearance in the royal crest on the Great Seal of England of Richard I which has a *lion passant*—walking—painted on a winged shape above the helmet. These wing shapes on helmets were used to break the force of a blow on the helmet, but they were later elaborated into fantastic forms and huge heraldic animals, worn in the tournament rather than on the battlefield. They inspired the heralds to the designing of armorial crests.

From the reign of Edward III to Henry VII the royal crest had been a lion *statant guardant, crowned*—standing on four legs, wearing a royal crown. This is the attitude which it still occupies in the crest of the Royal Arms today.

The lion has been a persistent, but not always exclusive, 'supporter' of the Royal Arms of England on the dexter side; it has had to partner such royal beasts as the falcon of Edward III, the antelope of Henry IV, the bull of Edward IV and the silver boar of Richard III. Occasionally the lion was discharged from duty: Richard II had two white harts and Richard III finally gave his favourite silver boars both positions at the sides of his shield. The lion's presence was also erratic under the Tudor sovereigns. Henry VIII sometimes favoured arms with a dragon and a bull, or a greyhound and a silver cock. During Mary's marriage to Philip of Spain the royal arms were impaled with his own, and the supporters were an eagle and a lion. Elizabeth I restored the lion to its dexter place opposite a red Tudor dragon. When James I came to the English throne, however, the lion became the dexter supporter of the Royal Arms in England again,

The Three Swords of State in the English Regalia: *left* the Sword of State in its scabbard with the Arms of William III and Mary II; *centre* the *Curtana*, or Sword of Mercy with the blunted point, alongside its scabbard; *right* the Jewelled Sword of the Offering with its scabbard

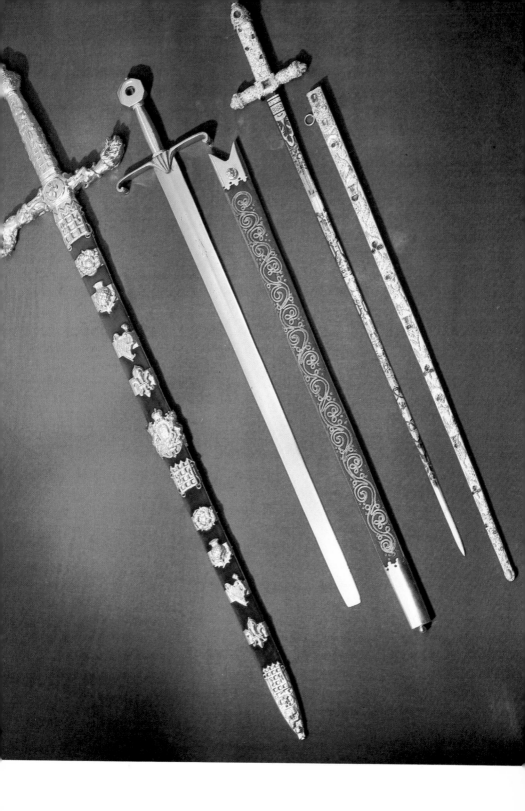

but changed places with the unicorn when domiciled in Scotland. The Royal Beasts came and went so frequently that the heraldic experts hesitate to call them 'supporters' until the lion and the unicorn are firmly settled in their places.

THE ROSE AND THE CROWN

It was, appropriately, a very beautiful woman who brought the rose to the English Crown—Eleanor, daughter of Raymond Berenger, Count of Provence, the troubadour's land of 'music, song and roses'. When she married Henry III the golden rose of Provence became a badge of the English kings; it was also adopted by their sons, the future Edward I and Edmund Crouch-back, Earl of Lancaster, who changed its colour to red. The golden rose of Edward I was changed to white by his descendants and when the Lancastrian heiress, Blanche, married John of Gaunt, she carried the red rose to him. The white and red roses were worn on the liveries of the Houses of York and Lancaster respectively and gave rise to rivalries and quarrels long before the scene in the Temple Gardens in Shakespeare's Henry IV and so splendidly depicted in the great painting in the House of Lords.

The changing fortunes of York and Lancaster were reflected in the royal heraldry of the Wars of the Roses, as the red and white roses came and went on the badges and liveries of their kings. After the Yorkist victory and his coronation, Edward IV super-imposed the white rose on the sun—the *'white rose-en-soleil'*. Holinshed recounts that before the battle of Mortimer's Cross, Edward IV saw the sun 'like three sunnes and suddenly joined altogether in one: at which sight he took courage that he, fiercelie setting on his enimies, put them to flight; and for this cause men imagined that he gave the sun in his full brightness for his badge'. This badge had fatal consequences at the battle of Barnet in 1471 when Warwick the 'Kingmaker' mistook the white star of his ally de Vere, Earl of Oxford, for the king's badge and charged his own side. The result was the death of Warwick and the victory of York.

Henry VII, the ultimate red rose champion, married Elizabeth of York and united the rival houses. The rival roses were also joined in the red and white emblem of the Tudor rose. The Badge

St Edward's Crown: the Coronation Crown, made for the Coronation of Charles II, and by tradition used only for the crowning of the Sovereign. It was placed on the Altar of Westminster Abbey but because of its size and weight was not used at the Coronations of Queen Victoria and King Edward VII. It was reinstated for the Coronations of King George V, King George VI and Queen Elizabeth II. It is set with about 440 precious and semi-precious stones

of England is still the red and white rose united, 'slipped and leaved proper'.

The armorial rose was presented in the form in which the heralds saw it—the wild dog rose of the hedgerows, with five simple petals. They emblazoned it with its centre seeds and the tiny green spikes and described it as 'barbed and seeded vert'. The Tudor rose of Elizabeth I on her Royal Badge had a stalk with two leaves—'slipped and leaved'—very similar to the royal rose of her namesake and descendent, Elizabeth II.

In 1960, a new chapter began in the history of the Rose and the Crown when, after 750 years, the golden rose of Eleanor of Provence appeared again as an armorial design for a queen. In that year the Queen adopted a flag for her personal use before her visit to India and Pakistan. It was intended for her use when the Royal Banner—whose symbols were associated exclusively with the United Kingdom—was not quite appropriate. This new flag consists of the Queen's personal initial 'E' ensigned with the Royal Crown within a chaplet of gold roses on a square blue flag with gold edges. It is a design of graceful elegance, worthy of the ancient symbols of a land of beautiful women and troubadour's songs.

THE GOLDEN LILIES OF FRANCE

The symbols which surround kings are among the most tenacious of temporal things. They cling like burrs to the royal robes and are impressed from age to age on the regalia, and on the gates and walls of palaces.

The lily shape of the fleur-de-lis appeared long ago on a cylinder seal of the Pharaoh Rameses III. Later, throughout the shifting kingdoms of the Middle East, it appeared on walls and on pottery. It possibly reached France through contacts with the Saracens. In the Eastern motif the three leaves were separate, the French heralds formalised it by tying the three leaves together with a band.

The symbol made a miraculous entry into the arms of France. It was, say the legends, the lily emblem of the Virgin, who sent her flower by an angel to Clovis, king of the Franks, at his baptism. This account was solemnly advanced by the French bishops at the Council of Trent as the reason for giving precedence to the French king.

The fleur-de-lis first appeared as a heraldic device on a royal seal of Louis VII (1137–80), who divorced his wife Eleanor of Aquitaine; she afterwards married Henry II, and so began the long wars for the throne of France. Louis VIII (1187–1226) formally adopted the device as the arms of France on a shield '*azure, semé de lis or*'—a blue field strewn with golden lilies. The French arms were among the most beautiful ever to be emblazoned. They tempted Edward III, who, claiming the throne of France in 1340, began the Hundred Years' War and placed the golden lilies in the first quarter of his royal arms.

Edward III was entitled, as the son of Isabella of France, to quarter the fleur-de-lis with his three lions in the second and third quarters of his shield. He had, however, placed the emblems of France in his first and fourth quarters, giving them precedence over the lions of England. In armorial terms it was a clear statement that he was king of France. At the same time Edward took as his royal motto: *Dieu et mon Droit*—'God and my Right'; this was possibly an expression of his 'right' to the French throne. The motto is still, after 600 years, in the Royal Arms, but with a very different connotation.

About 1365, Charles V reduced the number of fleurs-de-lis in the French arms to three—to 'symbolise the Trinity'; but he may have wished to differentiate his arms from those of the English king. He did not succeed; for in 1405 Henry IV of England also reduced the number of fleurs-de-lis to three in each of the French quarters of the English arms. The claims of England were still armorially proclaimed. The old and the new arms of France are described as France Ancient and France Modern.

Henry V's 'hot alarms' in France were symbolised by the flaming beacon which was his badge. When, after Agincourt, he was recognised as the *heretere de France*—the future king—his armory included a shield bearing the three fleurs-de-lis by themselves. The three English lions were left at home!

Henry VI, the feeble king, continued to display the arms of France and England separately, but on his seal the two shields are not supported by the warlike images of his father—instead he summoned up an angel who somewhat disinterestedly props up these two emblems of earthly ambition.

A passage in Shakespeare refers to the growing alarm as the tide of war turned against the English.

> Awake, awake, English nobility!
> Let not sloth dim your honours new begot.
> Crop't are the flower de luces in your arms;
> Of England's coat, one half is torn away.

At the accession of James VI of Scotland to the English throne—as James I— the Royal Arms of Scotland were marshalled with those of England. The prominent fleurs-de-lis were diminished in scale by the incorporation of the lion rampant of Scotland and the harp of Ireland. In 1707 at the Union of the kingdoms of Scotland and England the royal arms were re-marshalled but the fleurs-de-lis continued to be displayed in the second quarter. It was not until 1801, following the Union with Ireland that the lilies of France were taken from the Royal Arms.

The long claim to France has still left its impressions in England. The fleurs-de-lis, next to the Crown, is the most ubiquitious of the royal symbols. There was a time when miles of city streets and enclosed parks had iron railings surmounted with the barbed lily, until wartime salvage campaigns swept them away. They present themselves on the marbled tombs of great cathedrals and small village churches and they have lingered in gold on the walls of council chambers in solid Victorian town halls.

These lily symbols have remained close to sovereignty. At the coronation of the Queen there was a breathtaking moment when she was invested with the splendours of the Robe Royal of Cloth of Gold. As the Mistress of the Robes put this shining robe on the Queen, which each sovereign wears only once in a lifetime, I could see upon it all the flower symbols of the 'royal garland' which the centuries had brought to Elizabeth II—the red and white Tudor roses, 'slipped and leaved', the green shamrock, the purple and green thistle, held together in branched patterns by alternate coronets and the silver threads of the fleurs-de-lis.

THE HARP OF IRELAND

English ideas rather than Irish traditions have been responsible for the emblems of Ireland on the English arms and regalia. The first sight the Irish had of their future national emblems was on the banners of their invaders!

The only Englishman on the Papal throne, Adrian IV, issued a Bull in 1155 in favour of Henry II giving him the entire right and authority over Ireland. The kings of Munster, Leinster, Meath, Ulster and Connaught were not consulted! Gilbert de Clare, the spendthrift Earl of Pembroke, surnamed Strongbow, led the English forces to the invasion of Ireland. The English landed under the banner of St Edmund, a ninth-century king and martyr, whose insignia was the three gold crowns of the Saxon kings. Strongbow had as his lieutenant Maurice Fitzgerald, a Welsh knight, who carried on his banner a red saltire cross. The three Saxon crowns and the red saltire were to serve in turn as the heraldic representations of Ireland.

Much later Edward IV appears to have had some doubts about the proper arms for Ireland and appointed a commission of enquiry. They supported the three crowns and Edward IV put them on his Irish groat.

In 1544, Ireland, which had been styled a lordship, became a kingdom under an Act of Henry VIII. He substituted a harp for the three crowns, because, it was said, they reminded the Supreme Head of the English Church of the triple crowns of the Papacy. Tradition also says that the Pope had given Henry an actual harp of the High Kings of Tara on account of his orthodox

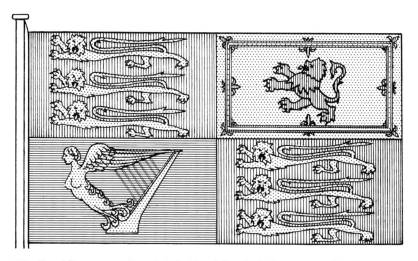

The Royal Banner, usually called the Royal Standard, flown on royal residences and ships when the Queen is present. The colours are: first quarter, Lions are gold on a red background; second quarter, the Rampant Lion is red on a yellow background and the lines of the border are also red. Note that the fleurs-de-lis do not show inside the border lines; third quarter, the Harp is gold on a dark blue background, the strings of the Harp are silver

religious zeal, which had also earned him the title 'Defender of the Faith' which is still part of the royal insignia.

Elizabeth I made a crowned harp one of her badges for Ireland and placed it on her Great Seal for Ireland, where it appeared on a banner held by a lion rampant, opposite it a dragon held another banner charged with the familiar three crowns. From then on, the harp—which had the merit of some association with Irish traditions—came more prominently into its own on coins, seals and badges, although it did not appear in the Royal Arms until the Union of the Crowns in 1603 when James I placed it in the Royal Arms in the third quarter of the shield where it has since remained.

In 1960 the Queen adopted a persona flag intended for use outside the United
Kingdom where the emblems of the Royal Standard were not appropriate. It
consists of the Queen's initial E within a chaplette on a square blue background
fringed with gold

An example of how the Queen's personal flag can be used on a visit to a
Commonwealth country: it is shown here on the fesse point of the arms of Jamaica

The Welsh knight Maurice Fitzgerald, founder of the great Irish feudal house of the Geraldines, had to wait a long time for his heraldic hour: in 1801 the red saltire on the arms of his descendents was lifted by the heralds and solemnly laid on the Union flag as the 'Cross of St Patrick.'

The Irish harp still keeps its place in the Royal Arms by virtue of Northern Ireland being part of the United Kingdom. The frame of the harp has shown a tendency to change its fashion, and has occasionally been altered from the 'winged lady' design back to the ornamental curve at the top of the frame, known as the Celtic harp. On her accession, the Queen expressed a preference for the Celtic harp, but in 1958 exercised her prerogative as a woman and Sovereign to bring the winged lady back into the Royal Arms.

A sardonic politician long ago remarked on the appearance of the harp in the Royal Arms: 'The best reason that I can observe for the bearing thereof is that it resembles that country in being such an instrument that it requires more cost to keep in tune than it is worth.'

THE ROYAL STANDARD

By the ancient rules of heraldry the Royal Standard is technically the Royal Banner, bearing the same quarterings as those which are on the Royal Arms—1 and 4, the lions of England, 2 the tressured lion of Scotland, and 3, the harp of Northern Ireland. The crest, supporters and other additions do not appear on the Royal Standard.

Flags with symbols were flown a long time before coats of arms were painted on shields. The heralds, once they arrived on the scene, soon applied their armorial rules to the assorted flags of kings, nobles and knights in the battle array and on the jousting field. They systematised them into three groups—the banner, the standard and the pennon.

The banner was square or oblong and charged with the arms of its owner; like the Royal Standard today it carried no other devices. In time these rectangular flags became longer in the hoist than in the fly, to prevent them becoming entangled on the battlefield. Their size was rigidly controlled by rank; an emperor's banner was 6ft square and that of a king 5ft. A prince or royal duke had a banner 5ft by 4ft and the lesser nobility had a mere 3ft square of emblazoned cloth.

The standard, on the other hand, was a long triangular flag

six times as long in the fly as in the hoist. It was swallow-tailed, tapering to a division, and the two ends were curved. In England the standard bore the Cross of St George next to the hoist (staff) and the rest of its length carried the crest, badge, motto and other devices of its owner, but not his arms, which appeared only on his banner. Its length was also regulated by rank, from the 8 yards of a king down the degrees of nobility to the knight who had 4 yards.

The personal standards of the English kings, as distinct from their banners, were magnificent productions. Henry VII had a swallow-tailed standard with St George's Cross at the head followed by a white swan, the red roses of Lancaster, gold stocks of trees for Woodstock and a fox's tail placed on the white and blue livery of Lancaster. These long elaborate standards were obviously intended for pageantry and the displays of the tournament.

The third flag was a pennon, which was a small standard, carried on a lance; it was emblazoned so that its device was in the correct position when the weapon was lowered for the charge. At all cost a knight had to save his pennon. He was cautioned that: 'From a standard or streamer a man may flee, but not from his banner or the pennon carrying his arms.' A knight who had carried his pennon through some valiant encounter could be made a banneret on the battlefield. The fortunate knight had to be rich enough to sustain his new dignity and this required him to provide at leasty thirty of his own armed retainers. The ceremony could only take place on the battlefield beneath the Royal Banner; the act was simply done—the king took the knight's lance and cut away the points of his pennon so that it became a rough banner shape. 'Sir,' said Sir John Chandos in 1367, as he received his curtailed pennon from the royal hand, 'I thank God and you that I have land and heritage to maintain it withal.'

Edward III made John de Coupland a banneret for taking David Bruce prisoner at the battle of Neville's Cross and, much later, Charles I honoured Col John Smith for rescuing the Royal Banner at Edgehill. George II, the last king of this country to appear in person on a battlefield, made several English officers bannerets at Dettingen.

The Royal Standard is flown over a royal residence only when the sovereign is there. When the monarch is embarked on a ship of war, three flags in combination are flown: the Royal Standard at the main, the Admiralty flag—an anchor in a horizontal position—at the fore, and the Union Jack at the mizzen mast; if a ship does not have three masts, the flags are flown as ordered.

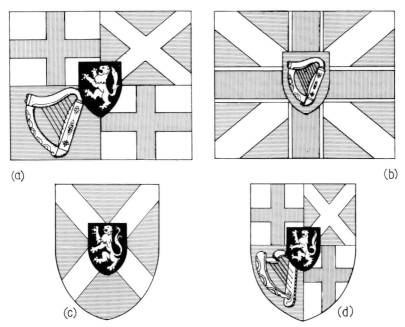

(a)   (b)

(c)   (d)

Above left The Union flag of 1685 displeased all three nations and infuriated
officers of the Royal Navy; *above right* first attempt at a Union flag: banner of
Oliver Cromwell as Protector of the Commonwealth of England, Scotland and
Ireland; *below left* Cromwell's Scottish Arms for the Commonwealth: a cross
gules (England) repeated top left and bottom right, azure a silver cross
(Scotland) and azure a harp stringed silver (Ireland) on an escutcheon sable a
lion rampant silver (Cromwell)

FLAG OF UNITY

The bright red cross of St George on a white ground was the
symbol which led English soldiers to victory at Crecy and Agincourt; it flew before them in bitter skirmishes in Scotland. In the
fourteenth century troops were ordered to wear a surcoat emblazoned with the cross of St George and rushed into battle with
shouts of: 'St George! St George for England!' It was with the
cross on his mainsail that Drake sailed round the world and it
blazed on the banners of Elizabeth's army standing ready to repel
the Armada. The feeling of the English for their symbol was as
strong as that of the Scots for the saltire cross of St Andrew.

The Union of the Crown in 1603 under James VI of Scotland—
James I of England—provoked old enmities between the two
countries: English ships sailed into the ports of Leith and Aberdeen with the Cross of St George flying on the mainmast above
the Cross of St Andrew—signifying a victory over the nation of
the lower flag; while Scottish vessels coming up the Thames or
into Portsmouth flew the flags in the reverse order.

Three years after his succession, King James tried to allay these rivalries with a proclamation:

Whereas, some differences hath arisen between our subjects of South and North Britaine travelling by seas, about the bearing of their Flagges: For the avoiding of all contentions hereafter, Wee have, with the advice of our Council ordered: That from henceforth all our Subjects of this Isle and Kingdome of Great Britaine, and all our members thereof, shall bear in their maintoppe the Red Crosse, commonly called St George's Crosse, and the White Crosse, commonly called St Andrew's Crosse, joyned together in the forme made by our heralds, and sent by us to our Admerall to be published to our Subjects: and in their fore-toppe our subjects of South Britain shall weare the Red Crosse only as they were wont, and our subjects of North Britaine in their fore-toppes the White Cross onely as they were accustomed—1606.

The flag 'joyned together in the forme made by our heralds' did not commend itself to the Scots since it had been made by super-imposing the Cross of St George on the Cross of St Andrew; they felt this placed their cross in the underneath and inferior position. The English did not like it as their familiar red cross was no longer prominent, while the king's 'owne shippes' did not take to it since common merchant ships could fly the same flag as the proud vessels of the king's navy. The King's 'flagge' was unpopular with everyone.

The agitation went on until, in 1634, Charles I had to issue another proclamation 'for the honour of Oure Shipps in Oure Navie Royall' whereby those ships alone had the right of hoisting the 'Union Flagge'.

The King's Flag was hauled down during Cromwell's Protectorate and replaced by the Great Union and later by the Commonwealth Ensign. These flags carried quarterings of the two crosses and the harp of Ireland; the ensign also had a rampant lion in 'an escutcheon of pretence'. These quarterings were not very visible at sea and the Navy felt it had been given a mere regimental banner of the despised soldiery.

At the Restoration, the Navy reverted to the Union Flag; and merchantmen were instructed to fly the Cross of St George or the St Andrew's Cross, as well as a Red Ensign with the St George on the canton—the first step towards the famous 'red duster' of the merchant fleet.

In 1801 when, by Royal Proclamation, Ireland 'was for ever

after to be united into the one United Kingdom of Great Britain and Ireland', the problem of the national flag once again came to the fore. How should Ireland be represented? The experiment of Cromwell's Irish harp was a bitter memory which the Lords of the Admiralty were not prepared to repeat, nor was the symbol of an ancient Irish crown acceptable to the crowned monarch of Great Britain. The solution was pure invention: the heralds placed a red saltire on a white ground and called it the 'Cross of St Patrick'; the saint who had loved the shamrock and the harp had never seen a cross like that alongside his crozier. Certainly, a red saltire had never waved over the battle hosts of Erin, though it is possible that the St Patrick's Cross had originated in the arms of the Fitzgeralds—one of the greatest Irish feudal families who bore in one of their quarters a red saltire on a white field.

The placing of the three colours and the three crosses on the united flag must have kept the heralds up o'nights; eventually the results of their labours were presented in their concise language: 'The Union Flag shall be Azure, the Crosses Saltire of St Andrew and St Patrick, Quarterly per saltire, countercharged

The Roman Britannia on coin to mark the completion of Hadrian's Wall (*RTH*)

Argent and Gules, the latter fimbriated of the second, surmounted by the Cross of St George of the third, fimbriated as the Saltire.' A distinguished expert has said 'it is impossible to describe the combinations which were used without a great excess of verbiage'. Let the flag speak for itself.

Public reaction was at first extremely vocal; from the agitation which arose it seemed that England and Scotland had lost everything, while Ireland had got something she did not want! Time brought acceptance, devotion and eventually pride. The Union Flag took its place as the symbol of three peoples, was embraced by the patriotism of war and demonstrated in itself the deep attachment of men to the symbols and insignia which they have created for themselves.

Until 1864, the Royal Navy was divided into the Red, the White and the Blue squadrons, each with the appropriate ensign in the maintop, but in that year this system was abandoned and the White Ensign was adopted:'All Her Majesty's ships of war in commission shall bear a white ensign with the Cross of St George and the Union in the upper canton, and when it shall be thought proper to do so, they may display the Union Jack at the bowsprit end'—that is, the jack-staff end, from which the Union Jack had already taken its name.

RULE BRITTANNIA

When the Romans had finished their monumental task of stretching the wall between Carlisle and Wallsend, the Emperor Hadrian commemorated the event by issuing coins which bore the figure of a large, heavily draped female, wearing a helmet and armed with a spear and an oval shield; beneath was inscribed 'BRITANNIA'. This figure has been taken to represent the Roman watch on the Wall by Roma Dea, the symbolic personification of the Roman state.

Roma Dea left with the legions, but twelve centuries later her sister figure made her appearance on a farthing of Charles II. This time she sat with spear and shield, not looking to the Pictish north but outwards from the island to the sea. 'Britannia' had returned to keep 'The Watch on the Sea Frontier'. John Roettiers, engraver to the Mint of Charles II, took for his model the beautiful Frances Stuart, afterwards the Duchess of Richmond. 'It is a pretty thing,' wrote Pepys sourly 'that he should choose *her* face to represent Britannia.' Afterwards Britannia ruled the waves for a long time on the 'tail' side of the English penny.

CHAPTER 13
SEALS OF SOVEREIGNTY

The seal was an important symbol of authority in the earliest civilisations. In Babylon, Assyria and Egypt the royal emblem of the king was first engraved on a stone cylinder; this was then rolled over tablets of clay, leaving a lasting impression of the symbol. The superb craftsmen of the pharaohs later engraved the royal cipher on such gemstones as chalcedony, jasper, agate and amethyst. These seals were often carved in the shape of the scarab, or sacred beetle, and were pierced so that the keeper of the royal seals could wear them strung from neck or wrist.

The Jewish people made much use of seals, both in practice and in biblical allegory: in Nehemiah ix.38, for example it was written 'we make a sure covenant and write it, and our princes, Levites and priests put a seal unto it'; and, in Esther iii.12, the importance of the royal seal is emphasised—'in the name of King Ahasuerus was it written and sealed with the king's ring'.

The emperors of Byzantium used lead seals for general administration purposes, but on more notable occasions seals—or *bullae*—of gold; these were impressed on thin golden laminae. Lead was also used by the Romans for their seals and later for the *bullae* of the popes.

By early medieval times it was becoming customary in Western Europe to use beeswax to take the impression of the royal symbols. The Great Seals of England and Scotland were impressed on both sides—the obverse or principal side and the reverse or secondary side. This was done by means of a tool like a pair of tongs; the flat face on the inside of each arm was engraved with the effigy, name and other devices, and these matrices, or moulds, were then brought together to leave an impression on either side of the wax. In some cases the matrices of the 'tongs' were closed up and wax was poured between them and left to harden. A document might be sealed by pressing the matrix onto a lump of wax, or by passing a cord through a scroll, splaying out its ends and applying the seal. The centre of the seal was protected by the raised rim of wax; sometimes it was coloured by dyes, and the early seals were often green.

The Great Seal of England has now been for nearly a thousand years the 'very act and deed' of the sovereign. It is the supreme symbol of the royal authority in action. 'It is considered the emblem of sovereignty', wrote Lord Campbell in his *Lives of the*

Obverse and reverse of the Great Seal of King William II, the so-called Red King, which set the pattern for later Royal seals (*Mansell Collection*)

Chancellors, 'the *clavis regni*—the key of the kingdom—by which on solemn occasion the will of the sovereign can be expressed. Absolute faith is universally given to every document purporting to be under the Great Seal, as having been duly sealed with it by the authority of the sovereign.'

One of the earliest royal seals of England belonged to Coenwulf, who was king of Mercia about the year 800. It is a lead seal, or *bulla*, bearing an impression on the lead of a small cross with the king's name COENVVULFI REGIS and another cross on the reverse. It is a solitary example of its kind since the Anglo-Saxon kings did not use seals but signed their documents with their name and a cross. Seven centuries were to pass before another English king, Henry VIII, was to use a metal for his royal seal; the Golden Bulla of the flamboyant Tudor king was attached to the treaty he made with Francis I, the King of France, at the Field of the Cloth of Gold in June 1527. The other kings and queens of England were content to leave the imprint of their Great Seals on white or coloured beeswax.

Edward the Confessor was the first king of England to make a large seal of state. It is described as a 'seal of majesty' since it shows the king in his robes of royal dignity seated on his throne; in his right hand he holds the sceptre of the royal power, and in his left hand the mound, or orb, of territorial sway. The other side of his seal carries the symbolism still further since the enthroned king holds the sceptre with the dove of peace and mercy in one hand and the sword of might and justice in the other hand. The symbolism of the seal is complete; it depicts all the attributes of kingship—territorial possession and royal authority, and the king as the sovereign fount of justice and of mercy. This concept of the sovereignty has continued to be expressed in the symbolism of the Great Seal of England for over 900 years.

William the Conqueror in his Great Seal expressed the same ideas but, as we might expect, with more martial vigour. On the reverse of the seal the king is shown seated on his throne in majesty, with sword and orb, but on the obverse the king is shown as the Conqueror clad in armour, mounted on his warhorse with lance and shield: the emphasis is on the warrior, the triumph of his conquest of England.

His son, William Rufus, did not stress the warrior aspect of his kingship by placing it on the obverse, the first position, on his seal; instead he placed first the impression of the robed, crowned and sceptred king and on the reverse side he appears as the mounted warrior in the armour, conical helmet, lance and shield of the Norman knight. This type of seal, with few exceptions, was to remain the prototype of the Great Seals of England down to that of Queen Elizabeth II. On one side we have the sovereign enthroned in majesty of the royal power and on the other side the equestrian figure of the warrior monarch, together representing the symbolism of the sovereign as the ruler in peace and in war.

From the beginning the kings were concerned that the symbol of their royal authority should not be wrongly used and the Great Seal was entrusted to the personal protection of a special officer of the Court, the chancellor. At a time when literacy was mainly confined to the clergy, the chancellor was usually a cleric; he combined the duties of king's chaplain, private secretary and keeper of the Great Seal. All the charters and documents requiring the use of the Great Seal had to be prepared by the chancellor and his clerks, so that he became the centre of the machinery of government. The first of all his obligations, however, remained the protection of the Great Seal at all times; many chancellors slept with it under their pillows. There were chancellors who held the seal in their dying hands until a proper warrant arrived from the king authorising them to pass it to a successor or to 'place it in commission'—that is, to entrust its keeping to two or three officials until a new chancellor was appointed.

The Great Seals were protected from damage by an outer leather bag or case and an inner purse of rich material embroidered with the royal arms. As a further protection both containers were usually sealed with the chancellors own signet when the Great Seal was not in use. Today when the Lord Chancellor, who is also keeper of the Great Seal of England, walks in procession to the House of Lords to preside as Speaker of that Chamber he is followed by his Purse Bearer carrying the richly embroidered purse which still, in theory, holds the matrices of the Great Seal of the Realm.

The Great Seals of England are the important footnotes of history. Crowns have been melted down, lost in the Wash, seized by predatory or fanatical hands, but we can still trace the shapes of the English crowns on the matrices and wax impressions of nine hundred years. The figures of the kings on their seals may not always have been portrait representations but there were times when the engraver has obviously tried to depict his royal subject. The pointed beard, thin moustache, sloping shoulders and thin legs of the king on the seal of Edward the Confessor must surely have been taken from life; and the vanity of James I of England insisted that on his first seal 'the canopy over the picture of our face is so low that thereby the seal in that place thereof doth easily bruise and take disgrace'—the second seal gives us a clear impression of the royal visage.

The seals also provide an insight into the continuation of the ceremonies which have surrounded our kings. The seal of Henry I, the youngest son of the Conqueror, in 1103, appears to show the king in his coronation robes—the tunic, the dalmatic and the robe royal. Over nine hundred years later the young Queen Elizabeth II was invested in those three royal robes at her Coronation.

The symbolism of the seals speaks to us from century to century. On the seal of Richard I are two symbols which were to him of special significance—alongside the enthroned king is a crescent moon enclosing a star—almost certainly a reminder of his long absence on the Crusades—and on each side of the throne is a wavy sprig of foliage, interpreted as the broom plant, the *planta-genista*, from which the Plantagenet kings took their name. It is on this seal of Richard I that the art of heraldry makes its appearance on the seals; the equestrian figure of the king carries

The Great Seal of Elizabeth I—the 'Gloriana Seal'—from original design by Nicholas Hilliard (*RTH*)

Queen Elizabeth I as 'Queen of the Seas' on Golden Seal of 1502—the Gold Rial of Queen Elizabeth (*RTH*)

a shield with the lion rampant, the appropriate heraldic symbol for the 'Coeur de Lion'.

As the royal engravers became more skilled in their craft and as Italian influence made its impact on English design, the engravers not only created figures which were more lifelike, but were also able to increase the amount of symbolism on the Great Seals. The seal created for Henry IV in 1408 is a fine example of the engravers' craft. Henry V was obviously so impressed by his father's seal that he retained the design on his own seal; the equestrian figure, in full armour on the richly caparisoned steed with his uplifted sword, expressed to the full the martial vigour of the warrior king at Agincourt. The obverse of this seal is full of the symbolism of Christian chivalry: the king in majesty is surrounded by St George slaying the dragon, Michael the triumphant archangel, the lions of England, the eagle and the fleurs-de-lis, to assert his claim to the French crown. They were all symbols which spoke eloquently to their times.

The seals of some kings could be a symbolic representation of the state of the kingdom,—for example, a later seal of Henry VI, 1422–61, reflects the bitter conflicts of the Wars of the Roses, during his reign. The king is not enthroned in the customary seat of majesty; instead a half figure of the king appears above an embattled wall, with an entrance guarded by lions supporting the shield of France and the quartered shield of England and France surmounted by the royal crowns; it is an epitome of his reign.

The design of the Golden Bulla of Henry VIII was strongly influenced by the Renaissance. Henry is shown in the flowing robes of Estate, with cloak and tippet, wearing an arched crown,

The Royal Seal of Edward III, sixth seal, 1340–72 (*Mansell Collection*)

with sceptre and a large jewelled orb, seated on a shell-backed throne. He is a Renaissance figure. The reverse of this Great Seal also departs from the equestrian tradition, consisting mainly of a large shield, with France quartering England, surmounted by the arched crown, surrounded by a chain and the royal badge of the Tudor rose, each encircled by the Garter ribbon.

The long reign of Elizabeth I, 1558–1603, produced only two Great Seals: the first shows the queen seated on a curtained and canopied throne in her robes of Estate—the crown is unfamiliar and inexplicable, consisting of small crosses; on either side are the royal arms within the Garter ribbon ensigned with crowns. The reverse shows the Queen on horseback with richly embroidered skirt and polonaise, a long stomacher, ruff and sceptre, against a field set with sprays of roses and fleurs-de-lis. This is the famous 'Gloriana' figure appearing on her seal.

On Elizabeth's second seal she appears robed as the sovereign of the Garter with her cloak upheld by hands issuing from the clouds. On the reverse is the crowned harp of Wales, the English rose and the fleur-de-lis of France, all illuminated by the radiant beams of a cloud of glory. This seal was the one affixed to the death warrant of Mary Queen of Scots in February 1587.

Queen Elizabeth I on several occasions took her Great Seal into her personal keeping. She retained her first seal for a month until she decided to entrust it to Sir Nicholas Bacon. At a ceremony at Somerset House on 22 December 1558 she took the Great Seal

1 Reverse of The Great Seal of Queen Victoria (*RTH*); 2 The Great Seal of King George V showing him as an admiral on the bridge of a battleship—a departure from tradition (*The Times*); 3 and 4 The Great Seal of the Realm of Queen Elizabeth II, obverse and reverse (*The Times*); 5 and 6 Seal of Queen Elizabeth II for Privy Council Office (*The Times*); 7 The Seal of the County Palatine of Lancaster showing Queen's corgi running beside her horse (*The Times*)

from its white leather bag and red velvet purse and delivered it to the great Chancellor who was to keep it for twenty years. On his death in February 1578, the Queen was so anxious to recover her Great Seal that she immediately sent the two greatest lords of the realm, Burghley and Leicester, to collect it. Lady Bacon gave it to them in its bag still sealed with the late Chancellor's signet. Until the Queen had made up her mind about the new chancellor the seal remained in her own custody; the Close Rolls recorded every occasion it was taken out of its bag, which was sealed and resealed with a royal signet. Chancellor Bromly died in 1587 and the Queen was again anxious to get the seal into her possession as quickly as possible, so she sent John Fortescue, the Master of the Wardrobe, in haste to recover it.

Elizabeth was wise to take precautions. The Great Seal had more than once been lost or misused. One of its keepers, who followed Richard I to the Holy Land, had been drowned in a shipwreck with the seal tied round his neck. During the struggle of Henry III with the barons they got possession of the seal and used it for their own purposes; after the defeat of Simon de Montfort in 1265 the king regained the seal and immediately repudiated all acts which had been done under it.

There had been more than one attempt to forge the Great Seal and this was high treason under a statute of Edward III. In December 1298 two merchants were charged with this treasonable offence of counterfeiting the seal. In 1312 John de Redinges was hanged for the same crime. Elizabeth would also know of another attempt to forge the Great Seal by Henry and Richard Overton during the reign of her sister, Queen Mary. The seal's importance is demonstrated again by James II who, on fleeing the country in 1688, hoped to make government impossible by throwing the Great Seal into the Thames.

The thin circle of wax between four and five and half inches in diameter, is a spotlight on history. It is a royal symbol which illuminates the continuing concept of the kingship. It proclaims, long after the heralds have gone to dust, the sovereign titles under which they ruled their kingdoms and sometimes the names of the realms to which their ambitions also aspired.

The Great Seals have thrown a clear light down the little byways of history. The developments in the medieval armour for men and horses are shown in precise detail on the equestrian sides of the Great Seals. The heralds can read on the seals the significance of the symbols of sovereignty which their predecessors at the College of Arms had designed for their royal lords. We have a minuscule history of the engravers and goldsmiths of the royal seals, skilled craftsmen like Walter de Ripa, who made the first seal of Henry III in 1218, Henry Coldeville who engraved the first Great Seal for the youthful Edward VI, and Charles Antony who flattered the vanity of James I. There were families of engravers like the Wyons who made the seals for George IV and Queen Victoria.

In comparison with the ornate seals of the sovereigns from Queen Anne to Edward VII, those of the House of Windsor have an elegant simplicity, with plain fields on both the obverse and reverse sides. King George V made a departure from the traditional equestrian figure of his Great Seal; instead, the 'Sailor King' is shown, on the reverse side of his first Seal, in naval uniform with sword on the bridge of a battleship.

The Great Seal of Queen Elizabeth II continues the symbolism of the sovereign in peace and war, but it too has an innovation that runs contrary to tradition: the equestrian figure of the Queen is on the obverse side, with the monarch enthroned on the reverse —as it was the case with William the Conqueror's seal. This departure was made because in Gilbert Ledward's design for the sovereign in majesty the Queen's robe impinged on the border, limiting the space for the royal style and titles which must be included on the obverse; the equestrian figure thus changed sides.

The device for the obverse is a portrait of the Queen on horseback, wearing the uniform of Colonel-in-Chief, Grenadier Guards. The Latin legend is the royal title, to be translated as 'Elizabeth II by the grace of God of Great Britain and Northern Ireland and of Her other realms and territories Queen, Head of the Commonwealth, Defender of the Faith.' The reverse shows the Queen enthroned and robed, holding in her right hand the sceptre and the orb in her left. On either side of the throne are the shields of the Royal Arms.

The Sovereign in person still delivers the matrix of the Great Seal into the custody of the Lord Chancellor. When a new matrix of the Great Seal has been made it is laid on the table at a meeting of the Privy Council and is touched in approval by the Sovereign who directs the Lord Chancellor to take custody of it. In the past the old seal was broken into pieces, but in recent times it is now defaced—or 'demasked'—by a special hammer with an indented head. One half of the matrix may be presented to the Lord Chancellor. The Great Seal of Queen Elizabeth II is of silver alloy weighing 18lbs with a diameter of 6in.

The sealing of documents now takes place at the House of Lords in the office of the Clerk of the Crown in Chancery. Traditionalists may be horrified to learn that cellulose acetate plastic is now used in place of the fragile wax which has for centuries been the only material. The colours vary from the dark green for the patents of peers to scarlet red for the appointments of bishops and Supreme Court Judges.

By the rules made under the Crown Act 1877 it is no longer necessary for documents such as royal proclamations, and writs of summons to Parliament to be handwritten on parchment: instead a new wafer of the Great Seal can be used with the impression taken from the obverse side.

PRIVY SEALS

The Great Seal was not the only seal of the sovereign. In time the Great Seals were reserved for major matters of state, and a small, or privy seal, came into use for the domestic business of the royal household. Later the Keeper of the Wardrobe assumed responsibility for the privy seal when it was brought into more general use. The king sought to extend his royal prerogative by using the privy seal to avoid the restrictions imposed on the use of the Great Seal. In 1311, in an attempt to exercise more control over Edward II, the Lord Chancellor placed the privy seal in the care of the Lord Keeper of the Privy Seal, who ranked below the Chancellor, and the privy seal became the instrument which authorised the use of the Great Seal.

There came a time when the small seals had smaller seals behind them. As the kings lost the control of the greater seals they began to use other types of seals, like the *novel* seal and the *griffen* seal, giving rise to the new office of the Keeper of the Signet. By the reign of Edward III these seals in their turn ceased to be applied to precepts of importance. The conflict over the seals reflects the history of the struggle for constitutional government— they were the potent symbols of the temporal authority within the realm, of the King, the barons or of Parliament.

The office of Keeper of the Signet was abolished in 1851. The title of Lord Keeper of the Privy Seal was retained, however, and its holder is now a member of the Cabinet. The Lord Chancellor continues the long tradition of being Keeper of the Great Seal.

The symbols on the privy seals and other signets were usually those of the royal arms of England. Some sovereigns, however, like Henry VIII, used the royal badge on their signets in place of the royal arms. Oliver Cromwell outdid royalty by having on his signet his family arms with six quarterings, five of them of Welsh origin.

The privy seal of Queen Elizabeth II is single-sided and it is used to make an impression upon paper and to affix a wax seal. Like the Great Seal it is made anew for each reign. The symbols on the present privy seal are a combination of the rose, thistle and shamrock, crowned and supported by the lion and the unicorn.

The Departments of State each have their distinctive seals bearing the royal insignia. There are occasions when a certain informality has crept into the royal seals of this reign. The obverse of the County Palatine seal shows one of the Queen's pet corgis running beside her horse!

The second Britannia on coin of Charles II, 1672 (*RTH*)

CHAPTER 14
SCONE OF THE HIGH SHIELDS

Three places in the British Isles are the traditional sites for the raising of kings to their royal dignity—the Abbey Church of Westminster, the Rath of Tara and the Hill of Scone.

In England since 1066 the inauguration of kings and queens has taken place within the grey walls and between the high pillars of Westminster Abbey, with a solemn service which has held its form for over a thousand years.

The green mound of Tara in Ireland has been trampled by the feet of cattle for over 1400 years since the High King Diarmait mac Cerbaill celebrated the last royal festival in 560 AD. The pagan rituals at Tara wilted away before the solemn curse of St Ruadan of Lorrha. Tara thereafter was abandoned by its kings.

The Hill of Scone came further along the path of history. It was the place of king-making in northern Britain from Pictish times until that New Year's Day in 1651 when the unhappy Charles II was crowned as King of Scotland and lead out on to the windswept hillside to the roar of a royal greeting which may have echoed around that hillside for two thousand years.

The royal mound of the Celtic kings at Scone was situated close to the river Tay, about two miles upstream from where Perth now stands. The Picts, in their confederacy of southern and northern tribes stretching from the Forth to Caithness, were once the most powerful people in Britain. They were a Celtic people who had occupied northern Britain at the time of the great Celtic migrations in the first millenium BC. They came over the horizon of recorded history in 86 AD when the advancing legions of Julius Agricola in the northern part of Britain were fiercely beset by tall, red-haired men with long swords. They halted the northward progress of the legions and, when Agricola was recalled to Rome, his policy of attempting to reduce the people he called the 'Caledonii' by occupation garrisons came to an end. In recent years the probing trowels of the archaeologists have uncovered the evidence of the legions' precipitious retreat from their great fortress of *Pinnata Castra* near Inchtuthil as the Picts surged forward to recapture the mound of their kings. The Romans left their half-

Copper coin of the Emperor Hadrian, builder of the wall against the Picts and the Scots. The reverse shows Britannia (*RTH*)

filled granaries and stores, pounded their glass and pottery into fragments in the gutters and hastily buried a million nails to deny their iron to the Picts. Eventually the Picts were to drive the Romans back behind the bastions of Hadrian's Wall.

At the climax of their struggle with the Romans the Picts sent across the narrow sea to Ireland where another Celtic people, the Giodelic Gaels, had for centuries been conducting their own internecine wars. They came eagerly to the prospect of a new fight. In their own land these Gaels were known as Feni, but Scot was the name they were to bear in their new land. Scot, it is claimed, is the corruption of an Irish name for a raider. If so they were aptly named. They poured across the sea in their long leather-skinned boats with blood-red sails, landing on the rocky beaches and along the deep sea lochs of what is now Argyll. The new allies of the Picts impressed the Romans. A panegyric to the Roman general Stilicho describes their arrival:

> The Scots stirred up the whole of Ireland
> And the sea foamed with hostile seamen . . .
> Icy Ireland wept heaps of Scots.

In 367 the Celtic allies burst over Hadrian's Wall and ravaged the Roman province as far as Londinium. In almost the last spasm of Roman power in Britain they were finally driven back beyond the Wall, which was always to remain a significant line drawn across the landscape of Britain.

Many of the Irish Celts who had come as allies remained as settlers along the shores, lochs and among the islands of Argyll. About the year 500 three brothers, Fergus, Aengus and Loarn, princes of the *Dalaraidhne* of Antrim, arrived to bond the settlers together into the new kingdom of Dalriada. It was a precarious kingdom facing the great Pictish nation. On several occasions the Picts grew impatient with the growing incursions of the Scots and drove many of them back to their beaches and their boats.

It was at such a time of defeat in 563 that Columba arrived from Ireland. He came seeking a place of exile among the islands of the Inner Hebrides. On 12 May 563 his small boat with twelve companions landed on the beach of the island of Hy, to be known to later generations as Iona.

Columba was in direct line of descent from the great Nial of the Nine Hostages, the High King of Ireland. Columba was of royal blood on both the spear and the distaff sides since his mother, Ethne, was of the royal house of Leinster. The Prince of the Ui'Nial grew up to be a priest and a student of literature and music under the great bards of Ireland. The resources of the Nials gave him the prestige and the means to plant the monasteries which were to grow like great oaks at Derry, Durrow and Kells.

At the pinnacle of his prestige as abbot, silver-tongued preacher, poet and musician he had a dispute with Finnian of Moville over a copy he had made of the Vulgate which Finnian had brought from Rome. Their dispute was taken to the High King Diarmait, who decided against Columba with the words: 'To every cow belongs its calf—to every book its copy'.

Columba would not accept the judgment. The Abbot was submerged in the warlike prince. He summoned his kinsmen of Clan Nial to battle and at Culdreimhne near Sligo they won a bloody victory over the High King. Columba had prayed with uplifted arms for the victory of his clan, but when at last he looked down on the field of the dead and the dying, all his passion had drained away. In that moment of agonising remorse he imposed his own sentence—exile from Erin.

Columba found his countrymen in a desperate situation. Gabran, king of Dalriada, and his kinsman had been killed in battle by Bruide, king of the Picts, and Conall, son of Gabran's brother, was little more than a vassal of the Pictish king. The Picts had the power to drive the Irish settlers finally into the sea. Here was a cause for both the prince and the priest beneath the coarse woollen habit of Columba. With two companions he set out on the long journey to meet the Pictish king in his capital, now Aberdeen.

The legends depict a pagan king cowering before the spiritual force of the Christian saint. The reality may have been different. Nonetheless it seems that King Bruide was impressed by the tall, austere man speaking with an eloquence which reached across the barriers of language and custom. The king granted Columba the living space—and the breathing space—for which he pleaded. He gave Columba the grant of the Island of Iona for himself and his disciples and promised peace between the small kingdom of Dalriada and its powerful neighbour. It was the moment when the

A page from the Lindisfarne Gospel, possibly made in Iona and used by
St Columba (*RTH*)

foundations of Scotland were laid and it was also the covenant by
which the Picts unknowingly consented to their own disap-
pearance as a people.

For the next eleven years Columba was busy with his
evangelising and his statesmanship. They were not peaceful
times. The white-sailed ships of the Angles had appeared on the
east coast of Britain above the Humber. They were part of the
great invasion of Teutonic tribes who had seen the former Roman
province as the promised land. While the Saxons were carving out
their kingdoms south of the Thames, the Angles, leaving their

timbered farmhouses in Denmark, were plying their swords to the same purpose in the north. The Britons, another Celtic people, were driven westwards into the future kingdom of Strathclyde and into the principality of Wales. Then horn-helmeted Angles turned northwards and even the Picts had to fall back on their natural frontier of the Forth. The invaders were to create the kingdom of Bernicia, lay the foundations of Northumbria and make their citadel on the mighty rock of Bamburgh.

During these events Columba prevailed on his countrymen to keep the peace and to gather their strength for the greater battles to come.

In 574 the death of King Conall was followed by a period of confusion in Dalriada. The clan of Conall claimed the succession for Eogan, the son of the late king, but sons did not usually succeed their father among the Celtic peoples. In Ireland the *deirbfhine*, or family group, could extend its relationships and its rights for five generations so that the succession could involve a complex move on the chessboard of Celtic genealogy. Several, therefore, came forward to claim the royal succession.

So great was now the influence of Columba that the issue was entrusted to him for decision. Columba had become the kingmaker of Dalriada. Yet at this crucial moment his choice vacillated between Eogan and the other claimants before it fell on Aidan M'Gabran, son of the king who had been slain by King Bruide. His early biographer, the Abbot Adamnan of Iona, saw the deeds of Columba in a supernatural light and he wrote that the choice of Aidan was by command of an angel:

> When therefore this angel of the Lord had appeared on three nights and enjoined the same commandments of the Lord concerning the ordination of the King, the Saint, following the word of the Lord, passed over to the island of Hy and there ordained Aidan king . . . And he laid his hand on his head and ordained him with benediction.'

The consecration of Aidan is the first record of the inauguration of a king by Christian rites, not only in the British Isles but in Western Europe. It was, in Britain, the beginning of the deep involvement of the Church in the affairs of the kingship. With Columba we have the first account of a priest-statesman shaping the policy of a king in Britain. The relationship between king and prelate was often to be the hub on which the wheel of history was to turn.

Columba died in 597—the year Augustine came to Canterbury.

The Brechennach containing the relics of St Columba. They were brought to
Scone by Kenneth mac Alpin and carried for centuries by the Scots on their
battlefields (*National Museum of Antiquities, Scotland*)

After him came the whirlwind and Adamnan wrote that 'the
years were filled with the dreadful clashing of war'. Picts, Scots,
Britons and Angles were at each other's throats. The Picts were
at the centre of the storm with the Angles pressing into their
southern territories, the Scots of Dalriada raiding from the West
and the princes of Strathclyde waiting to take any flesh which
might be left on their bones. In 685 the Picts drove Ecfrith of
Northumbria back beyond the Forth. It was the historic battle of
Nectanesmere and there never would have been a kingdom of
Scotland if the Picts had lost that battle.

Then the Picts had to turn to meet an even more terrible foe.
The Vikings had begun their devastating raids in a savage arc of
destruction which included Ireland, the north of Scotland and the
Western Isles including the sacred sanctuary of Iona. In 794 the
Irish annals bleakly record 'the devastation of all the islands of
Britain by the heathen'. The annals do not record any clear
sequence of events until they unexpectedly mention that in 843,
Kenneth, son of Alpin, king of Dalriada, had taken possession of
the Pictish throne. The chroniclers were unable to explain this
sudden event; they relate with wonderment that 'the Scots were
inferior to the Picts in every way'. It is now accepted, however,
that Kenneth succeeded to the throne through his mother, a
Pictish princess, since the Picts followed the matrilineal line of

succession. Be as it may, Scots and Picts were united in the kingdom of Alba. The Scots, swarming in from their narrow kingdom of Argyll seem to have absorbed the Picts with remarkable speed. It is an historical enigma that this great people with their ancient culture and long traditions, their immense vitality and courage should so quickly have lost their national identity as well as their language and the records of their history. Only the battle frenzy of the Picts, which once appalled the Romans, may still have lingered in the Scottish blood to inspire on many future battlefields the headlong fury of the Highland charge.

In 843 Kenneth mac Alpin brought with him to the 'kingdom of Scone' a royal stone and the relics of St Columba. He placed the royal stone of his race in the church built on the hill by the Pictish king Nectan IV after his conversion to Christianity. It was to be taken from the Church only for the raising of a future king with the ancestal rites of the Dalriadan people.

The relics of the saint were to have a more restless history. The reliquary shrine of Columba, the *Brechennach* was a small casket carried on the breast supported by a strap fixed to clasps at each end. It was richly decorated in bronze and silver with gold medallions. Experts consider that it was made about 700, over a century and a half before it was carried in triumph into Pictland. The Abbot of Iona who had prayed so earnestly for the victory of his kin on the battlefield would have approved of the use made of his relics—they were carried by the Scots into their battles. Nearly 500 years after Kenneth mac Alpin, the *Brechennach*, attended by the Abbot of Arbroath, was still in the midst of the Scottish army at the battle of Bannockburn.

For the next five hundred years each new King of Scotland came to the Hill of Scone to be 'raised on the stone'. The blessing of the king preceded the ancestral rites. The form of the service has not come down to us. There was, however, the Mass, the Communion, and we hear of 'seven priests' reading the seven Penitential Psalms over the King—a strange echo of one of the early accounts of the conversion of the Picts. Christianity, it said, came to the Picts with the arrival of seven prelates with seven presbyters, seven deacons, seven exorcists and seven doorkeepers— a legend of Scotland which dismisses the work of the scores of missionaries like Ninian, Kentigern and Drostan who had laboured among the Picts.

When he came from the church service the new king was dressed in white, to show, said the chroniclers, that 'he would be a light to his people'. White is almost everywhere the symbol of purity and integrity. The kings of Ireland wore white for their

investitures; in Rome the aspirants to office were robed in white—
they were *candidati*, the 'whitened'—a name which has held a
stubborn place in our tongue. The Emperors of Byzantium also
wore white on their 'day of joy and glory'. The French kings added
the Gallic refinement of appearing for their coronations in
magnificent robes of silver. In 1953, the young Queen Elizabeth II
was garbed in the white of the *Colobium Sindonis* before she assumed
her magnificent Coronation robes.

The King was led to the royal stone, 'spread with the richest
covering the times could afford', and seven men stepped forward
to stand close beside him. The kingdom had been divided into
the territories of seven overlords, the great mormaers. They were
blood relatives of the king, claiming the right to choose his
successor and to raise by their hands the new king for the acclamation of the people on the Hill of Scone. In due time in the Scottish
kingdom the seven mormaers were succeeded by the 'Seven Earls
of Scotland' who, like their Pictish predecessors, divided most of
the land between them and claimed the right of electing the
kings of Scotland. Foremost among them was the Earl of Fife who
claimed the exclusive right of raising the king to his seat above the
royal stone on the day of his inauguration.

If we could recover the records of early Scotland, we would
certainly find that the Earls, like the great magnates in England,
would have had hereditary rights to bear the items of the regalia.
One of them would place into the king's hand the most potent
symbol of Celtic sovereignty, the long white wand of royal
power—the ultimate symbol of royal authority in Scotland. The
enduring significance of this symbol was made evident in 1296,
when John Balliol, King of Scots, was ruthlessly stripped of his
royal regalia by Edward I. He surrendered his kingdom with the
'qwhyte wand, and gave up until Edwardes hand of this kynryk
all the recgt'.

The rod also had its personal symbolism for the king. It was
straight to signify that the king should be upright and just in his
judgments; it was smooth so that the king should be calm and
deliberate in his actions; and it was white, the symbol of purity
and truth. Words of this symbolism were heard by a long line of
kings in Scotland. At the coronation of Charles I in Scotland in
1633, the Rod of the Sceptre was placed in his hand with the
words 'receive the sign of Royal Power, the rod of the kingdom,
the rod of virtue, that thou mayest govern thyself aright . . .' The
words and symbolism of the centuries seem to crowd together at
the investing of kings.

There are oblique references to an ancient rite of which the clerical chroniclers disapproved but did not actually condemn. Some form of these early pagan rites appear to have lingered late at Scone, for King David in 1124, on his return after living at the English court, was appalled by what he had to do at his inauguration. He 'abhorred the obsequia' and his magnates had difficulty in persuading him to undergo the ceremony.

It is unlikely that the Abbot of Scone would have condoned the fertility rites of their remote ancestors. What may have happened was the ritual slaughter of a beast and the king being required to drink or be smeared with the blood.

When the ancient rites were done, the king, wearing the robe of majesty, seated on the royal stone and holding the symbols of his power, was presented to his people. It was surely a moment when the great roar of acclamation would rise from the Hill of Scone, until the human voices were drowned in the fierce clashing of the naked swords on the bosses of a thousand upraised shields. From Rome to Orkney it was the immemorial sound of warriors greeting their new emperor, king or chief. An even fiercer metallic sound may have greeted the Pictish kings on that hill, since Dion Cassius in 206 AD wrote that the Caledonians had 'a short spear at the lower end of which is a ball of brass; with this they are wont to make a noise to frighten their enemies'—a device which could also be made to resound with acclamation. In the eleventh century Berchan in his prophetic writing referred to Scone as the place 'of the high shields' and again as 'Scone of the melodious shields'.

The *Tanaise*, the Inheritor, had been made king and he could now be so proclaimed. Through the gathering around the king would come a man whose role and garb came out of the far past of the Celtic race. He was usually described as an old man, white haired and long bearded, wearing kilt and sandals with a red cloak hanging from his shoulders. He was the *sennachie*—one of the bards and genealogists of the kings and chiefs of the Celtic race.

'These men', wrote Posidonius of Athens from his observations of the Celts in 150 BC, 'pronounce their praises before the whole assembly and before each of the chieftains in turn. These are the

Opposite above: Queen Mary's Crown. During this century a new crown has been made for each Queen Consort and set with the Koh-i-Noor. This crown was worn by Queen Mary, Consort to King George V, at their Coronation in 1911

Opposite below: Queen Elizabeth's Crown. The Queen Mother's Crown is based on a circlet of Queen Victoria's and was worn when she was Consort of King George VI. At the Coronation of her daughter, Queen Elizabeth II in 1953, the Queen Mother wore the circle of this Crown as a diadem without the arches and the monde

poets who deliver eulogies in song'. Caesar, that astute observer of people he sought to conquer, wrote of their immense powers of memory and that 'they continue their studies for twenty years. They consider it improper to commit their studies to writing'.

At that far-off scene the *sennachie* of the royal house bent on one knee before the newly vested king and began to proclaim in Gaelic the royal lineage back to the eponymous founders of the kingdom—to *Aedain, mhic Ghabhrain, mhic Dhomhangartaidh, mhic Fhearghais.*

As the Celtic centuries were left behind and the Normans became officers of state and the kings spoke Norman-French, the appearance of the *sennachie* became less frequent. By a strange coincidence, however, this ancient figure appears again at the great turning points of Scotland's history. He was there at the investiture of Alexander III in 1249, the last of the ancient Scottish line, on the threshold of Scotland's long struggle for independence. Once again in the person of the Lord Lyon King of Arms and High Sennachie of Scotland, he was at the last royal investiture at Scone, when the long roll of the royal line was recited before King Charles II on that dark New Year's Day in 1651. It was as though at a time of desperate danger, when Scotland was being over-run by Cromwell's forces, that even the grim-faced Covenanters wished to recall the long antiquity of their kingdom and of their race.

The ancient rituals completed it was 'away to the feast'. It is said that in 1249 before the magnates left the hill, however, they bent down to take off their boots. The fiercely independent nobles of Scotland had each placed some earth in their boots, so that 'each stood on his own ground during the ceremony'. This earth was piled in a heap and in the course of time formed the mound called by the populace 'Boot Hill' and by the more dignified chroniclers *omnis terra*, 'everyone's land'. Perhaps the story is not altogether a figment of the vivid Celtic imagination!

The early kings of Alba and of Scotland were not anointed, as were the English kings from the eighth century. Nor did the early ceremonies on the Hill of Scone include the wearing of a crown. The sacred symbolism of the anointing and the state symbol of the crown were both to become the great issues in Scotland's claim to sovereignty.

The Imperial State Crown; the symbol of royal majesty, worn on State occasions such as the Opening of Parliament. A crown of dazzling splendour set with about 3,250 precious stones

CHAPTER 15
THE SYMBOLS ON THE STONES

The Picts have left us the incised imprints of their symbols which are as strangely beautiful as they are enigmatic. These symbols were placed on small standing stones, in caves, on boulders, sandstone discs, and on stones not much bigger than pebbles. Their distribution ranged from Perthshire to the Shetlands, the extent of the Pictish kingdom.

The symbols were highly stylised and not casually engraved in isolation; they were found in different combinations in which fourteen of the symbols are repeated over and over again. These common figures include a crescent with a V-shaped rod, a double disc with a Z-shaped rod, a mirror and comb, a serpent and a fantastic animal with a long snout, drooping body and finlike legs. They are not artistic doodles; the skill of the engraving implies that they are part of a long tradition. These symbols are found in combination with freely drawn and lifelike representations of fish, bulls, serpents, stags, boars, deer, eagles and wolves.

The interpretation of these Pictish symbols has presented a greater enigma than the deciphering of Linear-B. What is certain, however, is that the repetition of these shapes on stones is intended to convey a symbolic meaning and that the conveying of that message was the prime motive of the artists' patient chiselling or gouging the shapes on the stones.

They could have been the symbols of rank in the Pictish kingdom, conveying their status meanings as clearly as did the stylised hieroglyphics on the cartouches and scarab seals of the Egyptian priests and Pharaohs. There is evidence which points to this suggestion: the Romans called the inhabitants of north-east Britain *Picti*, the painted ones; the Greek historian, Herodian, writing in the third century, described the Picts as having 'the likenesses of animals' and 'with all sorts of drawing on their bodies', and Isidore of Seville, the Spanish encyclopaedist, stated that the marks on the bodies of the Picts represented the personal ranks of their bearers. It is reasonable to assume, therefore, that their body insignia was transferred to their commemorative stones. In every land the priests, warriors and kings lie beneath the symbols of the rank and race which they bore in their lifetime.

The lifelike animal outlines which appear with the abstract symbols point to their being totemic emblems of the tribe, or,

The mysterious symbols on the Pictish stones, possibly badges of rank and clan

more remotely, of class, like the oak tree insignia of the Druid orders. Animals were the first subjects to stir the artistic abilities of men. In prehistoric times the fierce pursuit of the hunt was the most intense of life's experiences, one which first moved the creative imaginations of men at least twenty-five thousand years ago. An identification of the hunter with the hunted grew into the adoption of an animal for the strength, fierceness or speed which the primitive social group wished to have for themselves. The totemic animals were painted on the caves of France and Spain as the glaciation of the Ice Age receded and these, the oldest of all man's symbols, are still emblazoned on the emblems of class, clan and sovereignty today.

The stylised symbols in association with the animals on the Pictish stones may, therefore, be pronouncing not only the rank of a chieftain, but also the name of his clan by the totemic emblem, or even proclaiming the titles of the *Ard-Ri*, the High King of Pictavia himself. Unfortunately, the meaning for us is still locked in the uncommunicative stones.

The Pictish symbols are not confined to stones. They have been found engraved on beautiful silver plaques, hand-pins and other articles of silver of a superb artistic merit which is evidence of great skill and practice in metal work combined with plentiful sources of supply. It is also significant that the symbols appear on some of the massive silver chains which could have been the ceremonial badges of office for the Picts. The kings of another Celtic people in Britain, whom we now call the Welsh, wore silver neckchains instead of crowns for the symbols of their sovereignty.

I suggest that the 'mirror and comb symbol' had a special significance. In Pictish tribal society descent was traced through the mother's line, and there must be a strong presumption that a mother sign would be among the symbols. This could be the 'mirror and comb' which is to be found on so many of the Pictish stones—'I am the son of my mother who was the daughter of a king'.

When the Picts were converted to Christianity they used their great skills in stone carving to create the beautiful crosses which have no parallel in the whole of Celtic art; many of them still carry, however, the early symbols; this again points to their being status emblems. Among the stones of the Picts there may be found the earliest symbols of sovereignty in northern Britain.

At the time the Picts were cutting their early symbols on stones, another Celtic people, as I have described, were getting their first precarious foothold on the western coast of what is now Argyll. These Irish immigrants established their fort on a twin-topped hill rising from the Moss of Crinan, accessible to the sea by river to the Sound of Jura. Archaeologists in their excavations at Dunadd have confirmed in broad outline the account given in the Irish annals of the founding of the kingdom of Dalriada. The hill-fort was occupied from the fifth to ninth centuries, a period corresponding to their arrival from Ireland to the triumphant departure of

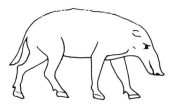

Boar carved on rock at Dunadd, Argyllshire, in 6th–7th century. Redrawn to show full outline

Kenneth mac Alpin to take possession of the united kingdom of the Picts and Scots. The fort of Dunadd became a formidable citadel with twelve feet thick walls protecting five enclosures for men, their beasts and their water supply. It has been described in the Irish annals as the inauguration place of the kings of Dalriada and it would seem that those kings have left on that deserted hillside the imprint of their sandal, their ritual bowl and the symbol of their clan.

The 'raisings' of the kings of Ireland were accomplished with certain mystical rites which usually took place around their ancestral and sacred stones. The people of Dalriada, therefore, cut into the rock of Dunadd the three ritual requirements for the installation of their own kings. The outline of the footprint at Dunadd had been carefully cut out of the rock to a depth of half an inch. The shape is that of a foot wearing the soft Gaelic sandal. By tradition it was the footprint of Fergus mac Erc, the first of the

royal line at Dunadd. As each new king of Dalriada was 'raised'
to his kingship he would place his foot in the imprint on the rock
to show that in peace and war he would walk in the footsteps of his
predecessors.

The footprint at Dunadd is not unique. Men have stepped into
the ritual footprints of their ancestors in many parts of the world.
There were temples in India, the Bishn-pad, the foot of Vishnu,
in which people stood in stone footprints 'to tread in the steps of
our great ones'. The footprints in stone have also been found
scattered all over the Celtic lands—in Britanny, Scotland,
Orkney and Shetland and in many of the Western Isles.

Near to the royal footstone there is the shape of a boar; its back
has been weathered by the centuries, but it is quite evidently the
work of a talented craftsman. It is clearly more than decoration; it
has significance. The boar was the great cult animal of the Celts
in every land they inhabited. They carved its shape on rocks,
moulded it in bronze, placed it on the boss of their shields and
often made its figure the crest for their helmets. Its flesh was their
favourite meat, which they also buried with their chiefs for their
ritual feasting in the other world. A great boar of supernatural
powers was the recurrent theme of Celtic mythology. The boar
had courage, ferocity and sexual prowess—all qualities which the
Dalriadians would expect of their kings, when strong and vigorous
leadership was essential to their survival.

The boar, about 3ft wide in the rock at Dunadd, had its own
significance. The ritual slaying of a white bull, a red boar or other
animal is frequently mentioned in the early accounts of pagan
Ireland. As late as the thirteenth century, Giraldus Cambrensis
was writing of the 'abominable rites' with which the Celts
inaugurated their kings, referring to the sacrifice of a white mare

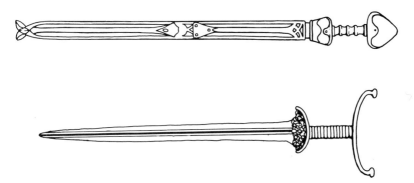

Celtic ceremonial swords, typical of those found in rulers' graves

in a fertility rite; this involved the king bathing in the broth and eating the flesh of the sacrificial animal. The regal inauguration of the kings at Dunadd could, therefore, have required the ritual slaughter of a boar whose significant figure still remains on the rock as the evidence of the far-off rites and symbolism of a people who were eventually to place their kings and queens on the thrones of far greater kingdoms.

The Celts had an obsession with stones and they saw magic in stones of all sizes. The folklore of Ireland is filled with accounts of stones which rose in the air, were mysteriously transported from place to place or which sealed the entrances to the other-world. Such legends of the stones persisted into Christian times. St Patrick, it was said, had a stone which floated a leper across the sea to avoid contaminating his companions in the boat and Columba had a pebble which floated on water and cured all ills. This veneration for the pebble was a persistent custom going back to the Bronze Age burials when a small pile of pebbles was placed in each grave. The monks who were buried on Iona also had a handful of pebbles beside them.

The most enduring of all the legendary stones may be the one which today rests in Westminster Abbey beneath the Coronation Chair. It was placed beneath that chair by Edward I who, on his invasion of Scotland in 1296, may have thought he was carrying away from Scone the royal stone on which the kings of Scotland from the time beyond recall had each been placed at their inauguration. This *Lia Fail*, the Stone of Destiny, was brought to Scone by Kenneth mac Alpin when he took possession of the united kingdom of the Picts and Scots in 843.

W. F. Skene, the historian of Celtic Scotland, has described the stone in Westminster Abbey as 'a solitary waif from the sea of myth and fable'. It has been carried far on a flowing tide of mythology. The stone begins its legend as the pillow on which Jacob laid his head when he saw the angels ascending to Heaven. Later it came into the possession of Scotia, the daughter of the Pharoah who found the infant Moses in the bullrushes. She married a Greek prince, Gathelus, and they brought the stone to Spain where it became the seat of Kings. Their descendent, Simon Brec, carried the stone to Ireland where it again became a royal seat for the High Kings at Tara. Fergus mac Erc, the founder of Dalriada, brought the stone with him across the narrow sea and on it he and all his successors were invested with the royal powers. Kenneth mac Alpin then brought it to Scone on the union of the kingdoms and on that stone the kings of the Scots were inaugurated until 1296 when it was hidden to prevent it falling into the hands of Edward I or, as others claim, it was brought to Westminster. Be that as it may, the legends followed a stone to Westminster with a distich which John Fordun wrote down in clerical Latin in the fourteenth century:

Ni fallat fatum, Scoti quocunque locatum
Invenient lapidum, regnare tenentur ibidim.

Sir Walter Scott has provided an elegant translation:

Unless the fates are faithless found
And prophets' voice be vain
Where ere this monument is found
The Scottish race shall reign.

We should pause before we smile at the legends. The legendary itinerary of the stone follows the route taken by some of the Celtic people from the Mediterranean to Spain, on to Ireland and from there to mainland Scotland. On 2 June 1953 those close to that Stone saw a young Queen, whose genealogy reached back to Fergus mac Erc, being crowned above it.

CHAPTER 16
THE MAKING OF THE NATION

The kings of Scotland, each in his time, came to receive the symbols of the royal dignity on the Hill of Scone. They were the inheritors of an expanding kingdom. The Anglian province of the Lothian was annexed; the Britons of Strathclyde, by dynastic changes and by force, were joined to the Celtic confederacy; Galloway was brought into unruly subjection, while Argyll and Moray were held in precarious yokes. After the battle of Largs in 1266 the Norse gave up the Western Isles, but Orkney and Shetland were not joined to Scotland until 1469.

During this time of growth, Scotland was a turbulent kingdom and its kings must often have felt that the ground beneath their royal feet was as treacherous as their native peat-moss bogs. When the king of Scots looked southward, he did not see a frontier but territory to claim, plunder to gain, cattle to be lifted and an enemy on whom he could quench the Celtic thirst for battle. So kings of the Scots united the loyalties of their subjects behind them by pointing their swords at the rich rewards to be gained in Northumbria, Cumbria and beyond.

Kenneth mac Alpin, founder of the kingdom, invaded England six times before his death in 858. His successors also plundered in northern England until the growing power of Wessex brought Athelstan, grandson of Alfred, to put a stop to the savage ploy by the victory of Brunanburh.

The Saxons made a great song about their victory, but the singing did not last for long. A new generation of Scots renewed the harrying of England until they saw the glint of chain mail and a thicket of tall lances when William the Conqueror rode into Scotland to dictate the peace of Abernethy.

The Anglo Saxon Chronicle recorded that Malcolm III, the King of Scots, 'came forward and made peace, gave hostages and became King William's man'. They were new and fateful words for Scotland; under the feudal system which William was bringing to England 'to become a man' was to do fealty and homage to a superior lord for land and possessions, to give service and to provide reliefs. From then on the Norman kings were to regard Scotland as a fief of the English Crown and its king as a vassal of the English kings.

After the death of the Conqueror in 1087, Malcolm thought he would test the mettle of his successor. The reaction of William

Rufus was swift. On his knees Malcolm swore to be William's 'man'. Malcolm took this quaint new procedure lightly, however, and invaded Northumbria five times before he was slain in 1093, plunging his kingdom into the turmoil of a disputed succession. For the next few years William Rufus was busy putting kings on the Scottish throne. An army from England allowed Duncan II to take his place on the royal Stone of Scone after he had done homage to William. When he was slain by Donald Bane after six months, another English army put another son of Malcolm III, Edgar, on the throne of his father. It was not surprising that Rufus should regard himself as the 'Lord Paramount of Scotland'.

Edgar was the first of the three sons of Malcolm III and his second wife, the Saxon Princess Margaret, to become kings of Scotland. They had grown up at the English court and had Norman ideas of kingship, law and church organisation. They brought their Norman friends to introduce these ideas into Scotland. When Edgar was succeeded by his brother Alexander, the chroniclers noted that 'he was generous beyond his means to newcomers'; his brother David was even more generous. He gave Robert de Brus of a Breton family 200,000 acres in Annandale, large estates in Teviotdale to Bernard, Lord of Bailleul, and appointed Walter Fitzalan his dapifer, or steward—a Balliol, a Bruce and a Stuart were to become kings of Scotland.

Behind the mailed hauberks of the Normans came the copes and habits; the old monastic orders of Celtic Scotland were gradually superseded by new monastic orders from England. There was a new Abbot at Scone and work was started on the building of a great new Abbey where the Stone of Destiny would lie before the altar. There were Norman officers at the Scottish court and new bishops at work on the organisation of new dioceses. In the twenty-nine years of his reign David worked unceasingly to establish a new concept of sovereignty and impose a feudal order on the ancient tribal society of the kingdom.

This Norman 'invasion' involved Scotland in the affairs of England. Robert de Brus held 80 manors in Yorkshire and the Bailleuls, Fitzalans, Comyns, de Grahams and others often held estates in both kingdoms. This double allegiance of the nobles was to be a fatal flaw in Scotland's sovereignty; the kings themselves also had a double perspective. In 1114 David received in marriage from Henry I, Maud, the daughter of the Earl of Northumbria; she brought him the earldom of Huntingdon with vast estates in the Midland shires. David, King of Scots, became the greatest of English magnates.

The entanglements with England grew deeper. Henry I had

married David's sister, Maud, whose daughter Matilda claimed the English throne against the rival claims of her cousin Stephen. Matilda was David's niece; but Stephen had married another niece, daughter of David's sister Mary. It was a double dilemma. David placed his wagers both ways; he sent his son to negotiate secretly with Stephen and summoned the Scots to arms ostensibly in support of Matilda. It was in 1138 that a proclamation of David 'summoned the whole nation'—a striking phrase which recognised the diversity of the people under his rule and united them in a new concept of sovereignty, the 'nation'. In effect, it was a 'nation' which responded to the summons. The host which gathered around the king was a multi-racial array of tribes and races, each with their own customs and traditions, with bitter recollections of past feuds, outrages and wars, speaking a variety of languages and bearing different weapons. The terrified Ailred, Abbot of Rievaulx in Yorkshire, saw them as a wild and savage horde. There were Scots from the Tay valley, mountain men from Argyll, Lothian spearmen and Flemings from the new towns, the wild kerns of Galloway, the axe-bearing descendents of the Norse invaders from Sutherland, and, drawn by the lure of battle, even men from the faraway islands of Orkney which were not yet under the king's rule. In the centre near to the king were about two hundred mail-clad and very unwelcome Normans.

Those men certainly had no ideas in their heads about the 'nation'. They had come for the plunder, responding to the fierce urge to battle, and those from Moray, Galloway and Argyll also came with a hatred of the Norman 'strangers'. The Normans doubted where their loyalties really were in such a situation.

The only power on earth which could have brought these discordant and diverse people together was their acceptance of a king's leadership. In all those races—Scot, Briton, Galwegian, Lothian, English, Flemish immigrant and Norman newcomer— there was a deep and instinctive response to the battle summons of a king. The king was the only unifying force out of which in the stress of battle and invasion the future kingdom of Scotland could be forged.

These primitive forces of war and the kingship were beginning to promote a long process of change in men's ideas. The diverse people of northern Britain were to submerge their ancestral memories slowly in a deep feeling of national identity. The Picts forgot their language, the Scots forgot they were Irish, the Britons the names of their former princes and eventually the Normans who cast their loyalties within Scotland like the Gordons, Frazers and Comyns, were to be absorbed in the fierce loyalties

ita eft fup ripam fluminis tyeve. in loco qu

David I and his grandson who succeeded him as Malcolm IV. Miniature from the Charter of Kelso Abbey, 1159. The style and regalia were copied from the English model and were unlikely to have been used at his inauguration on the Hill of Scone (*National Library of Scotland*)

of the patriotic Highland clans. The nobles and chiefs would often rise in rebellion against the Scottish kings, but the centuries-to-come were to show that it was still a king of Scotland which most of them wanted to put in his place.

It would have been impossible to see any omens of those changes in the wild horde which was plundering and savaging its path through Northumberland in 1138. The Scots and English met at Cowton Moor near Northallerton. Here the dual loyalties of the Normans were displayed; Robert Bruce and Bernard de Balliol came riding out of the English army to negotiate with the king who had granted them their great tenures in Scotland. David refused to forgo his claim to Northumbria, and Bruce—the grandfather of the future king—renounced his feudal allegiance to David, crying that it was shame on him for leading a horde of mixed savages against the gentle Norman chivalry. Bruce's son, however, remained with the Scottish army and was conveniently taken prisoner by his father in the battle, so that the Bruce estates in Scotland were secured to the family.

The 'gentle Norman chivalry' raised a tall symbol of their faith and feudalism; a pole as tall as a ship's mast on a great cart, after which the Battle of the Standard was named. From the mast were suspended the banners of the patron saints of York, Beverley and Ripon below the Sacred Host in a silver shrine. Beneath this standard the compact mass of mailed knights supported by archers awaited the impact of the wild men from the north. Across the moor David was flying the great Dragon of Wessex, the symbol of his mother's Saxon house of Cedric, proclaiming his right as her inheritor to at least a share in the kingdom he was invading.

The Galwegians at the last moment disrupted the Scottish line of battle by demanding the central place held by the Norman knights on their side. They got their way under threat of rebellion; then, drawing up the saffron skirts of the Gall Gael high on their hairy legs, they charged with wild shouts of 'Alban! Alban!' The repeated charges of the thin-clad men failed to break the ring of armour. The Abbot Ailred, with a zestful turn of phrase, said that the 'arrows buzzed like bees and flew like rain' so that 'men lay like hedgehogs with quills'. After a succession of furious onslaughts the Scots withdrew, in sufficiently good order, however, to begin a siege of Wark castle.

There was a triumph concealed in the disaster. Stephen, beset by enemies, made peace with David, conferring on his son Henry the whole of Northumbria, except the castles of Newcastle and Bamburgh. The Kings of England and Scotland were to play a long and bloody game of shuttlecock with Northumbria.

David I forced open the reluctant doors of change in Scotland. His father had been the warrior chief of a tribal society, the greatest of the great mormaers, ruling amid a diversity of tribal laws and customs, taking his revenues out of the direct produce of his royal estates, venison, hides and grain; when the royal resources were exhausted he moved on to the next thaneship or monastery under tribute to provide *cain* and *conveth* for the upkeep of the royal dignity. Malcolm had been a king whose writ went as far as his strength could reach and whose reputation was measured by his personal prowess in battle and the plunder he could gain for his followers. It was a kingship and society not far removed from that of the migrant peoples of the Bronze Age and still close to the ideas and customs of the regality which Columba had conferred on Aidan 500 years before.

David I brought to his kingdom a new concept of sovereignty which he had acquired during his formative years at the court of his brother-in-law, Henry I. In the system which the Normans had imposed on England the king was the source of power and the fount of justice; men were not linked together in the tangled web of Celtic consanguinity and every man knew his place in a society which climbed in hierarchic steps from the serf to the king. The service of each man was defined; his place in society was fixed by his relation to the land on which he lived—land held of a superior lord, who held of a still more superior lord, who held of the king. The act of homage was acceptance of obligations and the oath of fealty was the bond which held society together.

The Normans in England had forced their system on a land swept bare of any Saxon opposition. In David's kingdom there had been no such scouring of the land. The Celtic ferocities of Moray, Galloway and even the Mearns had not been subdued. The tribal passions, the furious entanglements of consanguinity and even the ancient matrilinear claims to the throne could bring their eruptions along the lochsides and down the mountain passes—as David himself discovered when the great-great-grandson of Lady Macbeth made a wild bid for the throne.

Beyond the Forth, his kingdom was wild and primitive, blanketed by vast forests, saturated with mires, fens and peat bogs, with barriers of trackless mountainsides and with the patchwork of a primitive husbandry in sheltered valleys and by lochsides. The scattered townships, like the monasteries, were found near fertile land with communal grazing and cultivation rights. Trade was limited by barter, but smiths, carpenters and tanners were kept busy. Herdsmen guarded their cattle. The elk still roamed the north and wolves, bears and lynxes prowled around the wood and wattle habitations. Yet withal it was a land of high courage, close kindred, fierce loyalties and old tribal laws, of long tales of a heroic past, of harp music and an obdurate resistance to change, as David already knew.

The Normans whom David had brought to Scotland built their fortresses on man-made mounds and hills, with timber towers behind palisades curtained with a ditch. In England these castles had dominated the land; among the unsubdued people of northern Britain their role was often to be self-protective. Even in David's reign, however, some Normans became so infected by their Celtic ambience that they were absorbed into the clan system and were ready to fight for ancient wrongs committed long before their time. The greater lords were to become the successors of the mormaers as the great Earls of Scotland, with a *sennachie* who conveniently discovered Celtic ancestors for them. Others were to remain the flawed strands in the kingdom, with lands in Scotland and loyalties in England.

Feudalism spread slowly across the kingdom like a green lichen with the solid rock of Celtic custom lying closely underneath, especially in the north, the west and in Galloway. It became a new and convenient cloak for the ancient tribal rights and customs. The charters by which the king granted tenures of land by knight service served to put on record the older system of Celtic land ownership. The clan system with its close family relationships and the fierce loyalty to its chief, was a stronger bond than the formalities of feudal homage and fealty. The businesslike Normans and Bretons recognised the practical value of the clan organisation within their fiefs, and the feudal lords at court readily became the Highland chiefs and chieftains in their own glens. It was in the drawing together of some of these lords around himself as king that David was more effective in creating his ideas of sovereignty. He appointed them to the feudal offices of justiciar, chancellor, chamberlain, constable and marischal and these officers of state, with their host of clerics and clerks busy with charters, tenures, grants, fines and briefs to the sheriffs, began to create the complex fabric of a national administration. In England the grip of the Norman king could reach down to the meanest serf, in Scotland the king established the forms of feudalism without its inflexible power of control.

It was through the Church that David came closest to achieving his ideals. The new orders of monks he summoned to Scotland brought both their asceticism and their vigour to the kingdom. They brought wealth as well as the word of God. The monks were as busy as the bees from their hives; the Cistercians created great sheep farms—the 'golden fleeces' of the future—and introduced new farming methods. Other monks saw the future for coal and became busy underground. They wove cloth, brewed beer, tanned leather, illuminated manuscripts, made gold and silver chalices and raised on high the square-faced churches and Abbey buildings above the squat buildings around them.

The new bishops, mostly Normans, worked to create the new dioceses and to promote the building of cathedrals. The Church grew into the texture of society. In times to come it would often be the voice of the Scottish Church which would speak for the whole realm. David kept the appointment of bishops in his own hands, resisting the claims of York and Canterbury, as well as those of the distant Pope in Rome. He appointed them to his Council, made them officers of state as his Chancellors and saw his kingdom growing closer together in the organisation of the Church.

David has left us an impression of how he saw himself on the seals attached to his charters. He presents himself clad in the

Norman armour of the period, with scaled coat of mail, conical steel cap, spurred boots and his lance flying his *pennoncelle*. It is a knight of the Norman chivalry who rides before us. This armoured king must have seemed an unfamiliar figure when he rode out among his Celtic subjects. He was a Norman king on a Celtic throne.

David took another step away from the Celtic past when he moved its capital from its ancient heartland to the rocky mound of Edinburgh. The Scots no longer looked back to their origins in Dalriada and the great Celtic devotion to St Columba was beginning to fade. A new saint was capturing the devotions of the Scots—St Andrew, the brother of St Peter who had been martyred far away at Patras in Achaia in 60 AD. The new monks, looking back at the apostolic centre of their faith, had fostered the growth of the devotion to St Andrew. David's mother, Margaret, herself to be canonised, encouraged the growth of pilgrims by providing the Queen's Ferry across the Forth. St Andrews became the ecclesiastical centre of the kingdom, the seat of the High Bishop and the source of a legend which overshadowed the Celtic Cross of Iona.

It was claimed that the relics of St Andrew had been brought to Scotland from Constantinople by Regulus in the fourth century. This belief was so strongly accepted that on that basis the Church of Scotland would later claim to be antecedent to the English Church and therefore free from its authority.

It was the time when the banners of the saints were raised along the battle lines, as at the Battle of the Standard, as well as the old totemic banners of the tribes and clans. It was to be nearly two hundred years, however, before the symbol of St Andrew, the white inverted cross on the blue ground, was to appear as the Banner of Scotland.

We know that David himself when he invaded England had borne on his battle standard the great Dragon of Wessex, the symbol which the royal house of Cedric, his mother's family, had borne to the unification of England. It might have been more than pride of blood which made him display the Dragon of Wessex to the English usurper, Stephen. The Anglo-Saxon Chronicle says that 'the king of Scots thought he would claim this land'. If that was his ambition, it was to remain a dream of sovereignty of which the fulfilment lay beyond centuries of wars, invasions and the deaths and sufferings of countless human beings.

CHAPTER 17
'JEO DEVEIGNE VOSTRE HOMME'

The lives of thousands of men and the resources of two kingdoms were centred on four words in Norman-French: *Jeo deveigne vostre homme*—'I become your man'. Few words have embraced a greater symbolism. They were the definitive words of the status between man and man, vassal and lord, lord and superior, subject and king. When spoken between kings they marked the distinction between vassalage and sovereignty. It became the unrelenting ambition of the English kings to have the kings of Scotland kneeling before them while they spoke the words which acknowledged that they were the 'Lords Paramount of Scotland'.

William the Lion, King of Scotland, was red-headed, burly and impetuous. On 13 July 1174 he rode out of the morning mist near Alnwick, saw a small force of English knights and setting his lance in advance charged upon them. In the skirmish William's horse was killed, pinning him to the ground. The leader of the English knights looked down with amazement at the Scottish king; here was a prize beyond all expectations! They tied his legs beneath the belly of a horse and led him off in triumph, and he was taken in captivity in the train of Henry II when the English king returned to carry on his war in France. He secured his release only by signing the humiliating Treaty of Falaise, becoming the 'Liegeman of his lord the King' and agreeing to perform fealty 'as did other vassals'. Henry II was declared the 'Lord Paramount of the whole Kingdom of Scotland'. It seemed that the issue of Scotland's sovereignty had been finally settled. For fifteen years the yoke of England lay on Scotland, provoking yet another unsuccessful rising by the Celtic lords, which William quelled by 'licence' of the English king.

Henry II was no sooner in his tomb than William the Lion was on his way to England to get a revision of the treaty which Church, nobles and people regarded as an act of shame. William carried

Opposite above: English Regalia: detail of the Jewelled Sword. One of the richest and most beautiful swords in the world, it was made for the Coronation of George IV. The scabbard is encrusted with diamonds, rubies and emeralds which form the emblems of the Tudor Rose, the Thistle and the Shamrock

Opposite below: English Regalia: the Coronation Orbs. The larger Orb was made for Charles II and is delivered only to a Sovereign Regnant. The smaller Orb was made for Mary II as joint sovereign with her husband, William III, and has since been used as the Orb of the Queen Consort

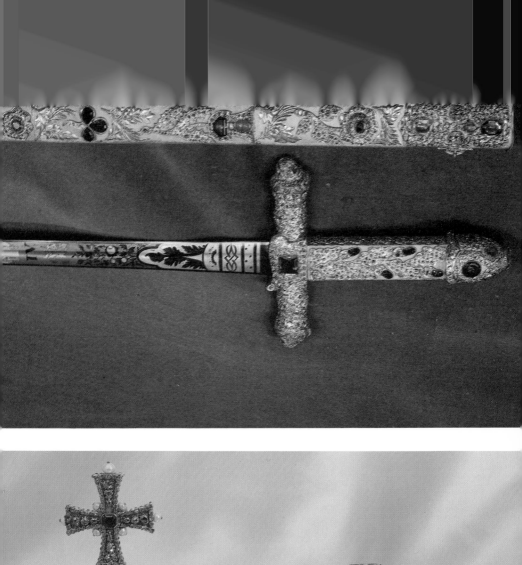

Scottish Regalia: the handle and guard of the Sword of State. Oak leaves and acorns, the emblems of Pope Julius II, are heavily sculptured on the pommel and handle of gilded silver. The traverse guard is two dolphins looking towards the handle with their tails ending in acorns and oak leaves

the Sword of State at Richard Coeur de Lion's coronation as a vassal service but judged the time was ripe for negotiation. Richard I was desperate for money to support his departure for the Crusades and, by the Quitclaim of Canterbury in December 1189 for a payment of 10,000 marks of silver, he ceded to William the castles surrendered in 1174 and renounced his feudal overlordship of Scotland.

It was to be a temporary quitclaim. On the death of Richard I, his successor, King John, began to take an increasing interest in Scotland. William the Lion, who had grown old and weary in wars to maintain his sovereignty against his own rebellious subjects, became apprehensive that the ancient claims of England might be renewed. He tried to mollify John. He arranged for his young son, Alexander, to be knighted by King John and sent his two elder daughters to be married to King John's sons with a dowry of fifteen thousand marks. On the death of William in 1214 King John pocketed the dowry, forgot about the marriages and contemptuously announced that he intended to 'hunt the red fox cub from his den'.

In fact it was the red fox cub—Alexander—who came out of his den to support the English barons against King John, and at the same time he renewed his great-grandfather's claim to Northumbria. The king of Scots, wrote the old chronicler John Fordun, 'with a grate army invaded the country with fire and the sword'; it was a brief excursion which ended in a retreat in which Alexander 'sped safely home without loss and with great honour'.

After the death of King John the two young kings—Alexander II and Henry III—met in an attempt to settle the disputes between the two kingdoms. They made amicable arrangements: Alexander married the Princess Joan, daughter of King John and the sister of the young King Henry. The English king did not renew his claim to the overlordship of Scotland, while Alexander renounced his claim to Northumbria in exchange for the honour of Tynedale and the manor of Penrith—to be held of the English king for the rent of one red falcon presented each year at Carlisle Castle. A joint English-Scottish commission eventually fixed the border between the two countries along the Tweed to Solway line. If that settlement had held there was every prospect that Scotland might have grown into a great and prosperous nation.

Unfortunately, the amity between the two kings began to fade after the death of Alexander's wife, Joan, which was followed later by his marriage to Marie, the daughter of the Sire de Coucy. Old animosities began to smoulder. Henry, having lost his

fraternal influence, revived the old claims of England's supremacy.
The armies began to muster again. Through the intervention of
the Archbishop of York, a precarious peace was arranged and
Alexander was free to pursue his own claim to be Lord Paramount
of the Isles, which were then subject to the Norwegian Crown,
but death came to him suddenly on the green islet of Kerrera,
opposite Oban, leaving as his successor his son Alexander who was
not eight years old. In later times the people of Scotland would
look back on the reign of Alexander III as the Golden Age. That
golden prospect was not there at the beginning: people looked
with fear on the dangers within and without and exclaimed:
'Woe unto the land whose king is a child!'.

The earls and barons of Scotland assembled at Scone in haste
only five days after the death of Alexander II. The investiture was
quickly prepared to forestall any intervention by Henry III. That
intervention came, however, from within. The most powerful of
the men at Scone was Alan Durward, Justiciar of Scotland and
hereditary *Ostarius*, or doorward of the kings. He was the leader
of the nobles who leaned towards England and he now demanded
that the investiture should be postponed on the grounds that
Alexander was not yet a knight. On the open hillside, with the
Stone already spread with its rich coverings, the issue was debated
between the nobles who were, like others of that age, obsessed
with the conventions of chivalry. On the other hand, Walter
Comyn, the leader of those who wanted to keep England out of
Scotland's affairs, argued that kings had often been invested
before they were knighted. When Durward saw that opinion was
moving to Comyn he tried to touch upon the superstitions of the
times, urging delay because the day itself was unlucky.

Comyn replied, 'No day can be unlucky for deeds which depend
on the arbitrament of men; it was mere superstition to think so'.
He continued, 'A realm without a ruler is tossed about like a
ship without oars among the waves of the sea. I loved beyond
measure the king who is now dead; and so I shall love his son, not
only for his father's sake, but because he is our natural and rightful
lord. Let us therefore advance him to be our king as quickly as we
may.' His appeal succeeded and, wrote John Fordun:

> ...they immediately led the future King Alexander to the
> Cross which stands in the churchyard at the east end of the
> church; and having placed him in the regal chair, decked with
> silk cloths embroidered with gold, the Bishop of St Andrew's, the
> others asssisting him, consecrated him king, the king himself as
> was proper upon the regal chair—that is, the Stone—and the

JEO DEVEIGNE VOSTRE HOMME—'I become your man'. The inscription describes Alan of Brittany paying homage and allegiance to William the Conqueror for the lands of Edwin, the former Saxon Earl of Mercia

earls and other nobles placing vestments under his feet, with bent knees before the Stone ... And behold, everything being completed, a certain Scottish highlander, suddenly kneeling before the throne with bent head, saluted the king in his mother tongue in these Gaelic words—*Benach de Re, Alban Alexander, mac Alexander, mac William, mac Henri, mac David*, and thus, repeating the genealogy of the Scottish kings, rehearsed them to the end.

The old chronicler goes on to record that the Earl of Fife was there to perform his ancestral duty of raising the king to the Stone and that the 'nobles, clergy and people had consented with one voice to his being made king'.

Two years after his succession the ten year old Alexander came to York for his marriage to Margaret, the youngest daughter of Henry III and Queen Eleanor, which had been arranged in his father's reign. On Christmas Day 1251 Henry invested Alexander with the belt and sword of knighthood and, on the next day, the feast of St Stephen, the young king of Scotland married the eleven years old Princess Margaret of England amid scenes of great splendour—500 oxen were slain for the first meat course.

The king of Scotland was then required to do homage to the king of England for the manors which had been granted to his father in Cumbria and Northumbria. Henry III, looking down on the young boy, thought he could prevail on his youthful inexperience and told him that he must also do homage for his kingdom in Scotland as his forbears had done to the English kings. But Alexander had a prudence beyond his years, as the *St Albans Chronicle* says that he answered civilly: 'I have come hither in peace, for your honour and at your command, to be allied to you by marriage, and not to reply to you about so difficult a question. For I have not held deliberation concerning this with my chief men, as so difficult a matter demands'. Henry III, looking at the determined boy and the grim faces of the Scottish lords standing around him, passed over the matter in silence.

The early years of Alexander's long reign were troubled by the rivalries between the Comyns and the followers of Alan Durward who continued his intrigues with the English king. Alexander and his bride were kidnapped, but released under pressure from Henry III whose proclamations sounded to Scottish ears like the tutelage of a Lord Paramount of Scotland. Armies mustered but did not cross the new frontiers.

Henry III died in 1272 and two years later Alexander and his queen journeyed to London to be present at the coronation of

Edward I on his return from the Crusades. Alexander must have already distrusted Edward I for before he would leave Scotland he obtained a written assurance from Edward that he would not be prejudiced by his attendance or by any service asked of him.

Despite his assurance, Edward asked Alexander to carry the sword of State at his coronation. Alexander refused this service of vassalage and returned to Scotland without even waiting to do homage for the English manors he now held. Edward sent frequent embassies to Scotland to demand homage for the manors held by the rent of the red falcon and eventually Alexander agreed to return. He came prepared for some subterfuge. The ceremony took place during the sitting of the English Parliament in the king's chamber at Westminster. Two accounts have been preserved of what took place in the presence of English and Scottish lords and the officers of Edward's council.

In the register of Dunfermline Abbey it was written that Alexander did homage to the king of England in these words: 'I become your man for the lands I hold of you in the kingdom of England, for which I owe you homage: reserving my kingdom'.

Then William of Middleton, the Bishop of Norwich, immediately interjected: 'And be it reserved for the King of England, if he have the right, to your homage for the kingdom.'

Alexander must have recalled the day twenty seven years earlier when, as a boy, he had done homage to the king's father. He answered the bishop, speaking clearly so that all might hear: 'To the homage for my kingdom none has the right save God alone; nor do I hold it save of God alone'.

The king of Scotland had refused to do homage to Edward for his kingdom, but none the less the English king, by the voice of his bishop, had made his claim to the overlordship of Scotland.

The account in the English records is quite different. The Close Roll, the sixth of Edward I of 1278, records that the king of Scotland did homage in the king's chamber at Westminster on the 29th day of September in these words: 'I, Alexander, King of Scotland, become the liege man of the Lord Edward, King of England, against all men.'

These were the words of unconditional homage and care was taken to confirm the record by the witness of the members of Edward's council. Despite this high authority, the authenticity of the record is open to question. Alexander could not have sworn on 29 September since it has been shown that Edward was not at Westminster from July to 24 October in that year. An expert examination of the Roll has also revealed that the account was written over an earlier record which had been erased. Furthermore, it was most unlikely that the experienced king would concede what as a young boy he had refused.

On his return to Scotland Alexander became absorbed in the affairs of his own kingdom. He travelled widely throughout his realm. 'This was his custom every year' says the *Scotichronicon*: 'With a strong force of knights and nobles he would pass through his kingdom and spend in each quarter of it an equivalent time of the year, having with him his justiciar to administer justice to every man . . . and so the king had pleasure of his people and the people also rejoiced in their king.' He gave Scotland peace, prosperity and the strength to endure the storm which was to come.

The Marquis of Argyll, Chief of Clan Campbell, who insisted on Charles II signing a declaration of 'all his own sins and the sins of his father's house' and condemning the 'idolatry of his mother' before his Coronation in Scotland (*National Portrait Gallery*)

CHAPTER 18
THE ANOINTING OF SCOTLAND'S KINGS

The anointing of kings is a very ancient rite. Among the ruins of the palace of the great Pharoah Akhnaton at Tel-el-Armana, has been found a cuneiform tablet describing the anointing of the kings of Syria in the fourteenth century BC. The ritual cleansing of the kings on their succession by anointing became a general practice among the ancient kingdoms of the Middle East.

The rite found its place among the Hebrew people of the old Testament, who anointed their priests and later their kings. Aaron and his sons were anointed as priests by Moses, and the first king of Israel, Saul, was so consecrated when 'Samuel took a vial of oil and poured it on his head'. It was, however, the anointing of Solomon which formed the pattern of the Christian rite in Western Europe: 'Zadok the priest took an horn of oil out of the tabernacle and anointed Solomon; and they blew the trumpet and all the people said God save King Solomon.'

The earliest accounts of the anointing of kings in Western Europe are to be found in the Acts of the Fourth Council of Toledo in 633 where it is referred to as the established custom for the Visigoth kings of Spain. In England the 'sacring' of the king was included in the coronation ritual from early times. The Pontifical of Archbishop Egbert (732–767) shows that the kings of Northumbria were being anointed at their inaugurations in the eighth century. In 787 the Anglo-Saxon Chronicle recorded that Offa, King of the Mercians, designated his son Ecfrith as his successor and that he was hallowed to be king'. The ecclesiastical Synod of Celchyth in 786 referred to the unction as the essential element of the kingly office and emphasised the honour and dignity of the *Christus Domini*—the Lord's Anointed. In England the anointing of the sovereign with holy oil has remained at the centre of the coronation service for over thousand years.

The anointing not only bestowed 'the spirit of the Lord', it also sanctified the royal person. 'How was thou not afraid to stretch forth thy hand against the Lord's Anointed!' was the angry retort of David, to the Amalekite who brought him the news that Saul had been slain. What had been conferred could not be taken away. Centuries later Shakespeare was writing:

> 'Not all the water in the rough, rude sea
> Can wash the balm from an anointed king.'

The privilege could only be granted by the Popes; it implied that the sovereignty of the anointed king was not a subordinate kingship or vassalage. When Scotland first came to recognise the significance of the rite only five of the monarchs of Christendom had the papal approval for their anointing—England, France, Jerusalem, Sicily and the Holy Roman Empire. Twenty-two of the states of Europe had been refused the privilege by the Pope.

The appeals of the Scottish kings to the Popes were countered by the powerful objections of England. The kings and bishops of England protested to the Popes that Scotland's requests were mere strategems to avoid the obligations which they owed to their overlords, the kings of England.

From reign to reign the patient churchmen and the more impatient nobles of Scotland travelled down the long roads of France, crossed the high Alps and rode down to Rome with their pleas, their petitions and the letters of their kings. They made little progress. The officials of the Curia politely spread their hands, and shrugged their shoulders, and the Popes themselves were unresponsive.

In 1127, when a hearing of the Scottish case was arranged by the Curia, David I, certain of defeat by the English objections, refused to allow his bishops to attend. In 1221 Alexander II continued his predecessor's appeals to the Pope to be crowned and anointed, but Pope Honorius III accepted the representations of Henry III that Scotland was subject to the English king and the Pope wrote to Alexander that the unction would, therefore, only be possible with the consent of Henry III, his council and his prelates. Alexander was persistent but in 1223 another application was successfully opposed by the Archbishop of York.

When his son, Alexander III, sent his own embassy to Rome he had the bitterness of knowing that several more of the states of Europe had been granted the privilege which his predecessors had been denied. Magnus V of Norway had been anointed in 1163, Knut VI of Denmark in 1170 and in Sweden the anointing had been introduced at the coronation of Erik X in 1210. The pleading of these precedents did not advance his cause. Conversely, each rejection of the Scottish claim strengthened the position of the English kings.

The unction was the symbol of the sovereignty of the kingdom, but it was also a matter which involved the supremacy of the Scottish Church. Who should be the minister of the anointing when, as the Scots obstinately believed, the right was conceded— the Archbishop of York, or of Canterbury, or the Bishop of St. Andrews? This was a very ancient issue.

When Augustine had been consecrated Archbishop of Canterbury in 601 he had been endowed by Pope Gregory with authority over all the churches in Britain. When Paulinus was appointed the first Archbishop of York in 625, however, the northern See would not accept that the primacy of Canterbury extended beyond the Humber.

This issue was not settled until William the Conqueror put an end to the ancient rivalries. In 1072 the Archbishop was compelled to acknowledge the primacy of Canterbury. The northern See was partly compensated by the concession of all episcopal rights from the Humber to the limits of Scotland.

Thomas of York returned to his see to assert his primacy over the Church in Scotland. He knew the fierce independence of the Scots and he made a cautious approach on the periphery. He consecrated one Ralf to the bishopric of Orkney. Nothing more was heard of this unfortunate bishop who disappeared into the island mists. Fifty years later the Archbishops of York were still trying to get their bishops into Orkney since we find the Pope issuing bulls requiring the parishioners of Orkney to receive them.

When York demanded the right to consecrate bishops to the vacant sees in Scotland the claim was vigorously rejected by the Scottish Church. The issue was taken to Rome where Pope Adrian IV upheld the claims of York. The next Pope Alexander III was more sympathetic to the Scottish Church and he appointed William of Moray as the papal legate to consecrate a bishop to the vacant see of St Andrews. When it seemed that the Church in Scotland was about to secure its independence from York its progress was thrown into jeopardy by William the Lion's acceptance of the Treaty of Falaise which contained the stipulation that 'the church of Scotia shall make such subjection to the Church of Anglia as it ought to make and was wont to make in times past'. When William the Lion and some of his nobles did homage to Henry II at York in 1175 there were conspicuous absentees among the bishops and abbots who took the oath of fealty, and other churchmen in Scotland firmly disputed the power of the king to bind the Church.

Henry II was determined to settle this ancient ecclesiastical dispute: he summoned William and his bishops and abbots to a council at Northampton in 1176. Henry informed them that by the terms of the treaty and the customs of the past, the bishops and Church of Scotland were subject to the primacy of the Church of England. The Scottish bishops rose to speak with angry tongues. Their predecessors had never been so subject and they themselves owed no such subjection to the Church of England. A cleric called

Gilbert attacked the English with passionate eloquence. The English, he said, were a race who tried to impose their yoke by violence on nations older and worthier than their own. He called on the Venerable Bede to witness that the Church of Scotland was the mother of English Christianity and had once held the primacy of all England north of the Thames.

The indignant Scots appealed to the Pope, declaring that the English king was attempting to make them swear obedience against their will. This was, they claimed, an offence to the papal dignity and the supremacy of the Pope over the Church. As the Scots had shrewdly foreseen, Pope Alexander did take offence at the action of the English king, and declared that it was not the business of kings and princes to meddle in the affairs of the Church. There would be 'injury to God and contempt of us and supression of ecclesiatic liberties' by this unwarranted action. He ordered the Archbishop of York not to exercise any jurisdiction over the Scottish bishops until the matter had been settled by the Pope himself. So the matter rested until in 1189 Richard I ceded again to William the Lion the sovereignty of Scotland for the sum of 10,000 marks. The way was now clear for papal action. In 1192 a bull of Pope Celestine III declared the *Ecclesia Scoticana* to be the special daughter of the Holy See directly subject to the Pope or his legate. No appeal might be taken to any other authority. It was the end of the claims of York and a notable victory for the Church in Scotland.

The kings and bishops of Scotland continued, however, to send their appeals to the Popes for the privilege of the sacred unction, but their expectations were to be for long deferred. In the end it was to be the sword of the Bruce and the victory of Bannockburn which finally convinced the Pope in 1329 that the Scottish king was a sovereign lord within his own realm.

CHAPTER 19
THE RAPE OF SOVEREIGNTY

Tragedy does not spare kings. For Alexander III the year 1281 was darkened by the death of his youngest son, David; then, within two years, he lost both his daughter, Margaret—who had married King Erik II of Norway and had a daughter by him—and his eldest son, Alexander, Prince of Scotland and heir to the throne.

The king moved swiftly to safeguard the succession, summoning all lords and bishops to a parliament at Scone. There, on 5 February 1284, they set their seals to a proclamation to 'all Christ's faithful of the Kingdom of Scotland' pledging themselves —if issue of the king should fail—to receive as true heir to the crown of Scotland 'the noble maiden Margaret, daughter of our Lord the King's daughter Margaret, of good memory, formerly Queen of Norway, begotten by the Lord Erik, illustrious King of Norway'.

Taking further steps to secure the succession, the forty-three-year-old king married in November that year the daughter of the Count of Dreux, but six months later Alexander himself was dead—killed when his horse stumbled and fell from a cliff path during a storm.

A small kingdom of 400,000 people was left leaderless. Scotland's new sovereign was the 'Maid of Norway', a sickly child in a foreign land, and other contenders for the throne began assembling their supporters. With feelings of increased anxiety, the Scots recalled what had been said when Alexander III, as a young boy, had been led to the Stone of Scone: 'Woe to the land whose king is a child'.

Now it was not only a child, but a girl. The idea of the Maid of Norway becoming the first queen regnant of Scotland violated both the Celtic and Norman concepts of the royal succession. Women begat kings but did not rule—the consort was simply the 'wife of the king' in Celtic Scotland, not a queen; while those of Norman descent would be reluctant to kneel in homage to a woman on the Scottish throne.

Robert Bruce of Annandale, grandfather of the future king, boldly declared that a woman could not inherit and put forward his own claims as a descendent of former kings. John Balliol, also of royal descent, declared that he alone was the true heir to the kingdom. The nobles hastily appointed six Guardians of Scotland to govern the realm and keep the rival claimants apart.

Edward of England was the Maid of Norway's uncle and the bishops of St Andrews and Glasgow wrote to him for advice. His response was immediate; Margaret, Queen of Scots, should marry his eldest son, Edward of Caernarvon, and be brought up in England by his consort, Queen Eleanor—so would the two kingdoms be united and have permanent peace between them.

The Scots refused to allow their young queen to be a ward at the English court, but a marriage treaty was drawn up and signed at Brigham in July 1290. 'The kingdom of Scotland was to remain separate and divided from the kingdom of England, free of itself and without subjection', and failing heirs of the marriage, the kingdom of Scotland was to return to the nearest heirs within the kingdom.

The Guardians wrote to King Erik of Norway urging him to hasten the departure of his daughter. Edward also tried to hasten her arrival, and in September 1290 the Maid of Norway saw the low roofs and the tall masts of Bergen falling away astern. The rumours ran before the official messengers. The Bishop of St Andrews wrote in haste to King Edward: 'There has sounded through the people a sorrowful rumour that our Lady is dead . . . on which account the kingdom is disturbed.' The bishop had cause to be fearful. In Orkney the child queen had died in the arms of Bishop Narve of Bergen. The ship returned to Norway where the first Queen of Scots was buried beside her mother in Christ's Kirk in Bergen.

Scotland became an armed camp of claimants and their supporters; thirteen nobles of Scotland claimed the throne, and Balliol issued a proclamation as 'heir to the Kingdom of Scotland'. Two of the Guardians were known to favour Balliol so the Bruce appealed to the Seven Earls of Scotland who, by ancient custom, had the right of 'making the king'. The Seven Earls responded by issuing a protest against the Guardians to prevent them choosing a king. Bruce then placed himself under the protection of King Edward and appealed to the crown of England for his rights. Edward got ready to arbitrate; he prepared the English Fleet for a blockade of Scotland, created a war chest of 10,000 marks and called on the feudal barons and shire levies of northern England to muster at Norham Castle on the English side of the Tweed.

The hearing of the Great Cause of Scotland is without parallel in the history of judicial and royal proceedings of the British Isles. It took place before an extraordinary court of 104 auditors: 24 barons and ecclesiastics appointed by Edward from his council and 40 assessors selected by Balliol and 40 appointed by Bruce.

The Great Seal of John Balliol, the 'vassal King of Scots', seated in majesty on a throne from which he could wield no power (*Scottish Record Office*)

On 17 November 1292 judgement was given in Edward's name in the great Hall of Berwick: John Balliol was formally declared King of Scotland. He did homage for his realm and swore fealty to Edward and was given the ominous injunction to govern justly 'least the lord superior of Scotland should be obliged to apply a guiding hand'.

On St Andrew's Day in 1292 Balliol was led out by the nobles and prelates to the royal stone on the Hill of Scone. There was a humiliating prelude: a warrant was read from Edward authorising the ceremony to be held and certifying that John Balliol was the proper person on whom it should be performed. Balliol was solemnly raised to the royal stone by John de St John, a relative of the Earl of Fife, who was a child. The vassal king was the last of the royal line to be seated on the ancient stone at Scone. He was given the sword and the sceptred wand of a hollow royal authority.

Balliol arrived at Newcastle for Christmas to pay homage, and to learn that the English king had used his authority to grant the appeal of a Scottish merchant against the Justiciars of Scotland. When Balliol protested that this contravened a provision of the Treaty of Brigham which forbade the hearing of such appeals outside the kingdom of Scotland, Edward made his position brutally clear: the Treaty of Brigham had been a marriage treaty, and its terms had died with the Maid of Norway; the right to hear appeals from Scotland belonged to him as sovereign lord of that realm.

Litigants, dissatisfied with judgements in the Scottish courts, were encouraged to appeal to Edward. When Balliol, unable to bear the indignity of appearing in person in the Court of the King's Bench, failed to attend, the English Council ruled that his failure to enter an appearance would mean that the King of Scotland would 'lose his homage and lordship and these could lapse to the overlord'. This rule was formally entered in the Rolls of Parliament for the Easter Term of 1293.

The yoke of England became too heavy for the Scots to bear when Edward, preparing for war with France, demanded the military service of the Scottish king, eight earls and twelve barons with all their retainers and prohibited the outward sailings of all ships from Scottish ports to France. At a Parliament at Stirling in July 1295 the government was taken out of Balliol's hands and a council of twelve elected to manage the direction of affairs. They began secret negotiations with France and a treaty was signed in Paris in October 1295 which was to remain the basis of the 'Auld Alliance' of France and Scotland.

The Scots mustered for war but there were gaps in their ranks when their forces assembled at Caddonlea; nobles with great estates in England had gone to join Edward. The old Bruce was dead, but his son and grandson crossed the border to swear fealty to Edward and to join the forces of the English king.

Edward's reply to the Scots was swift. With a large force he crossed the Tweed to Berwick, the thriving centre of Scotland's trade, which was protected only by a flimsy palisade. Edward ordered the destruction of the town and all its inhabitants, including the colony of Flemish merchants and their families. The horror of Berwick bred a hatred in Scotland which was to be replenished during the next three hundred years.

The support for Balliol began to ebb away. At Dunbar on 27 April 1296 the Scots remaining in the field were defeated and Balliol, deserted by all but a few, fled to the glens of Angus. Edward continued to advance into Scotland, killing when opposed, taking the surrender of castles, receiving the fealty of those who hastened to him

Edinburgh Castle resisted the huge siege engines for a week. When it surrendered Edward seized the regalia of the ancient kings of Scotland, as well as all the state records of the kingdom. No trace of this regalia was ever found again and only a few of the lumbering cartloads of the documents which wended to London survived the transfer to Westminster. Scotland was to be a land without a king, without a crown and without a record of its history.

At Perth Edward received the fealty of its citizens before turning his attention to the hill of the kings at Scone. It seems that for a time Edward intended to level the hill to the ground. There may have been more in this intention, however, than just to level the pride of the Scots. He had ransacked the adjacent Abbey of Scone of all its treasures and records, and before the altar he had found a rough block of reddish stone. The terrified monks of the Abbey insisted that it was the fabled Stone of Scone, the symbol of Celtic regality, the palladium of their race. When Edward looked at that rough hewn block of sandstone he may have had serious doubts about its authenticity for his clerks would have known that the stone offered to the king was not like the stone described in the records. The suspicions have lingered down the centuries. Dr Richardson, a distinguished archaeologist and an Inspector of Ancient Monuments, published a very persuasive account in 1951 in which he compared the stone in Westminster Abbey with the impressions on the early seals of the kings on their royal seats; he could find no correspondence between them. He pointed out that it was strange that a relic of such significance should be unadorned and that Henningburgh's description of the stone on which Balliol was enthroned only a short time before Edward's arrival at Scone, refers to it 'as hallowed out and fashioned in the manner of a round chair'. Dr Richardson concluded that the genuine stone had been hidden by the Abbot of Scone.

Balliol surrendered to Edward to taste the last bitter dregs of his humiliation and a cruel farce was enacted: he was garbed in the royal splendour of robes, crown, wand, ring and sceptre; the crown was snatched from his head, the royal sword plucked from his hand, the ring was torn from his finger and the ermine was ripped from his royal surcoat. Finally he had to place in Edward's hand the long white wand, the immemorial symbol of the regal power of the Scottish kings. The rape of Scotland's sovereignty was complete.

The land appeared firmly in Edward's control. English soldiers garrisoned its castles, English judges administered its law, English clerics were taking over the ancient cathedrals and monasteries, and English officers collected the feudal revenues. Edward did not add the title 'King of Scotland' or even 'Lord Paramount of Scotland' to his royal dignities.—Scotland as a separate land did not exist.

The Scots, like the Irish, could nurse their hatred like a smouldering fire in the heart of the peat; William Wallace, an obscure man from Paisley, thrust his own brand into the fire and

Scotland was suddenly alight—'there flocked to him all who were
in bitterness of spirit and weighted down with English despotism'.
The little men came first—the serving men, the small lairds and
the mountain men came hurrying down from their glens; later the
great lords like the Douglases, James, the Steward of Scotland,
Andrew of Moray and others from the old Celtic core of the
kingdom joined the banner of Wallace. The symbols of Scotland's
sovereignty were suddenly flying again before the battle array
which marched with the *Brechennach* in their midst. At Stirling the
English forces led by John de Warenne, Earl of Surrey, met with
a devastating defeat; Warenne fled to tell Edward that Scotland
was lost.

It was a brief triumph. Edward came hastening north and at
Falkirk in 1298 the triumph of Wallace was over, and it was his
turn to flee. For the next nine years revolts flared like sudden fires
among the heather and were extinguished, to break out elsewhere.
Edward had to march and countermarch his armies across moors
and mountains, besiege castles and throw bridges across turbulent
rivers. Wallace was betrayed to a shameful death at Smithfield.
Robert Bruce, inheritor of his grandfather's claim to the throne,
swore fealty to Edward, marched with the English armies and
conspired with the Scots.

An act of murder set Bruce on the road to the throne. In a
quarrel with John Comyn, the nephew of Balliol, in the Greyfriars
Church at Dumfries, Bruce in a blind rage stabbed Comyn to
death before the high altar. The sacriligious deed set the seal on
his resolution. Before the long arm of Edward could reach him,
Bruce gathered his adherents and took the road to Scone. The
Stone of Destiny was not in its place but Scone was still the
seat of the Scottish regality. Bishop Wishart of Glasgow gave
Bruce absolution for his crime before he was led out to a substitute
stone on the Hill of Scone on Friday 25 March 1306. He was
enthroned with the ancient ceremonies of the kingdom. Duncan,
the Earl of Fife, was in the power of Edward but his young sister,
Isabel, wife of the Earl of Buchan, stole her husband's horses and
fled from England to Scone for Bruce's inauguration, so that the
'right of the MacDuff of Fife might be exercised by the blood of
one of that ilk'. She paid a terrible price for the privilege: captured
by Edward, she was imprisoned in an open cage of iron and wood
and suspended from the castle walls of Berwick.

As Bruce rode away from Scone, his wife, riding beside him,
looked back at the Hill and exclaimed: 'We are but a summer
King and Queen, such as children crown with rushes in their
sports'. Before Bruce lay a long winter of flight from covert to

covert, with the bloodhounds trailing close behind him, sudden sorties, desperate feuds and the long months of exile.

In July 1307 Edward, borne northwards in a litter to pursue once again his implacable vengeance on the Scots, died at Burgh-on-Sands in Cumberland. His hatred did not diminish at the approach of death. He commanded his son, Edward, Prince of Wales, to boil the flesh off his bones and carry them with him in a leather sack to the final subjection of Scotland.

Edward II, however, had other interests. He arranged for his father to be buried in Westminster Abbey and returned to Carlisle while the Scots began to surge forward to claim more and more territory, moving from castle to castle, from glen to glen against the English garrisons. It was a dour and bitter struggle. On occasions Edward II shook off his lethargy and came north with an army, but the Scots cautiously retreated before him. It was another six years before the Scots met the English boldly at Bannockburn and struck the blow which drove the English out of Scotland and set a Scottish king firmly on the throne of his kingdom. Said the *Lannercost Chronicle*: 'And now Robert de Bruce was commonly called King of Scotland by all men, because he had acquired Scotland by force of Arms.' Bruce had forged his own sceptre.

That sovereignty was not yet acknowledged by England. In January 1327 Edward II was deposed and his young son, Edward III, led another array to conquer Scotland and wept boyish tears when victory eluded him. The extravagances of his father had depleted the young Edward's coffers and there was not enough money to pay his soldiers. Edward, therefore, proposed peace as well as the marriage of his six year old sister, Princess Joan, to Bruce's son, Prince David. Joan's dowry would be the recognition of Scotland's independence and sovereignty. By the Treaty of Northampton, Edward III solemnly declared that Scotland should be 'separate in all things from the kingdom of England, whole, free and undisturbed in perpetuity, without any kind of subjection, service, claim or demand.'

Eleven months later, by a bull dated at Avignon 13 June 1329, Pope John XXII granted to Robert, the illustrious King of Scotland, and to his successors, the right to receive the anointing and the crown. The long delayed indulgence of the sacred symbols came too late for Bruce; he had died six days before the issue of the papal bull.

David, Earl of Carrick, son of the Bruce, was married to Princess 'Joan-make-peace' with great splendour at Berwick. The groom was five and the bride seven. He was taken to Scone for his

The Battle of Bannockburn, 1314. A drawing from the *Scotichronicon*, a 15th century
source book of Scottish history by John Fordun. The fallen knight may be
de Bohun slain by Bruce himself (*Corpus Christi Library, Cambridge*)

royal inauguration with the ancient rites and the new sacring of the anointing and the crowning. 'He was,' says John Fordun, writing near to the events, 'the first king of Scotland to be so anointed and so crowned'.

He had not long to enjoy the peace of his kingdom. Edward Balliol, son of the John Balliol who had been dispossessed of his crown, suddenly appeared on the Border leading an array of Scottish nobles who had been 'disinherited' by Bruce for supporting the English and by English nobles eager to claim lands in Scotland. Edward III, forgoing his solemn undertaking at Northampton, had accepted the homage of Balliol to him as the overlord of Scotland; he gave Balliol the support of a powerful English army. The young king's forces, taken by surprise, were defeated at Dupplin near Perth. Like his father, Edward Balliol hurried to be crowned at Scone and left to do homage for his kingdom to the Lord Paramount of Scotland. English garrisons again occupied Scottish castles, English barons became earls of Scotland and the 'disinherited' returned to their forfeited lands. The boy king David and his queen had fled to France.

When in 1338 Edward III began to claim the richer prize of France, the Scots rose again, drove out Balliol and recalled their young king from exile. David answered an appeal from France for help against the common enemy, invaded England, was taken prisoner and remained a captive in England for eleven years.

Such was to be the history of Scotland for the next three hundred years. Peace was to be an interlude between battles. Royal marriages between the reigning families of Scotland and England failed to promote the ambitions of their kings. There were whole generations, say the monkish chroniclers of the times, when for sixty miles on each side of the border the corn could never be harvested.

England paid an immense price in bloodshed and suffering for the ambition of her kings, and the Scots paid a commensurate price for maintaining the sovereignty of their kingdom. For three hundred years they continued to display on countless battle-fields the symbols of their sovereignty and independence.

During that long struggle, countless thousands of Scots marched to a hundred battlefields behind the symbols of their nation; since the thirteeth century their battle standards had been emblazoned, white on blue, with the diagonal cross of St Andrew—the saltire. On 1 July 1385, the Scottish Parliament ordered everyone, Scots and French alike, in the army preparing to invade England, to wear a St Andrew's cross. Two legends seek to explain its appearance on Scotland's banner: the warrior's tale is that Angus, king of the Picts, before his victory in 740 over the Angles of Northumbria, saw a diagonal white cross in a clear blue sky and took it for his future battle ensign; the clerics told a more pious story, claiming that the cross was carried by St Regulus when he brought the relics of St Andrew from Patras to Scotland in the fourth century. The veneration of the Scots for the cross of their patron saint was to be deep and long-lasting.

CHAPTER 20
THE ROYAL ROAD TO SCONE

In 1559 the fires of the Reformation were lit in Scotland. In the Church of St John the Baptist in Perth John Knox poured out a fierce denunciation of the clergy and the general abuses of the Church. The congregation rose to destroy all its images and paintings, and went on to sack the monasteries of the Black and of the Grey Friars as well as the great Charterhouse. The treasures, the illuminated manuscripts and the records of the monasteries were destroyed. 'The palaces of idolatry,' wrote Knox, 'were made equal with the ground: all the monuments of idolatry that could be apprehended consumed with fire.'

Knox continued his incendiary preaching. On 11 June he entered St Andrews to urge the congregation to purge the church of its corruption. The building, the priory and all the monasteries around were destroyed. Knox described how he stood for three days in the centre of the town 'while their idols were consumed'.

The fervour for destruction spread across Scotland. The great Abbey of Scone was threatened; its commendator, the Bishop of Moray, pleaded with Knox and the Lords of the Congregation to spare the ancient shrine, but the fanatics, not to be appeased, began to march on Scone. Even Knox was appalled at the danger to the revered centre of the Scottish monarchy, but his intervention proved too late. The Abbey of Scone and the Bishop's Palace with all their contents were left in smouldering ruins. In that holocaust disappeared the records of the Scottish kings, accounts of their inaugurations and possibly also the manuscripts which would have unlocked the language and history of the great Pictish race which had once made Scone the centre of their kingdom. At the time it must have seemed that there would never be another king at Scone.

In 1567, when Mary Queen of Scots on the lonely island in Lochleven was compelled by threats and violence to abdicate, the thoughts of Knox and his associates did not turn to Scone. Mary's son, the infant James VI, was taken to the parish church at Stirling, where the Crown of Scotland was held above his tiny brow at his inauguration.

In the meantime the blackened ruins of Scone had passed into the possession of the Ruthven family, whose lords had lived short and dangerous lives. The fourth Lord Ruthven had plunged his dagger into David Rizzio at the feet of Mary Queen of Scots. In

John Knox preaching before the Lords of the Congregation. His fierce denunciation of the 'images of Popery' led to the destruction of churches and monasteries including the ancient Abbey of Scone (*Painting by David Wilkie, Tate Gallery*)

1581 he was created Earl of Gowrie and a royal charter appointed him Commendator of Scone. His tenure was short: he was beheaded in 1583 for an attempt to seize the King. The second earl died young and the third lost his life in another attempt to seize the King during the mysterious Gowrie conspiracy. Both the name and the estates of the Ruthvens were made forfeit by a formal act of the Scottish Parliament.

The stones of the Abbey of Scone had not been allowed to be covered with moss. The Ruthvens had them carried up the hillside to build a new palace at Scone, set around two courtyards with a long gallery which would be the scene of the last great royal occasion on the Hill of Scone.

Charles I, the last native-born king of Scotland, had grown up in England, and it was thirty years before expediency brought him back to receive the Scottish crown.

The Hill of Scone did not enter, however, into Charles's idea for his coronation. He chose the Chapel of Holyrood for a coronation which was alien to Scotland, foreign to presbyterianism in

its episcopal pomp, and neglectful of the ancient rituals of the
Scottish kings. The service had been prepared by William Laud,
Archbishop of Canterbury, who had followed the precedents of
the English coronation service. By royal command the Dean of
the Chapel Royal was instructed to use the 'form of our service
lately used at Westminster'.

The ministers of the Kirk and the Scottish lords beheld all the
ritual splendours of a great episcopal ceremony. Even the Yeomen
of the Guard had been brought from London to add another
touch of English pageantry. At the west door King Charles was
received by the Archbishop of St Andrews and five prelates in
violet silk cassocks, white rochets and copes of cloth of gold. As
the royal procession entered it was observed that 'at the back of
the church there was a rich tapestry wherein the crucifix was
curiously wrought; and as the bishops who were in the service
passed by the crucifix they were seen to bow their knee and beck,
which with their habit was noted and bred great fear of the
inbringing of popery'. It was an English rite translated to Scotland; the Lord Lyon as the High Sennachie of Scotland did
not step forward to proclaim the royal genealogy of the Scottish
kings, and there was none of the traditional fervour of the windswept Hill of Scone.

The Golden Ampulla used for the anointing of Charles I at his Coronation in
Edinburgh on 18 June 1633. Unlike the English Ampulla it was not preserved
among the Scottish Regalia

Charles went his way, alienating the affections of a people who wholeheartedly wanted to give him their devotion. He appointed Spottiswoode, Archbishop of St Andrews, as his Chancellor in Scotland, a committee of Parliament was selected by bishops, and he ordered the Kirk to use a new prayer book which brought the people out on to the streets to hunt down the bishops and beseige the Provost in the city chambers. Out of this upheaval in 1638 came the Covenant and the declared intention to oppose all changes which were not approved by a free Assembly and the Scottish Parliament. The old loyalties were still there, however, and the Covenant bound its signatories to 'stand to the defence of the King's Majesty'.

It was not surprising, therefore, that when the time came for the king to admit defeat in the Civil War that he should surrender himself into the keeping of the Scottish army at Newark. The Scots could not get him to sign the Covenant which required the imposition of presbyterianism on all three kingdoms of the British Isles. When Charles would not accept this impossible condition, the Scots decided that they would no longer fight for king or Cromwell, and that it was time to take their long delayed pay and go back across the Tweed again. They surrendered Charles to the English commissioners on the understanding that he would be treated 'with honour, safety and freedom'.

When the perils began to close around the king, there were bitter recriminations in Scotland. The charge was made that a Stuart king of Scotland had been sold for a few coins from an English purse.

The Scots acted to save their honour and their king: three Scottish commissioners saw Charles secretly at Carisbrooke Castle on the Isle of Wight and signed an engagement with him promising the help of a Scottish army in return for his undertaking to establish presbyterianism in England for a trial period of three years. The Covenant would not be obligatory. A majority of the Scottish Estates accepted this engagement and a Scottish army marched to liberate the king, but it was routed by Cromwell between Preston and Wigan. It was the last blood shed for Charles I, and he was brought to trial and executed seven weeks later on 30 January 1649.

Charles II was proclaimed as soon as the news reached Scotland. The Lyon King of Arms grimly noted in his records: 'King Charles behedit at Whytehall Gate, in England by that traiterous parliament and army ... Prince Charles proclaimed King of Grate Britaine, France and Ireland At Edinburghe Cross.'

Charles II at nineteen was confronted with a situation beyond the wit of any man. The Marquis of Ormonde had concluded a treaty which had united the Protestant Royalists and Catholics in Ireland; the English Royalists expected the King to be loyal to the principles for which his father had died, and the Scots wanted him to impose the Covenant on all three kingdoms. Charles II tried to cut the complicated knots with a sword; he sent the Marquis of Montrose to raise the Highlands to his cause and held long and bitter discussions with the Scottish commissioners who had come to meet him in Breda.

In the end Charles had to accept their terms—to sign the Covenant, impose religious uniformity on the three kingdoms and to ban all heretics. He was reminded by his cynical friend, Buckingham, that his grandfather had once considered that 'Paris was worth a Mass'. He sent messages to Montrose to lay down his arms; they never reached him—Montrose was defeated and betrayed by a laird for £20,000 pounds, part of which was paid in porridge oats. Montrose died with a dignity which earned him an enduring place in the heroic legends of Scotland.

Charles had a far less heroic part to play. When he landed at Speyside the people flocked to acclaim their king; they danced and sang, rang the bells, got intoxicated with joy, and housewives and fishermen kept the bonfires alight with their furniture and their fishing baskets.

As Charles rode inland the warmth of his welcome faded; the Covenanters closed around him. He had to dismiss all who had come with him from Holland, except Henry Seymour and Buckingham, whom the Covenanters believed to be 'replete with godliness'. At Pitcople the Marquis of Argyll was waiting for him— 'a man of craft, subtlety and falsehood,' was the opinion of the Earl of Clarendon, faithful servant of royal father and son. Argyll considered himself to be the real master of Scotland.

Charles was installed in the Palace of Falkland where he was isolated from all outside contacts and delivered to the theological fury of the Covenanting ministers, who had access to him at every hour of the day and night, even to his bedroom. The Sabbath must have been a great ordeal for Charles; he had to listen to as many as six sermons of inordinate length which included condemnations of his parents and his Stuart ancestors.

Charles bore his ordeal with composure; it was the price of his throne. Cromwell had no intention, however, of allowing him to ascend that throne. On 22 July the English army crossed the border, with Cromwell flinging at the Scots the words: 'I pray you by the bowels of Christ consider that you may be mistaken.'

The Scots prepared to fight, and the leaders of the Kirk began

by purging the army of all who were suspected of religious non-
conformity; 3,000 fighting men were cast out. While Cromwell
advanced the young king had to face his final humiliation; he
was required to sign a declaration of 'all his own sins and the sins
of his father's house' and to condemn the 'idolatry of his mother'.

He pleaded with Argyll, 'I shall never look my mother in the
face again if I sign it.'

The Marquis replied coldly 'It is necessary for your affairs.'

'I shall dishonour my father'. Argyll was silent; honour was not
a matter on which he felt strongly.

Charles made his last appeal: 'If you protect me I will make you
a duke and a gentleman of the bedchamber when I come into
my own.' He added the promise of £40,000. That was a different
matter. Argyll got some of the extreme words taken out of the
declaration.

Religious fanaticsm lead to the Scots' defeat by Cromwell.
They had the English army surrounded from their positions on
the hills above Dunbar, when the ministers heard the voice of
revelation and commanded that the Scottish army should come
down from their places. 'The Lord has delivered them into my
hands,' exulted Cromwell when he saw the Scots descend.

The defeat at Dunbar changed the position of the king. People
were shocked into sanity and moderate opinions began to prevail.
The King should be crowned immediately to unite the nation
behind him. Even royalists were recruited for the new army,
provided they sat on a penitential stool before they took up arms.

At the end of December 1650 Charles II came to the Hill of
Scone; when he entered the long gallery of Gowrie House there
were some who received him with sullen looks. 'Who but so good
a king,' exclaimed one of his adherents, 'would have exposed
himself to such men's trust at such a time.'

The preparations for his coronation had been entrusted to a
committee of the Estates; the Lord Lyon found that he had exchanged the dictates of the episcopy for the even stricter injunctions of the Kirk. In particular, there would be no anointing of
the king. Charles was formally offered the Crown of Scotland on
New Year's Day, in the Presence Chamber of Gowrie House, before
being led out in procession to the small church on the hillside.
The Marquis of Argyll walked behind the king carrying the crown
which he had sought to deny him.

The service began with a sermon by the Rev Robert Dowglas
which lasted three hours; it was an exposition of the principles of
the Scottish Covenant and the binding conditions which his
signature had imposed on the king. It ended with the familiar

The Flag of the Covenanters displayed their loyalty to the King. The slightly obliterated wording reads: Covenants. For Religion. King. And Kingdomes. (*National Museum of Antiquities of Scotland*)

diatribe on the sins of Charles, his parents and his predecessors— 'There are many sins upon our king and his family,' insisted the preacher. Charles knelt down to renew his undertakings to the Covenant, declaring 'by solemn oath, in the presence of Almighty God, the Searcher of Hearts, my allowance and approbation of the National Covenant . . . and faithfully oblige myself to persecute the ends thereof'. He bound himself to accept the acts of the General Assembly of the Church of Scotland and the Scottish Parliament under the Covenants, 'enjoying the same on my other Dominions.' Even as he swore, Charles must have known that this part of his oath was for ever beyond his attainment.

Seated in a raised Chair of Estate to be presented to the congregation, the king listened to another long sermon with repeated references to his fall from grace and the idolatry of his mother. He took the Coronation Oath which required him to maintain the true religion and to 'abolish and gainstand all other false religions contrary to the same' and also 'to root out all enemies of the true worship declared as such by the Kirk of God'.

He was now invested in the Royal Robes of a sovereign, the Sword was placed in his hand 'for the protection of the Kirk and of the true religion' and the Spurs were placed on his heels.

The Marquis of Argyll took up the Crown: the moment had come for which this king had endured insult and humiliation, condemned the religion of his martyred father, accused his mother of idolatry and had sworn what he knew he could never achieve. Argyll himself was about to do what he had used all his devious talents to prevent.

Argyll raised the Crown, the cold light of that winter's day striking a frosty gleam from its pearls, topazes and rock crystals— and brought it slowly down to rest on the king's head. Did the gaze of the two men meet at that moment of culmination?

In England the crowning was followed by the shouts of acclaim, the pealing of trumpets, the beating of drums and the ringing of the Abbey bells. There were no tokens of jubilation in the Church at Scone. The peers came soberly forward to kneel before the king and touch the Crown with the words: 'By the Eternal and Almighty God I shall support thee for ever'. The Sceptre was placed in the king's hand and this time the words were not distorted from their ancient symbolism: 'Sir, receive this Sceptre, the sign of the Royal Power of this kingdom, that you may govern yourself aright, defend all Christian peoples committed by God to your charge, punishing the wicked and protecting the just.' The king then sat down again to listen to another long sermon before the Lyon King of Arms came forward to perform the ancient custom of proclaiming the genealogy of the royal line of Scotland back to Aidan and Fergus mac Erc. It was the last time that the voice of the *Sennachie* would ever be heard on the Hill of Scone.

Robed and crowned and carrying the Sceptre Charles now 'went out of a door prepared for that purpose and showed himself to the people'. A great roar of popular acclamation resounded once more around a king on the Hill of Scone. Charles looked down on the moving sea of upturned faces, the waving arms, the uplifted muskets, with here and there a Scottish broadsword catching the light of that winter's day.

Charles had then to sit down on the open hillside in fading light of that winter's day to endure another long sermon from the inexhaustible preachers on the theme: 'If you break the Covenant, being solemnly sworn, all those who have touched your Crown, and have sworn to support it shall not be able to hold it on, but God will shake it off and turn you from your throne.'

At last he was allowed to go, returning in procession through the waiting crowds, his path lit by torches. The ceremony had lasted eight hours. The last king had been inaugurated on the Hill of Scone.

He was not, however, the last Stuart at Scone. Another Stuart was to come there for to be crowned. On 16 January 1716 James Edward Stuart arrived at Scone. He followed the precedents of the kings at that place, and made his proclamations from Scone, commanding prayers in all churches, summoning a meeting of the Estates, ordering all fencibles from 16 to 60 to repair to his standard. His final proclamation was about his forthcoming coronation.

It was not to be. Another Argyll was grimly closing in on another Stuart; the Old Pretender fled across the ice of the Tay, complaining with tears that 'instead of bringing him to a crown they had brought him to his grave'. Prince Eugene of Savoy, hearing of this, remarked that 'weeping was not the way to conquer kingdoms'.

At Scone the Scots had brought to Charles II the crown, the sword and the sceptre of the Scottish kings which they had carefully preserved in Edinburgh, Perth and Stirling Castles. In England the religious zealots had defaced and destroyed these hated symbols of kings; in Scotland they had been treated with a respect which amounted to devotion. The reforming zeal which had swept through Scotland, destroying images and the treasures of the churches and monasteries, did not lay destructive hands on the ancient regalia of the kingdom. When the Lord Treasurer had fled to Dalkeith Castle with the regalia and the Castle eventually fell into the Covenanters' hands they made a triumphant return to Edinburgh with them. The 'Honours of Scotland', as the regalia were called, were treated with all the traditional respect and with saluting cannonades from the Castle. A few months later the Honours were carried with even greater ceremony by the Commissioners to the meeting of Parliament, where they were placed in their customary place on a table, the constant reminder of royalty before the eyes of the Estates. The pieces of the regalia were decorated with images of the saints and the Virgin similar to those which had been destroyed in numerous churches; the sceptre had been blessed and conferred on James IV by Pope Alexander VI in 1494 and the scabbard of the sword was emblazoned with the name and arms of Pope Julius II. When the Scots looked at these symbols of their independent kingships the fires of the Reformation were subdued; they had a reverence for them despite the 'emblems of popery' which they so prominently displayed.

Their loyalty to their ancient symbols was a reflection of their loyalty to the king. There had been no treasonable intent in the Covenants. Their humiliating treatment of Charles II had been

inspired by a genuine zeal to convert him into a true Covenanting
king, purged of his iniquities, a royal pillar of the Kirk. Scotland
was again providing the reverse image of events in England. At
the Reformation it had been Henry VIII who had made his
subjects conform to his religious ideas; in Scotland it was the
subjects who were seeking to impose their religious ideas on the
king. It was not merely missionary zeal, however, which made
them try to bind Charles with hopeless oaths to ' conjoin the true
religion on all his kingdoms'. A uniformity of religious ideas was,
they thought, Scotland's best guarantee of her sovereignty within
the King's realms.

Parliament House, Edinburgh, meeting place of the Scottish Estates until 1707
(*RTH*)

CHAPTER 21
THE RESCUE OF THE REGALIA

Dunnottar on the coast of Kincardinshire looked an impregnable fortress; the great rock rose sheer out of the sea and could be approached on foot only by a narrow ridge which two good swordsmen could hold against an army.

Dunnottar had been both a fort and a sanctuary. Neolithic men had surrounded its flat top with earthen banks and sharp stakes; the Picts had made it a fortress. The kings of Dalriada in their incursions into Pictland had retreated when they saw its impregnable strength.

After many wars and sieges this great rock came into the possession of the Keiths. Herveus de Keith was the great marischal at the wedding of Alexander II and the princess Joan of England in 1220. The office of marischal seems to have been made hereditary in the family about this time. A later Keith was ambassador to England and his descendent was one of the Guardians of Scotland in 1305. It was a Keith who, as marischal to Robert Bruce, commanded the cavalry which routed the English archers at Bannockburn. It was another Sir William Keith, Great Marischal of Scotland, who took possession of the 'half barony of Dunnottar' by royal charter from David I in 1380 and raised the great fortalice on the rock.

The seventh Earl Marischal was both royalist and presbyterian and suffered on both accounts; he was out with Montrose in 1639, but stayed dourly in his fortress of Dunnottar when Montrose at Stonehaven in 1645 called on him to join the royalist forces. Montrose took his toll of Keith's estates, firing Stonehaven,

Standard of the Keiths, Earls Marischal of Scotland, bearing the motto TRUTH PREVAILS. This banner was carried from the field of Flodden and after nearly five centuries still shows the bloodstains of its bearer (*Faculty of Advocates*)

scattering his homeless tenants, burning barns, destroying the ships in the harbour and even setting fire to the woods at Fetteresso. The Earl and his wife 'watched the reek' from the top of the tower, while a minister of the Kirk tried to convince them

Dunnottar Castle, the impregnable fortress of the Marischals of Scotland. The last stronghold of the Scottish Royalists in the Civil War, it surrendered 'with honour' after the regalia had been smuggled out (*Scottish Tourist Board*)

that the blinding smoke would be a 'sweet smelling incense in the nostrils of the Lord!'

After the coronation of Charles II at Scone the regalia were kept in Stirling Castle, where a meeting was held in 1651 to consider the plight of the country. When the Parliament rose, without knowing when or where it would meet again, the Earl Marischal was instructed to 'take the Honours to his fortalice of Dunnottar thair to be keepit by him till further ordouris'.

How was he to get the Honours safely to Dunnottar? Cromwell's forces were penetrating deeper into Scotland and a large escort could be swiftly cut off.

Here we meet the first of the remarkable Scottish women in this account. We know little about her except that her name was Mrs Drummond, wife of the minister of Moneydue and daughter of Patrick Smith of Braco in the parish of Redgorton. Dressed as a

Opposite above: The Crown of Scotland, remodelled for James V in 1540 when the gold from earlier crowns may have been used

Opposite below: Scottish Regalia: The Great George, the Ring, the St Andrew and (*below*) a section of the Collar of the Order of the Garter

Scottish Regalia: the Sword of State and the Sceptre. The Sword was presented
by Pope Julius II to James IV in 1507 and the Sceptre was an earlier gift from
Pope Alexander VI, also to James IV in 1494

travelling woman, she made her way northward with a packhorse loaded with sacks of wool, apparently to sell at the market towns on her way. Inside each sack was an item of the regalia. Eventually, by what hazards we do not know, she passed through the lines of Cromwell's troops and handed her precious burden to the Earl Marischal, who had ridden swiftly by moor and forest tracks to his fortress. This courageous woman never received any recognition or reward for her part in securing the Honours of her native land.

The Earl Marischal had to appoint a Governor of Dunnottar to act in his absence. He chose George Ogilvy of Baras, from a local family, who had served as a soldier of fortune in the armies of the great Gustavus Adolphus. He was a tough, hard-headed soldier. The Earl Marischal's commission entrusting him with his command 'allowed fortie men, a Lieutenant and two serjeants to be entertained within it upon publict charge'.

The Earl Marischal left the recruiting of the men and the provisioning of the castle to the Governor and rode away to a meeting of the Committee of the Estates. He was captured by Cromwell's troops at Aylyth.

On the plea that he would need money for his support, he sent a messenger to his mother, The Dowager Countess Marischal, with the key of the treasure room for George Ogilvy and the command that he should 'hold Dunnottar for the King'. The Dowager Countess was a formidable woman. The daughter of the Earl of Mar, she had married the sixth Earl Marischal. On his death she had married the Earl of Panmure, but still continued to use the title of Countess Marischal and watched over the fortunes of her sons.

She went to Dunnottar, gave the Governor the key and his instructions and 'had not stayed two hours' when a messenger brought news of an approaching troop of Cromwell's horse. George Ogilvy was hurriedly left with his command, the key, the regalia and the problem of their defence. He was short of nearly everything for that purpose. He had not the 'fortie men', when he needed more than a hundred to defend Dunnottar. He lacked military stores, especially gunpowder, and was short of food supplies. He scoured the countryside for men and supplies and got very little of either.

By the end of September 1651 the English troops under General Overton had taken their position on the approach to Dunnottar. The English General, like many other invaders before him, looked at the towering rocks, the narrow ridge and the high stone walls and prepared for a long siege.

James Grainger, Minister of Kinneff, concealing the Scottish Crown Jewels below
his church pulpit (*Painting by J. A. Houston, RTH*)

In the meantime, Ogilvy used his sea route to send an appeal for help to King Charles who had reached Paris after his escape from Worcester. The letter was entrusted to John Keith, the Earl's youngest son, who had been sharing the siege. Out at sea in his small boat he was picked up by a ship bound for Holland. He seems to have dallied on the way because it was weeks before he gave the king the letter.

The English had brought up their heavy cannon, and their demands for surrender became peremptory; it was time to get the regalia out of Dunnottar.

The recriminations of later times have obscured the true account of how the regalia were smuggled out. Later the Countess Marischal, the Governor's wife and Mrs Grainger, the wife of the minister of the neighbouring parish of Kinneff, each had their accounts to give. The minister's wife, Mrs Grainger, was to say that she arranged with the Governor's wife to take the regalia away. She went to Stonehaven with her maid and bought some large bundles of flax. On the return journey she got permission from the English officer to visit her friends in Dunnottar. When she left there she had the Crown in her lap and the maid had the Sceptre and Sword concealed in the bundles of flax. She had been 'seriously incommoded' when the officer had insisted on helping her to mount her horse.

Another version is that Mrs Ogilvy arranged for the Graingers' maid to come each day to gather dulse and tangles opposite the rock until all suspicion of her was removed. The regalia was then lowered to her and she carried them away in her creel.

It is certain, however, that the regalia found their way to the manse at Kinneff, where the agitated minister concealed them at the foot of his bed, and when he could no longer sleep easily near them, he wrapped them in linen cloths and buried them in the church. At the end of March he went to the Countess Marischal and he gave her a receipt for the precious symbols.

The Honours had been removed by the Governor's authority, but he was not told where they had been hidden. It was a necessary precaution in a time when rough means were used to get information.

The Governor had one stroke of luck for which he was to pay dearly later. On an April night of light seas and temperate winds a merchant ship laden with goods for Bo'ness market anchored in the bay. A boarding party from Dunnottar swarmed aboard and she was quickly relieved of her cargo. It was a great moment for the hungry garrison.

The English long range guns began knocking holes in the tower.

The Countess Marischal, also alarmed at the damage to Dunnottar by the foraging English soldiers on her son's estates, began to send messages to the Governor urging him to surrender. He politely rejected these requests.

No help arrived from the King, but his messenger, Sir John Strachan, slipped through the lines with letters and good advice. He was full of hopes and an elaborate scheme for a landing from Norway, 'for there is room enough within this castle to receive an army and it is the very centre of the Kingdom'. The Governor was urged to hold out until the winter.

Ogilvy looked down at the heavy guns which had begun to pound the walls of Dunnottar. All that honour could do had been done. Dunnottar alone of all the Scottish strongholds had held out for so long against the invaders. On 24 May 1652 his small force marched out of Dunnottar after a siege of over eight months. They crossed the ridge with 'fleing colours, drums, arms and kindle matches and other things befitting men of honour'. The English were astonished to count only thirty five gaunt and haggard veterans when they had expected a garrison force of over one hundred.

The terms of surrender were honourable; Ogilvy's men would go free, his own liberty would be respected and his estates would be restored. This chivalrous attitude changed to fury when the English discovered that the royal regalia were not in Dunnottar. The Governor and his wife were immediately imprisoned. They insisted that the regalia had been taken away by John Keith when he had made his escape by sea. After seven months they were both released on parole, but suspicions still smouldered. They were taken in for further interrogations and were harassed by sudden searches of their house. In the meantime, the merchant whose ship had been relieved of its cargo by the night raiders from Dunnottar, was pursuing a claim for its loss. He was awarded £480 damages—a high price for Ogilvy to pay for sustaining his defence of the castle. Mrs Ogilvy died in April 1656, as a result of the privations of the siege, her imprisonment, the harassment, as well as the constant dread that the regalia might be discovered.

Young John Keith returned from Paris to Scotland. He was soon taken prisoner by the English, who found that he had a receipt for the delivery of the regalia to the King's officers in Paris. This was a contrived expedient which finally convinced the English that the Honours were beyond their reach. Ogilvy was thereafter left in peace.

For eight years the regalia lay concealed in Kinneff church anxiously watched over by the Graingers. Ogilvy had been told of their hiding place by his wife on her death-bed, and he came to Kinneff at intervals with fresh linen cloths. The regalia was lifted from below the church pavement, taken into the manse to be cleaned and to be 'ayred in ye night time before ane fire'. The three people who shared a fateful secret, watched the gleaming of the jewels in the old crown of Scotland and the firelight dancing along the great blade of the fine papal sword.

In May 1660, when King Charles came into his own again, greed and ambition reached out for their rewards. The Countess was the first to stir the royal pot; her part had been the smallest in saving the regalia but her anticipations were the greatest. She wrote to the King assuming all responsibility for the regalia and requesting to be favoured with His Majesty's personal instructions as to their disposal. Her letter did not refer to Ogilvy by name: 'the gentleman who commanded the Castle of Dunnottar discharged his duties verie honestly in putting them in the hands of a person who did show himself worthie of so great a trust'. This letter was given to her son John Keith, who went post-haste to deliver it in person to the King. Later, she was to allege that Ogilvy's surrender of the Castle had been 'a mean capitulation'.

The Governor placed his simple faith in the Earl Marischal, although his friends urged him to go post-haste to London. Importunity found its swift reward. The King appointed John Keith Knight Marischal and awarded him the handsome pension of £400 a year. When the news reached Scotland, Ogilvy sent his son to London with a belated petition to the King, pointing out that he had preserved the regalia 'at great hazard of his life and long and strait imprisonment'. This was news to the King, who told his minister, Stafford: 'By my lord Ogilvy's leave, it cannot be so for my Lady Marischal wrote to me that she and her son John had preserved the Honours.'

The King decided to test the strength of Ogilvy's claim by sending him an order for the delivery of the regalia—'for if the said John Keith hath kept the Honours, then the said George Ogilvy would not be able to deliver them, but if he could then he was undyniably the true Preserver'.

This move had been foreseen by the Countess who tried without success to get the minister of Kinneff to hand over the Honours to her. Ogilvy was now also about his own business. He showed the minister the King's order for delivery and suggested that they should go together to the Earl Marischal, who had returned to Dunnottar, and obtain his receipt for the delivery. On 8 October 1660 the two men who had done the most to save the regalia stood before the Earl Marsichal. The wrappings were removed, and the crown, sceptre and sword were laid on a side table. The Marischal carefully examined them before he took up his pen to write a discharge to George Ogilvy of Baras 'for the Honours of the Kingdom of Scotland, the Crown, Sword and Sceptre, the ancient monuments of this Kingdome entier and complete and in the same condition as they were entrusted by me to him'.

It must have been a great moment for George Ogilvy. The two men looked at each other and he knew that he had not misjudged the Earl Marischal. The Earl, in fact, had not known of the pushful action of his mother. When he later learned more he wrote to her: 'I leave to say no further than that it has been an ugly and unhandsome carried business'. A few months later the Earl Marsichal with a great escort of nobles and troops bore the Honours back to Edinburgh while the great guns of the Castle saluted the return of the symbols of Scotland's independence.

In March 1661, George Ogilvy was received by the King at Whitehall. He was made a baronet, received a warrant to include in his arms a lion with a sword defending a thistle crowned, and he was given the freehold of his estates. He was also awarded a pension of £200 a year 'how soon the King's revenues are settled' —they never were and George Ogilvy carried a burden of debt for the rest of his life.

John Keith made further progress in the royal favour; he succeeded his father as Great Marischal and became the Earl of Kintore.

After many petitions and supplications, Mrs Grainger, long after the death of her husband, received the sum of 2,000 merks. The old Earl Marischal had suffered, too, for the King's cause. His castle had been heavily damaged by the final cannonades and his estates were ruined. For the rest of his life Scotland saw little of him. He died shortly after his loyal friend, George Ogilvy, in 1671.

The rescuers of the regalia were not allowed to rest in peace. In 1699, Alexander Nisbet published his *System of Heraldry*. In describing the arms of the Keiths, he made a brief reference to the rescue of the regalia, which the old Governor's son and grandson felt did not do justice to the part which Sir George Ogilvy had played. The old animosities flared again. Sir William Ogilvy and son David rushed into print with *A True Account of the Preservation of the Regalia*. There was injured family pride and a strong emphasis on the contribution made by Sir George, but there was no real libel of the Keiths in that hasty pamphlet.

The Earl of Kintore, however, regarded it in that light, and he lodged a complaint with the Privy Council of Scotland; Sir William and his son were cited to appear to answer the charge of libel. The pleas and rejoinders in those proceedings make sad reading even after this long lapse of time. The legal language does not conceal the malice. Every detail of the siege, the rescue and the events at Kinneff were mulled over, distorted and exposed to slighting innuendo; some statements were manifestly untrue. The bright cloak of courage had become a dirty, tattered garment by the time the parties and the lawyers were done.

The pleadings were never really considered by the judicial committee of the Privy Council of Scotland; the Earl of Kintore was given the swift protection of his peers. Without calling any evidence and in the absence of the defendants, it was ordered that the offending pamphlet should be burned by the common hangman as 'injurious, ignominous and defaming the said Earl of Kintore'. A penalty of £100 was imposed on the principal author, David Ogilvy, who was ordered to be detained in prison until it was paid, and he was also 'further to remain therein during the Council's pleasure'. David Ogilvy had already put himself beyond sentence by departing for London. The old man, his father, remained in Scotland desperately trying to find the money to pay the fine and the lawyers' bills. An heroic episode in Scotland's history had come to a bitter and shabby end.

The Keiths continued on their fateful ways. The ninth earl opposed the Act of Union in 1707 and joined the rising of the Young Pretender. He fled abroad, his estates were forfeited and Dunnottar was sold to the York Building Company, who came north to sell off its ancient stones for new building works. The fugitive Keith became a high official of Frederick the Great. Through his influential friends he was eventually pardoned by the Government and came back to Scotland to buy back Dunnottar and his estates in the Mearns for £4,208. He was the last of the direct line of Keiths, who for nearly 500 years had been the Great Marischals of Scotland.

For a long time the rock of Dunnottar was left to the foxes and the seabirds, as Thomas the Rhymer, writing four hundred years earlier, had so strangely foretold:

> Dwnnotyr, standen by the se,
> Lairdles shall thy landis be;
> And underneath thy hearth stane
> The tod shall bring his birdis hame.

CHAPTER 22
'THE END OF ANE AULD SANG'

During the reign of William and Mary, Scotland had been a land in turmoil. The Jacobites had raised the standard of King James VII and the Highland clans had rallied to the Stuart cause. At the pass of Killiecrankie the forces supporting King William were swept aside by the fury of the Highland charge. The clans rushed on to Dunkeld to meet the fanatical resistance of the extreme group of religious zealots, the Cameronians, who faced the clans with pike and musket, with the blazing town at their backs. Those religious 'outlaws' helped to save the throne for William and Mary.

The Highlanders retreated chastened but not defeated. Soon the massacre of the Macdonalds of Glencoe, in which William seemed to have been implicated, nourished the hatred in the mountain glens. Persecution was also abroad in the Lowlands. The Scottish Parliament had abolished prelacy and its ministers were chased from their parishes; they reported that a third, or even a half, of their parishioners had died of hunger and disease. People lay dead at the roadside with grass in their mouths.

William, preoccupied with his own wars in Ireland and Flanders, looked with amazement at the turmoil and distress in his northern kingdom; to him it seemed absurd that two small countries should have separate legislatures. When he was dying in 1702 he sent a recommendation to Parliament: 'Nothing can contribute more to the present and future peace, security and happiness of England and Scotland than a firm and entire union between them'.

This valedictory wish became the first business of the English Parliament on the accession of Queen Anne. A Bill was passed to appoint commissioners to discuss the Union of Scotland with England with representatives of the Scottish Estates. It was a brief meeting. The Scots agreed to accept the Hanoverian succession to the throne as well as one legislature for the two kingdoms provided Scotland was given freedom of trade with England. The English were not prepared to concede anything and did not even bother to send a quorum to the meeting where the proposals were to be discussed. The Scots went home incensed, humiliated and determined to take action about their rebuff.

They made a powerful assertion of their sovereignty. A year before the death of William III the English Parliament had settled that, in the event of his successor, Anne, bearing no heir, the succession should fall on the Electress Sophia of Hanover, grand-daughter of James VI, and on her Protestant descendants. The Scottish Estates had not been consulted by the English Parliament and they now asserted the independence of the crown of Scotland by passing the Act of Security. This gave the Estates powers to name their own successor from the Protestant descendents of the royal line of Scotland 'and excluding the admitted successor to the crown of England, unless the honour and the sovereignty of this crown and kingdom, the freedom of Parliament and the religion and trade of the nation were removed from English influence'.

England seeing a separate Stuart king on the Scottish throne began to shout 'Treason!' By invasion or legislation Scotland had to be subdued. They attacked Scotland on her weakest point—her poverty. The English Parliament passed an Aliens Act by which Scotsmen were to be treated as foreign nationals and the im-portation into England of all goods from Scotland was to be prohibited, unless the Estates accepted the Hanoverian succession and agreed to appoint commissioners to arrange a 'firm and entire union' of the two kingdoms.

The Scots reacted with fury to the prospect of economic ruin. The mobs came out on the streets, while the Estates went into continuous session and the authorities reached out for the nearest available victims for the popular rage. They arrested the young officers of an English vessel, the *Worcester*, on a trumped up charge of piracy and after the pretence of a trial hanged them on the sands of Leith. In England, the Queen herself intervened to postpone the plans to fortify Newcastle and Tynemouth, repair the northern forts, call out the northern militia and march regular troops to the Border. She came in person to attend the sitting of the House 'both to hear the debates and to moderate by her presence any heats which might arise'.

On 1 February 1704, a Bill was passed by both Houses of the English Parliament by which the Queen was given powers to appoint commissioners to meet the representatives of the Scottish Estates, and the penal clause treating the Scots as aliens was postponed until December.

The Estates which met to consider the overture which the English had delivered with a clenched fist began its meetings in a state of high indignation, which subsided to anger and slowly diminished to the appearance of a rational debate. The abysmal poverty of the people, the extinction of her trade and the unequal prospects of a long struggle with England were factors too strong to be ignored. After long days of debate the Estates eventually agreed to treat with the English commissioners.

The representatives of England and Scotland met in the Cockpit at Whitehall! Both sides were now of a mind to enter into real negotiations. The Scots cleared the way for the discussions by accepting the Hanoverian succession, but failed to persuade the English to accept a federal constitution. Eventually they gave way on that point, and both sides began the immensely complicated negotiations on taxation, the equalisation of the national debt, customs, excise, salt and malt duties, colonial trade, navigation, joint armed forces and a score of other intricate and interlocking matters of concern to both countries. The complexity of those discussions was not to be equalled until the United Kingdom began the negotiations for entry to the Common Market two hundred and seventy years later.

The commissioners finished their work in a remarkably short time. There was no praise for them, however, in Scotland. Nearly every degree of opinion united to condemn the proposed terms of the Union. The presbyterians were furious at the prospect of 'intercommunion with the uncovenanted' and the Celtic nationalists were revolted by 'the sacrifice of the sovereignty of the ancient kingdom in the degenerate hands of the feeble descendents of its old protectors'. Scots were urged to go to Edinburgh Castle to take their last look at 'those ancient symbols of our sovereignty and independence—the crown, sceptre and the sword—before they disappeared for ever from Scottish eyes!'

When the Estates began their meeting in October, the English forces were moved to the Border, awaiting only a summons from Lord Queensberry, the royal commissioner in Edinburgh. The people of the city poured on to the streets to surround the Parliament House and sailors came marching in with significant ropes in their hands from the port of Leith.

Queensberry saw little prospect of carrying the Treaty of Union by straight votes. To gain support in the Estates all sorts of inducements were offered and many secret bargains were made. A sum of £20,000 was sent up from London for secret payments by the Lord Treasurer, the Earl of Glasgow. The arrears of salaries due to many office holders were made conditional on their supporting the union. The stockholders of the bankrupt Darien Company were recouped for their losses. As the hot debate continued, the cool work of 'management' went on quietly behind the scenes.

The anti-Union petitions began to pour in from nearly every town and royal burgh. The General Assembly of the Church of

The assembly of the Estates began with the Riding of Parliament when the Honours of Scotland were escorted to Parliament House in Edinburgh. This sketch shows the Constable seated on the Lady Steps awaiting the arrival of the procession (*National Library of Scotland*)

Scotland passed a resolution against the union. Riots broke out in Glasgow as ministers from their pulpits urged their congregation 'Wherefore, up and be valiant for the City of our God'. The desperate plight of the country influenced others; in the end the Treaty of Union was passed by forty-seven votes. The most important business which remained to the Scottish Parliament was the nomination of forty-five members and the fifteen peers who would in future represent Scotland at Westminster.

One of the last battles in the Estates had centred around the Honours of Scotland as they lay on the table before the members. Patriotic words were spoken over them. Lord Belhaven declared: 'Hannibal is at our gates. Hannibal is come the length of this table; he will demolish this throne, he will seize upon these regalia, he will take them as the rich spoils of war and whip us all out of this House never to return.'

Provision was made for the ancient Honours of Scotland in Article XXIV of the Treaty: 'the crown, sceptre and sword of state, the records of Parliament and all other records shall continue to be kept as they are within that part of the United Kingdom now called Scotland and they shall so remain in all time coming notwithstanding the union.'

The assent to the Treaty was taken with guards around the

The Duke of Queensberry, on behalf of Scotland, presenting the Treaty of Union
to Queen Anne (*BM*)

House and a battalion stationed on the outskirts of the city. The Sceptre was lifted from the regalia table and handed to the Lord Chancellor, the Earl of Seafield. He reversed the sceptre and laid its head on the text of the Treaty with the words: 'And there's the end o' ane auld sang'. There were Scotsmen who never forgave him for that remark. Over a century later Sir Walter Scott wrote that the Lord Chancellor 'deserved to be destroyed on the spot by his indignant countrymen'.

The anger in Scotland did not quickly subside. There were more riots in the towns, copies of the Treaty were burned in market squares and a song was heard in all parts of the country.

> Farewell to our Scottish fame
> Farewell to our ancient glory,
> Farewell e'en to our Scottish name
> Sae famed in martial story.

On 28 April 1707 it was really the end of the old song when the independent Parliament of Scotland was dissolved by royal proclamation. Its passing also brought to an end a colourful ceremony which had surrounded the regalia since feudal times. At the beginning of each session the Honours had been escorted to the House in the 'Riding of Parliament'. The streets were carefully cleaned, all vehicles were prohibited, the Royal Mile was railed on both sides and the civic and royal guards were stationed along the route. Each member of the Estates had to be mounted, the aged and infirm were lifted into their saddles.

The heralds mustered the procession, summoning the members by name from a high window of the Palace, in order of rank and precedence. There was a great mustering of robes, uniforms and liveries. All heads were covered except for those of the bearers of the Honours. The Lord Lyon with his heralds rode before the great Sword of State, while the trumpeters proclaimed the passage of the Honours to the assembly of the Estate. Afterwards the Honours were returned to the Crown Room in the Castle with an escort of officials, heralds, and guards under the command of the Earl Marischal to the welcoming salutes of the Castle guns. When the Honours were sent back for the last time, however, the ninth Earl Marischal, who had bitterly opposed the Treaty, refused to attend the depositing of the Honours in the Castle. He sent William Wilson, 'one of the under clarkis of session as our depute marischal', to deliver the regalia to the Lord Treasurer and the Governor of the Castle. Wilson read aloud to them his instrument of delivery in which the Marischal stated that the regalia were deposited 'without prejudice to our heritable rycht of keeping the said regalia both in the tyme of Parliament and in the intervals in the castle of Dunnottar or elsewhere in the kingdom as our ancestors have done'. The Earl Marischal demanded that the Honours should not be removed from the Castle unless he was present to see them safely transported to any other place within the kingdom, but that they should never leave the kingdom as Parliament had ordained. Another instrument of delivery contained a minute description of each piece of the regalia. Finally, the Earl Marischal demanded the right to inspect the Honours from time to time 'so that they may not pretend their ignorent (of their whereabouts) for which this presentis shall be to you a sufficient warrant'.

The Honours were placed in a chest in the vaulted Crown Room of Edinburgh Castle with its window protected by iron bars and behind an iron door and an outer door studded with iron nails. There the ancient symbols of Scotland's former sovereignty and the regalia of her kings were to lie gathering dust and slowly receding from the recollections of a people for whom they had once been of such great significance.

CHAPTER 23
'THE CROWN HAS BEEN FOUND'

On the first day of May 1707, Scotland ceased to be an independent nation. The sovereignty which she had sustained through centuries of wars and invasions had been ceded by the will of a majority of her own Parliament.

The Scottish peers and members who posted off to Westminster expecting influence, favours and honours were soon disillusioned. They discovered that their influence was negligible, the favours reserved for English gentlemen, and the honours were virtually unattainable.

The Scottish commoners were a minority of forty five in the House of Commons—they were lost among the 513 representatives of England and Wales. Their speech was almost incomprehensible to the bewigged English members, their manners were considered uncouth and they were bemused by the Parliamentary procedure. They were constantly derided by the elegant members on the benches around them. The Scots found that they had locked themselves into the confines of the Palace of Westminster and had thrown away the key.

Other Scottish expectations were also swiftly defeated. Believing that freedom of trade had been established by the Union a large fleet from Scotland sailed up the Thames laden with merchandise which included French wines and brandy. The ships and their cargoes were seized, and their officers were imprisoned for smuggling foreign cargoes.

The Scots were once again afire with protests—the English were trampling the Treaty in the dust. Other consequences of the Union also created anger in Scotland. A large number of commissioners of excise and customs descended on the country to apply the rigid English methods of revenue collection, which were infuriatingly incomprehensible to the Scots, who regarded the officers as 'a swarm of harpies let loose to suck the blood and fatten on the spoils of an oppressed people'.

Scottish pride was outraged and religious feeling inflamed when it was found that the list of justices for every Scottish county was headed by 'the most reverend father in Christ, Thomas, Archbishop of Canterbury, Primate of all England and Moderator thereof'.

Under the Union Scotland had retained her own laws and legal system, but it was soon clear that this concession was not absolute. The independence of Scotland's courts under the Treaty was set aside when the House of Lords on appeal reversed a judgement of the Court of Session.

There were economic grievances. Prosperity did not come with the Union; the tax on salt for example was increased and this damaged the Scottish fisheries. English peers and country gentlemen with the prelates of the English Church now made the laws for Scotland. The representatives of Scotland decided to get back their own Parliament and recover the sovereignty of their country. They promoted a bill in the House of Lords for the dissolution of the Union.

The first reading of the bill was moved by the Earl of Findlater, the former Lord Seafield who had contemptuously dismissed the last act of his own Parliament as the 'end of ane auld sang'. He now sang to a new tune, appealing for the return of what had been given away. There were many English members of that House who would have been glad to be rid of the Scots and all their woes, and agreed with Swift that:

> 'Strife and faction will o'erwhelm
> Our crazy, double-bottomed realm.'

But not quite enough of them were of that opinion and the bill was defeated by four votes; in any event it would not have got past the House of Commons which was certainly not prepared to let Scotland go her own way again.

The anger and frustration over the Union undoubtedly gave strength to the Jacobite rising of 1715. When James Edward Stuart was proclaimed king at Braemar it was declared that the Union had been a grievous blunder by which 'Scotland's ancient liberties were delivered into the hands of the English'. On the failure of the rising, the ensuing public executions, deportations to the plantations and heavy sentences of imprisonment laid the foundations of the still greater Jacobite rising in 1745. The defeat of Charles James Stuart, the butchery of Culloden and the

Opposite above The Royal Arms of England. The Lion occupies the dexter, the premier position, and unlike the Unicorn is crowned. In the shield the lions of England are in the first and fourth quarters, the rampant lion of Scotland takes the second quarter, and the harp, representing Northern Ireland, is in the third quarter. All the emblems are of ancient origin; compare with the Royal Arms of Scotland, page 208.

Opposite below English Regalia: the Armills, the symbolic 'bracelets of sincerity'. At the Investiture they are placed below the elbows and attached to the Stole Royale by golden cords. Beneath them are the Golden Spurs, the symbols of chivalry and honour, made for Charles II

systematic devastation of the Highlands seemed—even to many Scots not sympathetic to the Stuart cause—like the acts of an enemy army of occupation.

A piece of repressive legislation which struck deeply at the pride and lifestyle of the Highland people was the Act of 1746 for the 'Abolition and Proscription of Highland Dress'. For English ministers the tartan plaid was the symbol of Jacobitism; for the Highlander his traditional garb was the symbol of his kinship, his clan loyalty and his national identity and to forfeit his philabeg was as deep a humiliation as the loss of his manhood. 'Had the whole race been decimated,' wrote Stewart of Garth, 'more violent grief, indignation and shame could not have been excited among them, than by being deprived of this long inherited costume'.

The repressive laws against the Highland garb were not repealed until 1782, although many had reverted to the kilt when the enforcement of the laws was relaxed under George III. There were, however, now fewer people to wear the kilt since the clearances were under way and some chiefs placed a higher value on their sheep than on their clansmen.

At a time when the traditions and legends of the Highlands were being dispersed across the Atlantic to Canada, the creative imagination of a Lowland Scot kept alive the images of the highland people and their ways. Frank Adam, the historian of the Scottish clans, wrote: 'But for the vision of Walter Scott in re-capturing the spirit of clanship at the critical moment, Scotland today would have been as shadowy a name as Mercia, Bernicia and the other lost kingdoms of the heptarchy'.

The great stream of Scott's Waverley novels illuminated their past for his own countrymen and fired the imaginations of the world with the scenes of Scottish life and history. His narrative poetry, like Marmion, was infused with a patriotism which was like lilting music to Scottish hearts.

Walter Scott gave the world the impression of Scotland as a land with its own history and its own national identity. Scotland lionised him in his lifetime and after his death erected in Prince's Street, Edinburgh, the tallest monument to any writer in the world.

Walter Scott kept up his prodigious output while he was also

The Royal Arms of Scotland from the armorial of Sir David Lindsay of the Mount ca 1542. When used in Scotland the Unicorn is crowned and on the dexter—the premier position; the rampant lion is in the first and fourth quarters of the shield. The banners continue to display the historic opposition of St Andrew's Cross and the Cross of St George. Compare with the Royal Arms used in England on previous page (*The Trustees of the National Library of Scotland*)

active as the Sheriff of Selkirkshire and a Clerk of the Sessions. His intense interest in Scotland's past and his own researches led him to enquire into the whereabouts of the ancient regalia. It had been one of his predecessors as Clerk of the Sessions who had delivered the crown, sword and sceptre to their oblivion in Edinburgh Castle in 1707.

For over a hundred years the Honours had been kept out of sight. All enquiries had been met with silence. After the Union it had been rumoured that they had been taken to London 'as a token of the complete humiliation of the ancient kingdom'. The rumours and the public anger were ignored.

'Since the regalia were deposited,' protested an angry Scot, 'no governor of the castle, upon his admission, has made enquiry if they were left secure by his predecessor. No mortal has been known to have seen them.'

'The memory of the regalia,' wrote Walter Scott, 'became like that of a tale that has been told and their dubious existence was altogether forgotten.'

Scott was in a unique position to make enquiries through his friendship with the Prince Regent, who had told Lord Byron that 'he had thought it impossible for any poet to equal Walter Scott'. Later the Regent was to offer Scott the poet laureateship which Scott gracefully declined.

Scott interested the Prince Regent in a search for the regalia of Scotland. On 28 October 1817 the Prince Regent, on behalf of his father, George III, issued a warrant to unlock 'the Crown Room within the castle of Edinburgh, and to open, or cause to be forced open, the said chest, and inspect the contents thereof'.

On 4 February 1818 a dozen people assembled outside the massive door of the old building, among them the Duke of Buccleuch, the Lord Provost, the Solicitor General, the Lord Justice-Clerk, the Major-General commanding the forces in Scotland and one of the Principal Clerks of Session—Walter Scott Esq. The news of the search had been well publicised and a large crowd had gathered on Castle Hill to await the outcome.

The massive doors of oak and iron were unlocked and they entered the chamber in the dim light from the barred window. The undisturbed dust of a hundred years lay thickly on an old chest. The keys to open its triple locks could not be found, so the king's smith was ordered to force them open. Walter Scott has left us his account of the scene:

> The general persuasion that the regalia had been secretly removed, weighed heavy on the minds of all while the labour

The rediscovery of the Scottish Regalia in the Crown Room, Edinburgh Castle, 4 February 1818. Walter Scott is shown with his arm on the lid of the chest. (A contemporary pencil and brown wash sketch of the scene)

proceeded. The chest seemed to return a hollow and empty sound to the strokes of the hammer . . . The joy was therefore extreme, when, the ponderous lid of the chest being forced open, at the expense of some time and labour, the regalia were discovered lying at the bottom covered with linen cloths, exactly as they had been left in the year 1707, being about a hundred and ten years since they had been surrendered by William the ninth earl marischal to the custody of the Earl of Glasgow, Treasurer-Depute of Scotland. The relics were passed from hand to hand and greeted with the affectionate reverence which emblems so venerable, restored to public view after the slumber of more than a hundred years were so peculiarly calculated to excite.

At 4 pm on that misty February evening the crowds waiting on Castle Hill saw the royal standard run up above the castle; it was the signal they had been awaiting for. A great roar of cheers broke from the crowd. The Crown of Scotland had been found again! People were deeply moved to know that they still possessed the ancient symbols of Scotland's sovereignty.

The next morning the commissioners returned to the Crown Room with their families; Scott brought his daughter Sophia. When they had gathered around the old chest, Sophia felt so overcome by excitement that she nearly fainted. Suddenly she heard her father's loud exclamation of indignation: 'By God, no!' One of the officials had lifted the crown to place it on the

head of a young lady. There was a moment of acute embarrass-
ment. The thoughtless official replaced the diadem in the chest.
Scott whispered, 'Pray forgive me', and turned to see his daughter,
deathly pale, leaning against the door; he took her by the arm and
led her out of the room. The memory stayed with her: 'He never
spoke all the way home, but every now and then I felt his arm
tremble.'

There was popular clamour for the regalia to be seen and Scott
was already busy to that end. He put forward the name of his
friend, Adam Ferguson, as the Keeper of the Regalia. Ferguson
had been a distinguished officer in the Peninsular War, whose
devotion to Scott was such that he had read the sixth canto of
'The Lady of the Lake' to his troops while they were lying flat on
their faces in the lines at Torres Vedras with the French shot
striking briskly on the ramparts above them. He had now retired
on half pay.

There were, however, other eager claimants, including Keith of
Ravelstone, a descendant of the Earls Marischal. The Prince
Regent intervened to suggest that Walter Scott himself should be
given the appointment without emoluments but with the rank of
baronet. Scott gracefully declined, but suggested that should his
Royal Highness be disposed to give the Keepership to another
then he would consider the rank suggested for him an honour.

After some months of active lobbying the matter was settled to
Scott's satisfaction: Adam Ferguson got the post and a knighthood and Scott became a baronet. At his investiture, George IV,
who had at last succeeded his father, declared: 'I shall always
reflect with pleasure on Sir Walter Scott having been the first
creation of my reign'; his pleasure was such that he shook hands
with the new baronet 'repeatedly'.

The arrangements for the public exhibition of the regalia were
soon made. Two veterans of Waterloo, retired non-commissioned
officers, were appointed Yeomen Keepers and the Crown Room
was refurbished 'in the form of a tent'. The eager Scots began to
pour in to indulge their pride and curiosity by gazing on the
symbols of their ancient sovereignty.

George IV wanted to gratify his own curiosity about the
regalia and also to indulge the strong curiosity of the Scots about
their monarch. For most people the Stuart cause had now become
no more than the sad lilt of a few old songs. The old intensity of
feeling of the Scots for their kings was again aroused by the
prospect of George IV's state visit in August 1822. The chief
responsibility for the arrangements were entrusted to Walter
Scott; countless committees sat under his guidance. He settled a

hundred arguments on questions of pride and precedence. The Highland chiefs were locked in their ancient contentions about their positions in the ceremonies. The positions of their clans in the battle line at Bannockburn were, they held, the proper precedence for their places in the escort for the King from Holyrood to the Castle. Somehow Scott managed to placate them and three hundred Highlanders with their pipes were brought down from the north and awakened the weary author at dawn with their practising below his windows.

Highlanders and Lowlanders thronged the streets to welcome the king, filling stands for which some had paid a hundred guineas. The king was greatly moved when at the Toll House he read the banner—'Descendant of Bruce, thrice welcome!' The Lord Provost conducted the ceremony of offering and receiving back the keys of the City. The streets were decorated with all the old symbols of Scotland, the Cross of St Andrew, the thistle, the tressured lion, unicorn and the Royal Crown.

The presence chamber at Holyrood Palace was crowded with a colourful array of uniforms, peers' robes and lines of chiefs and chieftains in all the resurrected splendour of plaid, kilt, sporran, sword and skean-dhu, silver badges and shoe buckles. King George took his place on the throne to await the arrival of the regalia which were borne in solemn state into his presence—after an initial dispute over who had the hereditary right to carry the crown and the sceptre. The emotional monarch, who was at that moment more Scottish than any Scot, gazed at the old crown, the sword and the sceptre. There was a long silence while the king and the crowded chamber looked at the venerable relics of Scotland's kings and their history.

The royal visit was the beginning of what has been called the 'tartan explosion'. The polite society of Edinburgh tittered discreetly at the sight of the enormous figure of the King swathed in Stuart tartan, but many of them were soon to make the belated discovery of a Highland ancestor to justify their wearing the garb of the once despised Highlanders.

George IV had made a lasting impression on Scotland. The monarchy ceased to be so alien and remote as it had been since the time of William and Mary. The ancient loyalties were awakened. Victoria and Albert consolidated those feelings by making their summer home at Balmoral and by their keen interest in every aspect of Scottish life. Balmoral itself was part of the tartan explosion, with all its rooms carpeted with clan patterns and the walls heavily decorated with stags' heads, hunting horns, broad swords and skean-dhu.

The Honours of Scotland being presented to the Queen in St Giles Cathedral, Edinburgh, on 24 June 1953. The Queen hands back the Crown of Scotland to the Duke of Hamilton 'for safe keeping', Dr Charles Warr, Dean of the Thistle, is in the centre and (left centre) the Earl of Home holds the Sword of State

In the years which followed the kilt came into its own again; it was not merely as the Lord Lyon has said 'the most manly dress in the world', it was also for many Scots the symbol of their national identity and its tartan setts carried the revival of clan and kinship to every country where Scots have retained the consciousness of their race and its history.

The old regalia has taken its place on other royal occasions in Scotland since the state visit of King George IV. It was brought forth to honour Queen Elizabeth II when, after her Coronation in Westminster Abbey, she came to Edinburgh to drive in state procession to a service of thanksgiving and dedication at St Giles on 24 June 1953.

In its composition the Queen's procession resembled the 'Ridings of Parliament' which had last borne the Honours along that way when the Scottish Parliament had come to its end in 1707. For Queen Elizabeth II the years were rolled away and the ancient Honours were again borne before their sovereign along the Royal Mile in front of the Queen's coach. The old Crown of Scotland was borne by the Duke of Hamilton and Brandon: Lord Home, who had carried the Second Sword at the Queen's Coronation in Westminster Abbey, now carried the great Sword of State, and the Sceptre was in the hands of Lord Crawford and Balcarres as premier earl on the Union Roll of Scotland. The Queen's coach and the Honours were flanked on each side by the Royal Archers of the Queen's Body Guard for Scotland, while the Lord Lyon with the Scottish heralds were in their traditional places immediately before the regalia.

The ancient offices of Scotland were resumed for the day. Lord Dundee, Hereditary Banner Bearer of Scotland, descendent of a long line of his family who had discharged that duty in peace and war, carried the Royal Banner of Scotland, which was preceded by the national flag, the white saltire cross of St Andrew on a blue field, carried by the Master of Lauderdale, on behalf of his brother Lord Lauderdale—the Hereditary Bearer of the Flag. At St Giles, trumpets announced the arrival of the Queen with the Honours and as the procession moved down the centre of the cathedral crowded with one of the most representative gatherings in Scotland, one had an awareness of the deep national consciousness and the pride in their past which is part of the inheritance of the people of Scotland.

The bearers of the Honours passed into the sanctuary and there was a second when the gems in the old crown suddenly shone with points of light as it was placed on the Holy Table. The service held its own echoes from the past—the Declaration was paraphrased from the National Covenant of 1639 and the prayer for the Queen was attributed to St Columba who long ago had laid his hand in benediction on King Aidan, from whom the young Queen in St Giles could claim her descent.

In its own way that simple and evocative service in St Giles was as impressive as the great liturgical ceremony of the Queen's Coronation in Westminster Abbey. At its conclusion the Queen came into the sanctuary to receive from the Dean of the Chapel Royal, the Crown, the Sword and the Sceptre of her ancestors and to hand them in their turn again into the hands of their bearers. Another episode in the long history of the Honours of Scotland had been enacted.

CHAPTER 24
THE HONOURS OF SCOTLAND

The regalia in the Crown Room of Edinburgh Castle are the symbols of Scotland's ancient sovereignty: the sceptre and the Sword, splendid papal gifts, have a colourful history, but pride of place is given to an old crown, its gemstones dulled by age, concealment and neglect, which nonetheless has been an object of reverence for many generations of Scots.

THE CROWN

The Picts and Scots bound their hair with a leather band round the forehead; this later became a more ornamental circlet of bronze or gold worn by their chiefs or kings. At the royal installation ceremonies at Scone, however, sword and sceptre were the essential emblems of authority, not a crown. In the early part of the twelfth century Giraldus Cambrensis was writing with contempt of 'the Princes of Scots who are named as kings but are neither anointed or crowned'. It was possibly not until after 1329, when the Bull of Pope John XXII granted Robert Bruce 'the illustrious king of Scotland, the right for the kings of Scotland of receiving the anointing and coronation by the sacred hand of a pontiff' that the crowning became part of the inauguration ritual.

Before that, crowns had been worn on state occasions; David I, who adopted many English customs, added a crown to his royal ornaments and is shown wearing one in an illuminated charter to Kelso Abbey in 1159. Thereafter the crown depicted on Scotland's royal seals closely follows the design of England's royal crowns: the gold circle with the raised points became the crown with the trefoil, symbolising the Trinity; this was superseded by the crown with the lilies, often described as the flowers of the Virgin Mary; finally the diadem was enclosed with arches, indicating that it represented a sovereign state, and surmounted by the orb and cross, symbols of the Christian faith and an authority above that of the king. It is a crown of this last type that is in Edinburgh Castle today.

An earlier sovereign crown of Scotland was appropriated by Edward I in 1296 when he stripped John Balliol of his royal insignia at Montrose Castle—as was recorded in the *Cronykil of Wyntoun*:

'This John the Balliol dyspoyled he
Of all hys robes of royalté,
The pelure that tuk off hys tabart,
—Toom Tabart was he callid efftyrwart—
And all other insyngnys
That fell to kyngis on any wyse.
Bathe scepter, sword, crowne and ryng,
Fra this John that he made Kyng
Halyly fra him he tuk thare,
And made him off the kynryk bare.'

When Bruce raised the standard of independence, Scotland was a kingdom without a crown. A coronet of gold was made for Bruce's investiture at Scone, but this too was carried off to England after the defeat of Bruce at Methven three months later. This coronet was concealed by one Geoffrey de Coigners, who may have picked it up among the plunder of the battlefield. The theft was discovered but Queen Margaret of England pleaded for him and Edward issued a pardon from Carlisle on 20 March 1307. Bruce would, without doubt, have restored the symbol of Scotland's sovereignty sometime during the rest of his reign, although there are no surviving records of the making of a new crown. A small crown was specially made for his five year old son who succeeded him in 1329.

From the reign of David II to James IV the Scottish records do not give any details of the royal regalia, but the royal seals of Bruce and his immediate successors show the king wearing a diadem with the fleur-de-lis. In the fifteenth century the kings of the independent states of Europe began to close their crowns with arches to show their sovereign status. The rulers of states owing duty or allegiance continued to wear the open crown. From the evidence on his tomb in Westminster Abbey, Henry V, the victor of Agincourt, was the first English king to wear a crown with high arches, but Scotland did not soon follow the English example and it was not until 1493 that James IV was shown on his second coinage as wearing the arched crown of the sovereign state.

The crown which today rests in Edinburgh Castle is that of James V who succeeded his father in 1513 in the dreadful aftermath of Flodden Field, where the king lay dead among thousands of his followers. The arched crown of his father was held above the head of the eighteen month old child in what has been called the 'Mourning Coronation of Scotland' since the stricken land could not rejoice when:

The Flowers of the Forest, that fought aye the foremost,
The prime of our land are cauld in the clay'.

The boy king became the shuttlecock of his mother, Margaret, sister of Henry VII of England, and ambitious regents, until in July 1528 he rode in secret to Stirling and took possession of his kingdom. Shortly afterwards he began to consider the question of his crown.

The accounts of the Lord High Treasurer of Scotland show payments in 1532 and 1533 for gold to mend the crown, and on 15 January 1540 a substantial payment was made to John Mossman, a goldsmith of Edinburgh, for the making and fashioning of the King's Crown and for the supply of twenty three jewels for it: 'This crowne deliverit to the Kingis grace in palice of Halyrudehous the viij day of Februar'.

Sir Walter Scott, with his great interest in the regalia, thought that the alterations in 1540 were merely the addition of the arches and not the replacement of the circle and the jewels; he was captivated with the romantic idea that the circle of the crown with its jewels was the one made for Bruce after Bannockburn. As Scott noted, the arches were not part of the original crown but were attached to it by tacks of gold, and the gold of the rim and of the arches are of different quality; he also observed that some of the diamonds were examples of cutting done by fourteenth-century goldsmiths, possibly even before the time of Bruce. Unfortunately the evidence does not support Scott's romantic notion; a manuscript record by Lord Fountainhall states that 'the Crown of Scotland is not the ancient crown but was casten of new by James V'. This statement, taken with the record of the work commissioned from James Mossman, suggests the entire remaking of the ancient crown, with the possible exception of the arches.

Few experts even now would differ from the opinion of A. J. S. Brook, FSA, who made a detailed examination of the crown in 1889. He pointed out that the fillet, or circle, had been made to suit the exact space required for the setting of twenty-two of the gems supplied to the goldsmith, while the remaining stone—the amethyst—was placed in front of the cross patée on top of the mound above the arches; he suggests that the evidence points to 'an entire remaking of the ancient crown and an increase in its size and weight'.

The connection with Robert Bruce may not be completely lost, however, since the records show that $41\frac{1}{2}$ ounces of gold of the mint were added to the crown in 1540; this may imply that the gold of the ancient crown was used when the new crown was 'casten of new'. In its substance, therefore, the present crown may contain the gold which once ornamented the brow of the great Bruce.

There is an equally strong possibility that some of the gems were taken from the earlier crown. An inventory of the Royal Wardrobe and Jewel House in 1539 describes the ancient crown as having been adorned with twenty diamonds and sixty-eight pearls; and, as examination shows, the setting of these gems in the present crown was the work of a goldsmith of the earlier period.

Eight of the diamonds in the crown are cut in a style of some of the earliest forms of cut diamonds. The diamond of the Middle Ages was not the many-faceted brilliant of today; its latent splendour had yet to be fully revealed. The early stones were sober gems and, diamonds being the hardest of materials, their cutting and polishing presented great problems for the lapidaries. The first shaped diamonds were the table-cut stones; the early Indian lapidaries discovered that the tip of an octahedron diamond could be ground away to leave a square or rectangular face, which could be polished. Later a second soft direction for the cut was found by the patient Indian craftsmen—through the dodecahedron plane which involved the loss of half the weight but produced an attractive lozenge-shaped stone. Both of these early types are in the crown. Below the crosses and the fleur-de-lis are six table-cut diamonds in triangular settings and two diamonds of the later style,—one lozenge-shaped and the other circular. These diamonds were very possibly of Indian origin since it was not until 1727 that the Brazilian diamond fields were discovered. Much larger and finer diamonds are described in an inventory of King James V's rings and royal ornaments in 1542; this leads to the supposition that the diamonds set in the crown were regarded as being of historic interest and they may, therefore, have had their places on the crown of Bruce or even earlier Scottish kings.

The arches of the crown are also older than the fillet. The crowns shown on the coinage of James IV were closed with arches and surmounted by the mound or ball and cross. The arches on the Edinburgh crown are of a slightly inferior gold and craftsmanship than the fillet and they are fastened to it by gold tacks. These facts support the view that they were taken from the earlier crown. There is less uncertainty about the mound and the cross patée which surmounts the arches. James V was careful to place his enamelled cipher IR5 at the foot of the cross. The experts are unanimous that the mound, the cross, the leaf ornaments on which it rests and the enamelled oak leaves on the arches were the work of French goldsmiths—and thereby hangs a royal romance.

In 1536, the young James V, the most eligible prince in Europe, after casting his gaze around the princesses of Europe, let his choice fall on the beautiful but fated Magdalene of Valois, the eldest daughter of the French king, Francis I. He married his 'white damask bride' in a ceremony of great splendour at Notre Dame in January 1536 and stayed in France until the following May, passing the time in jousts and revels at the French court. He sailed for Scotland 'loaded with gifts, gold and sumptuous apparel and many other rich jewels.' One may assume that, having seen the jewelled splendours of the French court and of the Valois crown, he decided to add some of the same regal quality to his own crown and that is was then that he had the mound, the cross and the other adornments made by the renowned French goldsmiths. The expenditure would not appear in the accounts of the Scottish Treasury since Magdalene had brought him a 'tocher' of 100,000 crowns.

The pearls are the most numerous gems in the Scottish crown; there are sixty-one oriental pearls and eleven Scottish pearls, also four large oriental pearls in enamelled settings in the bonnet of the crown. Most of them have lost their lustre from age and from the viscissitudes suffered by the regalia—the long sojourn in the damp earth of Kinneff church must have greatly diminished their iridescent sheen. The pearls are set around the fillet of the crown on the crosses fleury and on the points of the rays. Before pearls from the Orient became available Scotland was regarded as the source for freshwater pearls of high quality. As early as 1120 the King of Scots was reputed to have more fine pearls than any man living. Scottish pearls were placed in the English crown in 1324, 1333 and 1605. Pope Pius II, who visited Scotland in 1435, spoke of Scottish pearls as one of the greatest exports of Scotland and about the same time goldsmiths in Germany were sending for the fine pearls of the Tay.

In 1621, the provost of Aberdeen brought a pearl found in a local stream to Charles I; it was reputed to be the largest pearl ever found in Scotland and Charles was so delighted that he 'gave him twelve or fourteen chalders of vituals about Dunfermline and the custom of merchant goods in Aberdeen for life'. Charles was so impressed by his treasure that he appointed a commissioner of the pearl fisheries in Sutherland so that 'his Kingis Maiestie hes als undoubtit right to all pearls breeding in watteris'. As an early conservationist the king also instituted a closed season for the pearl fisheries. Pearls are still found in Scotland and only a few years ago I watched a solitary pearl fisherman probing along the banks of the river Tay, below the Hill of Scone.

The large stones around the fillet of the crown are the carbuncle, jacinth, amethyst, white topaz and the rock crystal. As I have mentioned, their settings show that they were taken from an older crown. They could not have been stones of great value in 1540 and it is possible they were replaced in the crown because of their symbolic significance and historical association.

A carbuncle is a red garnet cut *en cabochon*—that is with a smooth curved surface—which was the only style, except inlaying, until faceting was introduced in the late Middle Ages. At the time these stones were first placed in a Scottish crown they were thought to be a protection against poison, the plague, sadness and evil thoughts—all perils which were often close to the Scottish kings.

The jacinths are cut in rectangular shapes with flat table surfaces and four side facets, with the exception of one stone which is slightly domed and of pyramid form at the base. The properties attributed to this stone in the Middle Ages were that it procured sleep, riches, honour and wisdom—not always possessed by the kings of Scots!

The four amethysts on the fillet are all of different cuts since this stone was not so intractable as the diamond; one is in fact cut so that it resembles a rose cut diamond of a much later period. The amethyst was rated for its magical properties: it protected the wearer in battle, was an antidote against poison, sharpened the wits and prevented its wearer from becoming inebriated—all valuable qualities in the Middle Ages and indeed even later.

There are three white topazes in the fillet. The topaz was one of the gems which had adorned the breast plate of the High Priest of Israel; the symbolism of this stone could have reflected the sacerdotal character of the kingship. It had magical properties indicating the presence of poison by becoming obscured by its touch; unfortunately this power waxed and waned with the moon.

The two rock crystals are of the type used in many types of ornament and might be described as the poor man's gem. They were used as charm stones with almost any magical attributes which their owner wanted them to have—an amulet against the evil eye, the perils of witchcraft, or conversely, as a charm stone to attract the interest of a lover.

Traces of green foil behind the two rock crystals suggest that the goldsmith was seeking to give them the appearance of emeralds. The carbuncles also show these traces of a green foil behind them. The medieval lapidary had to take what stones he had without the advantage of modern methods of cutting to increase their quality. He used various methods to heighten their brilliance and to enhance and even change their colour. A plain stone could be given a colour by the use of foil—a thin leaf of metal, usually made of different proportions of gold, silver and copper, which was placed behind the stone. Cellini in his *Treatise* gave recipes for red, blue and green foils to improve the colours of the ruby, sapphire and the emerald. The use of foils in the Scottish crown was a method of keeping up the royal appearances.

There is an old tradition that the crown of Scotland was set with Scottish stones and made with Scottish gold. Unfortunately it has less substance than most of the legends of Scotland—only eleven of the pearls, the rock crystals and possibly the three topazes could have come from indigenous resources, while the frame of the crown was certainly made from gold from Scottish mines.

The Romans came to Britain to mine gold, silver and tin and their various expeditions against the Picts may have been partly motiviated by the intention of securing precious metals, especially silver, which they would have seen the Picts wearing in the form of beautifully engraved chains, brooches and other ornaments and used on the finials of their chariots.

With the introduction of a national currency the silver and gold mines became of great interest to the Scottish kings. The working of the mines was encouraged; King David I in 1125 made a grant to the church of the Holy Trinity at Dunfermline of a tenth of all the gold found in Fife and Fothrik, while James I in 1425 took care to protect his interests in any gold or silver found 'in ony lordes landis of the realm'. The great mines on Crawford Moor were for a long time the most prolific sources of gold in Scotland. This gold was used for the early crowns as well as for the first gold coins minted in Scotland. In 1540, the year the present crown was 'casten of new', 130 ounces of gold from Crawford Moor was minted into gold coinage of James V. It is, therefore, certain that the gold for the earlier crowns and the present crown must have come from the oldest and the richest mine in Scotland.

Scotland also had abundant supplies of silver, extracted from the working of the lead mines. In January 1562 Mary Queen of Scots granted a licence to John Acheson to work the lead mines in Dumfriesshire on condition that he brought into mint 45 ounces of refined silver from every 1,000 stone weight of ore.

The Scottish hammermen excelled in silverwork and their art was almost at its prime at the time this new crown was made. They sometimes worked on massive silver pieces: maces for the royal burghs and the universities; macers, montieths, tankards and quaiches for royal and noble tables and superb monstrances and chalices for cathedrals and churches. The Celtic taste for cloak pins and brooches was abundantly catered for in the supply of silver clan crests and brooches for keeping the Highland plaids

The Crown of Scotland without the bonnet. The details of the stones and their mountings can be clearly seen

in their correct folds. Much of the church work of centuries was destroyed in the looting and the fires which ushered in the Scottish Reformation, and the needs of national defence later completed the holocaust of gold and silver work. In June 1639, the towns of Scotland ordered the 'haull plate' to be brought in to be melted down for the defence of the nation.

That is why, when you enter the Crown Room in Edinburgh Castle, you are not confronted with the dazzling array of massive silver pieces such as you see in the Jewel House of the Tower of London.

The main piece which Scotland has to offer is an old crown, its gemstones dulled by age, concealment and neglect, which nonetheless is full of historical significance and the object of reverence for many generations of the Scottish race. Most of Scotland's other royal treasures in gold, silver and precious stones went to pay for the wars of independence.

THE SCEPTRE AND THE SWORD

The Sceptre and the Sword in the Crown Room were papal gifts to James IV. For many centuries it had been the custom of the Popes to bestow crowns, sceptres, swords and other royal ornaments on the kings and princes of Christendom. They were more than gifts of honour, since it was once held that only the Pope and the Emperor had the prerogatives of bestowing the title of king. By the twelfth century kings were becoming reluctant to acknowledge that they reigned by favour of the papacy and the popes had to find more acceptable tokens of their favour to kings, such as sceptres, swords and ornaments like the famous Golden Rose.

The gift of a papal sword was also a long established custom. The sending of it was based on the precedent in the fifteenth chapter of the second Book of Maccabees where a sword of gold was handed to Judas Maccabaeus with the injunction: 'Take this Holy Sword, a gift from God, with which thou shalt smite the adversaries.' The papal sword was, therefore, a gift to kings and princes who had defended the cause of Christendom. The Spanish kings during their struggles against the Moors were the frequent recipients of the sword of the Faith: it was usually sent with a consecrated hat so that the head of the king might be armed with the grace of the Holy Spirit as his hand was armed with the sword.

The sword and the hat were often accompanied with an additional mark of papal favour—*La Rosa D'oro Pontificia*, the Golden Rose of the Pope. The sword and the hat were consecrated by the Pope at the midnight mass before the Nativity; the papal legate who was to carry the gifts to the king stood at the side of the altar with the hat resting on the point of the sword. The swords had hilts of gold, with the papal arms on the scabbard and the blades carried an inscription of the name of the pope.

According to Holinshed the first king of Scots to receive the papal sword was William the Lion in 1202; Pope Innocent III, by this account, sent the king a sword with a sheath of gold set with precious stones and a 'hat of purple hue'.

The sceptre and the sword in the Crown Room at Edinburgh Castle were both papal gifts to King James IV. The sceptre was the first of the papal gifts and there was possibly a special reason for Pope Alexander's choice of a sceptre instead of the sword. James IV, who was sixteen when he was crowned at Scone on 26 June 1488, had been implicated in the overthrow and the murder of his father James III. His deed became such a burden of conscience that, it is said, he inflicted on himself the penance of wearing an iron chain round his waist vowing to add one link for each year of his life. He became a paragon of the Church: 'He hears two Masses before transacting business and after Mass has a Cantate sung during which he sometimes attends to business'. He wrote to the Pope for absolution and Alexander VI replied: 'There is no man so safe, excellent and transcendent, who by an insolent nobility and a ravaging populace might not be compelled to perpetrate many things against his heart and intention.' For consolation the Pope sent James the sceptre, the royal symbol of equity and justice and the 'rod of royal virtue'.

The next king, James V, in his zeal to improve the regalia carried out alterations to the papal sceptre as well as to the crown. In 1536, the Treasurer's accounts show a payment to Adam Ley, an Edinbrugh goldsmith, for remaking the sceptre and adding 11½ ounces to its weight, for which he was paid £26 4s. It is possible that in this remaking the sceptre lost much of the delicate repoussée work which was characteristic of the Italian goldsmiths at that time.

The head of the sceptre is divided into three by dolphins in

The Mound and Cross Pattée on the Scottish Crown—front and back views. The back view shows the initials of James V—I R 5—at the base of the Cross

the form of scrolls, with leaves enfolding their back and front; their heads point upwards and their tails are curled up immediately above the capital of the rod, enclosing cinqfoils, three of which are now missing; the green enamelling of the leaves has also been worn away. There are three figures between the dolphins: the Virgin Mary with an open crown, holding on her right arm the Infant Child and in her left hand a mound with a cross; on her left is St James in robe and cope, holding book and staff, and on his left is St Andrew carrying his saltire cross, the top part of which has been broken off. The execution of these figures was beyond the capabilities of the Edinburgh goldsmiths of the time. They have obviously been recast from the original figures and the marks of the soldering of the two halves of the casting can be detected. The constant use made of the sceptre at the meetings of Parliament and its hurried removal with the rest of the regalia in times of danger must have been the cause of some damage to this gift of Pope Alexander VI.

The rod piece of the sceptre is of gilded silver, hexagonal in shape. It has been made in three divisions, the end part forming the handle. The second piece of the rod is ornamented on three sides with engraved fleurs-de-lis and thistles, while the top section has been decorated with grotesques, cups and foliage.

In 1507, another papal legate arrived at the court of James IV this time bearing a sword, a hat and a Golden Rose. There was also a flattering letter from the Pope describing James as the 'most peacefully disposed prince in Europe'. His father-in-law, Henry VII of England, might not have accepted that description after the recent defeat inflicted by Scottish seamen on his own fleet. The papal ornaments were delivered by the papal legate with a great solemnity in the Church of Holyrood. This papal sword became the royal Sword of State carried before the king and borne in the Ridings of Parliament until it was placed in the old oak chest in 1707. The blade of the sword is 3ft 3in long and 3in across its broadest part. On the blade are three gold-filled etchings of the apostles Peter and Paul, which were once concealed by ornamental leaves which have now broken away. In the centre of the blade is etched with gold infilling the name of the donor, Pope Julius II. The guard is $17\frac{1}{2}$in wide and designed with two dolphins looking towards the handle. Oak leaves and acorns, the emblems of its donor, are heavily sculptured on the pommel and handle of the sword.

The scabbard is covered with crimson silk velvet and mounted with silver gilt repoussée work. It bears the arms of Pope Julius II, with the oak tree, the crossed papal keys, surmounted by the

The Head of the Sceptre with the Globe of Rock Crystal and the Finial. The figure is that of St James. St Andrew occupies the third division of the Sceptre.

Scottish Regalia: the Head of the Sceptre. It is divided into three by by dolphins in the form of scrolls with leafage front and back, surrounding the figure of the Virgin and Child

papal tiara with three ducal coronets. This plate and other parts
of the decoration have also been marked by time, use and mis-
adventure. The back of the scabbard is mainly a repetition of the
oak and acorn design, while the enamelling near the tip has
broken away leaving only the little grotesque mask looking
sternly from the scabbard.

People who see this sword for the first time are often surprised
by its slender shape and the wide ornamental guard. The popular
idea of a Scottish sword is the claymore, or the heavy broadsword.
This sword is a rare and precious gift from Italy at the time of the
Renaissance.

The Sword belt which was part of the papal gift is a fine piece
of woven lace also ornamented with the oak leaves, acorns and the
arms of Pope Julius. Its existence had been forgotten until it
was found by Sir David Ogilvy in 1790 hidden in the wall of his
ancestors' house at Barras. It had been hidden by the gallant
governor of Dunnottar during his endeavours to get some credit
for saving the regalia. Obviously its possession would have shown
that the royal emblems had been in his care. It was eventually
restored to its place beside the sword in 1892.

THE MACE

The mystery of the mace still awaits its solution. It was found with
the rest of the regalia in the oak chest in 1818, but the Act of
Delivery and Deposition of 1707 does not mention it. Was it some
sudden and impulsive decision before the lid of the chest was
closed which committed the mace to a place with the Honours of
Scotland? Sir Walter Scott believed it was that of the Lord
Treasurer of Scotland and that it had been put in the chest by the
Earl of Glasgow who was present at the deposition. Others have
taken the view that it was a queen's mace; but it is $38\frac{1}{2}$in long and
weighs 20oz 12dwt and it would have been a cumbersome article
for a queen to handle. On the other hand the registers of the Privy
Council of Scotland show that the Treasurer in 1609 was ordered
to have a silver mace carried before him.

The date of its design is as obscure as its origins and the mystery is
not clarified by the maker's mark—F. G.—on the rod. The first
statute about goldsmiths in Scotland was that of 1457 which set
down the standards for work in precious metal and required that
in every town where goldsmiths worked there should be 'an
understanding and cunning man of good conscience' as deacon
of the craft. Every craftsman had to put his mark on his work,
but town marks were not obligatory until 1485. The presence of

only one mark might indicate that the mace was made prior to 1485, although the requirements about town marking were not always followed.

The mace is of silver gilt surmounted with an oval globe of rock crystal, cut with square facets and enclosed with four bands. Above the globe is the cross patée. The mace can be separated into three divisions and is worthy of its place in the Crown Room.

THE OAK CHEST

The oak chest which held the regalia is an early example of 'knock down furniture'. It was made of Danzig oak and constructed so that it could always be taken to pieces for transportation and for passage through narrow doorways. Its woodwork was made by Scottish craftsmen of the time of James IV, although it is possible that its lock and iron mouldings were imported from Holland.

THE INSIGNIA OF THE GARTER AND THE THISTLE

The insignia of the Orders of the Garter and of the Thistle as well as the Ring in the Crown Room are not part of the Scottish regalia, but a Stuart legacy, bequeathed by Henry, Cardinal York, the last male descendent of the Stuart kings, to George III. The last of the Stuarts had been impoverished by the French Revolution and the Hanoverian king sustained the cardinal with a generous pension of £4,000 a year for the rest of his life. The cardinal's bequest included the Stuart papers, the insignia of the Orders and the Ring—all of which were taken by James II of England in his hasty flight to France in 1688.

The Collar of the Order of the Garter consists of twenty-one garters in gold, having in the centres a double rose enamelled in red and green. The Great George of the Order is the familiar figure in enamelled gold of the mounted St George about to thrust the Dragon with his lance. The figures are studded with rose and table cut diamonds.

It is not certain which of the Stuart kings wore these insignia of the Garter; the George does bear some resemblance to the one worn by Charles II at his restoration, but the fact that James II took it with him on his flight does suggest that they were his personal insignia. The first king of Scots to receive the Order of the Garter was James V in 1535, at a time when Henry VIII was trying to persuade him to marry the Princess Mary and before his glance fell on the beautiful daughter of the French king.

The jewel of the St Andrew is a beautiful piece from the insignia of the Order of the Thistle. In its centre is an oval chalcedony cut with a cameo of St Andrew holding his saltire cross against a blue grey background. The narrow gold edge which surrounds the cameo has an outer circle of twelve large rose diamonds in silver grain settings.

On the reverse side a garter inlaid with gold enamel carries the motto of the Order: *Nemo me impune lacesset*—'No one provokes me with impunity'. Within the garter is a thistle on a lid covering a small compartment which holds a miniature painting on ivory— now thought to be of Louise, Countess of Albany, the wife of Prince Charles Edward Stuart.

The presence of this jewel of the Order in the Crown room is another acknowledgement of the pervading influence of James V. In 1534 he received the Order of the Golden Fleece from the Emperor Charles V; in the same year Francis I of France bestowed on him the Order of St Michael and Henry VIII made him a knight of the Garter. The thought must have struck James that Scotland lacked a noble order of chivalry and he 'revived' the ancient Order of the Thistle. How it was a revival is not clear. Some claim that the Order was founded in 807, long before the days of chivalry; others claim it was formed to celebrate a famous victory of the Picts and Scots over Athelstan of England. When new statutes of the Order were published in 1687 they stated: 'It is most certain by the consent of ancient and modern historians and by several other authentic proofs that the Order of the Thistle had existed in great glory and splendour for many hundreds of years'. The Order as revived by James V consisted of the king as sovereign and twelve other knights in 'respectful imitation of Christ and his twelve apostles'.

The Order fell into abeyance with the Reformation, was revived by James VII of Scotland (James II) and again became dormant until Queen Anne decided to remodel it on the general lines of the Garter, as Scotland's premier order of chivalry. In 1714 George I added the star to its insignia, and Queen Victoria increased its members by statute to include the Royal Family and sixteen knights of the Order. The chapel of the Order is in St Giles' Cathedral in Edinburgh.

THE RING

Another of the bequests of Cardinal York is the Ruby and Diamond Ring now in the Crown Room. The centre of the ring is a large but very thin ruby which, like some of the stones in the crown, has been foiled to enhance its colour. It has been engraved with a cross with its outline sunk slightly below the table of the ruby. It has a girdle of twenty-six small diamonds, very irregularly cut and also foiled to improve their colour. An unusual feature of this ring is that it is jointed like a bracelet, with a number of notches and a snap spring so that it could fit almost any finger.

This ring, according to tradition, belonged to the Stuart kings and was used at the coronation of Charles I, but there is no reference in the accounts of Charles's coronation of any ring being used. There have been occasions, however, when the accounts of the long and complicated coronation service have been incomplete. The ring had been part of the investiture of the regalia since the coronation of Edgar as King of all England in 973.

The coronation service for James I had been translated from Latin into English for the first time and Heylyn stated at the time that 'it was drawn in haste and wanted many things'. The same was certainly not true of the coronation of Charles I which was prepared by Bishop Laud who wrote 'I had a perfect book of the ceremonies of the Coronation made ready, agreeing in all things with the King's Book'. The King's Book was the *Liber Regalis* which in the fourteenth century set down from still older precedents the order for the anointing, investiture and crowning of the English kings. A 'perfect' order of the service would almost certainly include the investiture with the ring at the coronation of Charles I.

CHAPTER 25
SCOTLAND'S ROYAL ARMS AND SEALS

Heraldry was carried into Scotland on foreign shields. The progress of arms-bearing was not hastened by any visitations of the heralds which had promoted the use and registration of arms in England. The descendants of Norman and Breton newcomers to Scotland took the conventional arms of the feudal nobility, but the old Celtic families were not so eager to abandon their ancient tribal symbols. The pages of a monumental volume like Laing's *Ancient Scottish Seals* show on the quarterings the emblems and beasts of the Celtic past, and scattered on the shields of many families in the former provinces of the Celtic mormaers are the creatures of Celtic totemism and mythology: the great boar, the fleet hound, the proud stag, the potent rams and bulls, as well as those messengers of the earth and the underworld—the heron and the raven.

The boar of Aidan of Cenil Gabran carved on the rock of the royal citadel of Dunadd still appears on the arms of the dukes of Argyll whose title covers the territory of the ancient kingdom of Dalriada and whose family genealogists trace their origins to those early times. The shield of Lorne, named after the brother of Fergus mac Erc, the founding king of Dalriada, carries a galley—perhaps a distant reminder of the treaty Columba made so long ago with the High King of Ireland which gave Aidan the right of ship service to the narrow seas.

Many of the arms with the Celtic imprint changed, became conventional, and were quartered away by marriage and inheritance. But Celtic symbolism has had an obstinate survival in Scotland; the ancient Celtic symbols still appear on the crests of Highland chiefs and on the badges of their clansmen. Many of these clans can trace their descent from Celtic times and there are even some who claim a Pictish origin. The boar's head still appears on the crest of the MacAlpines whose territory once included Dunstaffnage, another citadel of the Dalriadic kings, and it appears again on the crest of the Mackinnons, who claim their progenitor was Kenneth mac Alpin, the Dalriadic king who founded the united kingdom of the Picts and Scots; and the MacIvers, also originally from the lands of that kingdom, carry the same potent symbol of the ancient kings.

The families of the north and west gradually accepted the conventions of the feudal shield, but they kept the symbols of their

Seal, coins and (alleged) skull of Robert Bruce (*COI*)

Celtic and sometimes Norse origins on their separate crests and badges. The kings of Scotland emblazoned the conventional charges of French and of English heraldry on their royal arms. All they took from their Celtic past was the native thistle to use as a royal badge and sometimes to decorate the compartment below their arms. The earliest Scottish Royal Badge seems to have been a trefoil. The heraldic trefoil is drawn as three circular leaves placed together on a stalk—like the ace of clubs in a pack of cards. The early adoption of this symbol may have been a remote link with the Irish origins of the Scottish kings; the trefoil plant, the Irish shamrock, was alleged to have been taken by St Patrick to illustrate his exposition of the Trinity. By the reign of King Alexander III (1249–1285) the trefoil began to appear on Scottish royal seals; on one of these seals the trefoil is ingeniously used to terminate the tails of two wyverns—small dragons— beneath the feet of the enthroned king.

The thistle on the royal seals appears for the first time on the second Great Seal of Robert Bruce in 1318; its adoption is attributed to the victory of Alexander III over the Norwegians in the battle which united the western Isles to Scotland in 1263. At this Battle of Largs, King Haakon and his men landed from their great invasion fleet and were moving barefoot in silence through the night for a surprise attack on the Scottish forces. In the darkness one of the invaders placed his bare foot firmly on a native thistle;

The Rampant Lion Banner of the Kings of Scots

his sudden shout of pain gave the alarm. Scotland was saved—by a thistle.

The thistle appeared on the silver coinage of Scotland in 1474 in the reign of James III (1460–1488), who formally declared that the thistle was to be the official badge and emblem of Scotland, being 'a native Scottish plant of which the self protective qualities most aptly illustrated the Royal motto "In Defence".'

It eventually gave its name to the premier order of chivalry in Scotland—the Most Ancient and Most Honourable Order of the Thistle. The founding of the order finally settled the heraldic shape of the royal thistle as it appears now on the insignia of the Order. In designing the insignia of the Order, the heralds paid their respects to the old tradition that the thistle had been the badge of the Celtic kings and that the rue—the herb of grace—was borne by the still older Pictish kings. On the golden collar of the Order, the thistle of the Celtic kings alternates with the rue of their Pictish predecessors, and the pendant badge of the Order presents the thistle again, below St Andrew's Cross.

After five hundred years the thistle remains the Badge of Scotland, 'slipped and leaved proper' and ensigned with the Royal Crown.

Great Seals of Scotland: Great Seal and silver coin of Alexander I and (below)
Great Seal and silver coin of David I (*COI*)

The unicorn seems to have crept into Scotland without any legendary claims for its ancient associations with the kingdom; the Scots seemed to have been sufficiently impressed by the legendary characteristics it had already acquired in medieval Europe. Like its companion, the lion, it has had a long association with kings. The huge royal bulls of Nineveh and Babylon were sculptured in profile with a single horn; even then the unicorn was shown in opposition to the sculptured profile of the lion. It was said that the unicorn was so huge and fierce that Noah did not take it into the ark; instead it was towed behind.

Later the unicorn began to shrink. In early Christian times it was described as the size of a kid, but still so fierce and fleet that no hunter could ever capture it. A virgin could succeed, however, by feminine guile. If she sat under a tree near to its path, it would eventually come to her, lay its head in her lap and fall into a deep sleep, when it could be made captive and slaughtered for its priceless horn.

The horn had special properties. It was believed that other animals would not drink at a new pool or stream until a unicorn had stirred it with his horn to remove any poison or pollution; water stirred by a unicorn became sweet and crystal clear. The horn was, therefore, regarded as the infallible remedy agaitns poison. In an inventory taken at Windsor Castle in the first year of Elizabeth I's reign a reputed piece of unicorn horn was valued at £10,000. The gullible James VI of Scotland—the 'wisest fool in Christendom'—paid a similar amount for another piece of horn. He put it to the test by stirring a cup of poison which he commanded a servant to drink; when the man died, James indignantly declared he had been swindled—it was not a genuine piece of unicorn's horn! The translators of his famous version of the Bible set the seal of Scripture on his belief by equating the Hebrew word for 'rhinoceros' with 'unicorn'.

The lion on the arms of Scotland may have crossed over from England early in the twelfth century, at a time when the kings of Scotland were introducing many Court customs and ideas from England. William the Lion (1165–1214) probably earned his soubriquet by the use of the lion on his shield and his royal banners. A rampant lion is shown on the Great Seal of Alexander II (1214–1249). His son, Alexander III (1249–1286) placed on his Great Seal a shield which appears to bear the lion alone, but the bardings—caparisons—of his horse are surrounded by a bordure charged with crosslets and have demi-fleurs-de-lis on the inner edge. This is the first indication of the 'double tressure' which was to be a consistent part of the Royal Arms of Scotland.

A tressure is a narrow border inset from the edges of the shield. On the Arms of Scotland it is a double tressure with the heads of the fleurs-de-lis pointing alternately outwards and inwards without crossing the space between the lines. The heralds have called this design a 'double tressure flory counterflory'. The lion rampant was placed in the centre looking towards the dexter side of the shield.

It is not clear how the lilies came to Scotland. The fleur-de-lis, the golden lily, first appeared on the arms of France during the reign of Louis VIII (1137–1180), but the Scots have sometimes placed a much earlier date on their acquisition of this symbol. They claimed that Achiaius, king of Scots, entered into an alliance with Charlemagne and that the Emperor of the West had surrounded the lion with the tressure flory to show that Scotland had defended the French lilies and would henceforth be encircled by the protection of France. The 'auld alliance' therefore began with Charlemagne—a fine Celtic legend which, alas, has no historical basis in fact.

It is possible that the golden lilies did come to Scotland as the result of some early association between the kings of the two countries. Later the Scots came to feel that the lion enclosed by the lily border implied their subordination to France and were not inclined to accept inferiority to anyone. In 1471, over two hundred years after the tressure appeared on the arms, the Scottish Parliament became sensitive about keeping their splendid rampant lion within its French bordure and an Act laid it down that 'in tyme to cum thar suld be na double tressor about the kingy's armys, but he suld ber hale armys of the lyoun without ony mair'. This Act was apparently ignored by James III and his heralds, as the tressure continued to embrace the reluctant lion—which does in some representations of the arms, appear to be clawing at the sides of a cage!

The arms of Mary Queen of Scots became one of the factors which sealed her fate. Elizabeth I continued the old claim to the throne of France by quartering the lilies on her shield, but she was not prepared to allow anyone else to display similar pretensions to her own throne. As an heiress of the English royal line Mary could claim to bear the English Royal Arms quartered with those of Scotland. After her marriage to the Dauphin, the Arms of Scotland were quartered with his own, which he could properly do. Over these arms, however, he next placed an 'inescutcheon of pretence' of the Arms of England—a statement that he regarded his wife as the heir to the English throne.

After the death of her husband, Mary returned to Scotland and placed on her shield the arms of Scotland and France with the significant addition of a half escutcheon of the English Royal Arms. The enraged Queen Elizabeth, who spoke the language of heraldry with great fluency, took this to mean that Mary intended 'to denote that another had gotten possession of the Crown to her Prejudice'. The Earl Marshal of England and his heralds were summoned for an opinion. They gave their formal judgement on the Arms of the Queen of Scots: 'we find the same prejudicial to the Queen's Majesty her State and Dignity'.

The tital of Elizabeth to the English throne depended on the legality of Henry VIII's divorce from Catherine of Aragon. In the precise language of heraldry the arms of Mary were stating that Elizabeth was illegitimate, and that she, Mary, had been falsely deprived of the English throne. The heraldic statement was not forgotten or forgiven; it was one of the articles in the indictment of Mary in 1572 during her captivity in England.

The granting of a tressure on a coat of arms remained a royal privilege, but this does not prevent it being borne by anyone whose ancestor was entitled to it in the past. The tressure when borne otherwise than on the Royal Arms indicates maternal descent from the Royal line. The Bowes Lyons, Earls of Strathmore, the family of Queen Elizabeth, the Queen Mother, have the tressured lion on the first and third quarters of their arms from the marriage of Sir John Lyon of Forteviot and Glamis to Jean, daughter of Robert II of Scotland, and the tressure is borne by her own descent in the Royal Arms of the Queen Mother.

The Union of the Crowns under James VI of Scotland and I of England presented great difficulties in the settling of the new Royal Arms; in the end, there had to be quite different arrangements of the arms in England and in Scotland. Since 1603 the tressured lion of Scotland has been quartered with the arms of England and Ireland, but in Scotland it always occupies the first and fourth quarters of the shield; the unicorn of Scotland is also presented on the dexter side of the shield as the principal supporter of the Royal Arms. In Scotland the shield is surrounded by the collar of the Order of the Thistle, in England by the collar of the Order of the Garter.

In Scotland each supporter holds a tilting lance from which flies a banner: the unicorn that of St Andrew and the lion the cross of St George. The Royal Arms of the King of Scots were without supporters until the reign of James I (1407-1437), when the unicorn appeared as a single supporter of his arms; it was not joined by another unicorn until James III (1460-1488).

James VI also took the unicorns as his supporters until his

accession to the English throne brought the two reluctant beasts, the lion and the unicorn, into confrontation on each side of the Royal Arms, while the question of their precedence was settled.

The tressured lion on its own is a coat of arms which is personal to the Sovereign. The Lords Lieutenant in Scotland are also entitled to display it as the Queen's Banner when, for example, they attend in their official capacity at Highland gatherings when it is raised to a fanfare. It also flies over the Scottish Office in London since the Secretary of State for Scotland is also the Lord Keeper of the Great Seal of Scotland. It has in its time been flown on fields far different from the bland frontages of Whitehall, as when William Wallace as 'Guardian of the Realm' raised it in 1297 as the *vexillium regium*—the flag of Sovereignty.

The Royal Crest of Scotland has been the lion, which made its first appearance on the helmet of Robert II (1371–1390) as a *lion sejant, affront, gules*—a red lion seated, gazing at the viewer—holding in his dexter paw a sword and in his sinister paw a sceptre. The royal motto on the crest is 'In Defence'.

THE SEALS OF SCOTLAND

The earliest Royal Seal of the Scottish kings is possibly that of Duncan II, who reigned for six months in 1094. This seal shows the extent to which the Norman ideas of kingship and their symbolism were influencing the Scottish kings. On his seal Duncan is shown mounted on a war charger wearing an armoured shirt of mail, conical helmet and the kite-shaped Norman shield; in his right hand he holds a lance with a small pennon. Edgar, the brother of Duncan, did not favour the equestrian figure and presented himself on his seal crowned in majesty, wearing the royal robe; the legs of his throne ressemble the talons of an eagle. He holds the two symbols of the royal authority, the sword and the sceptre. The legend on his seal reads: IMAGO: EADGARI: SCOTTORUM: BASILEI: Edgar's use of the title *Basileus*, or Emperor, instead of *rex*, or king, is possibly in imitation of the Great Seal of Edward the Confessor, from whom he was descended through his mother, Margaret, sister of the Atheling at the Norman Conquest.

King Alexander I (1107—1124) introduced the type of Great Seal of Scotland which was to remain the pattern for eight hundred years. One side presents the war leader—the sovereign—clad in hauberk of mail, conical helmet, holding in his right hand a gonfanon with three streamers and in his left hand a kite-shaped shield. The horse is furnished with a breast band, head strap and *nasale*, the protecting piece for its forehead. The other side of the

Cromwell's Great Seal for Scotland: the Royal Crowns and symbolism of seals, it will be noted, were retained (*RTH*)

The Great Seal of Scotland redesigned for Queen Elizabeth II (*The Times*)

seal illustrates the king in majesty, in civil state, with mantle, crown and sword. His style declares him to be DEO RECTORE REX SCOTTORUM—a style followed by his immediate successors.

The forty-nine years reign of William the Lion inaugurated a new epoch in the design of the Royal Seals. The delicate touch of the artist replaced the archaic stiffness of the figures on the previous seals. There is the suggestion of vigorous movement in the mailed figure on the great warhorse which is matched on the other side by the graceful delineation of the crowned king on an elegant throne.

His son, Alexander II (1214–1249) was the first king of Scotland to use his armorial bearings on his seal. The equestrian figure of the armoured king carries the lion rampant on his shield—the regal beast which has appeared on the Royal Arms of Scotland to the present day. The other side carries the usual presentation of the king in royal state.

The seal of his son, Alexander III (1249–1286), shows clearly the lion rampant within the double tressure of flory-counter-flory; in his second seal, which compares in design with the best royal seals of England, the king in majesty has his feet resting on two heraldic wyverns—lizard-like monsters.

When the death of the Maid of Norway plunged Scotland into the uncertainties of the first interregnum, the Guardians of the Kingdom used a fine seal for the 'Government of the Realm' which depicts St Andrew, the patron saint and protector of the kingdom, crucified on the saltire cross of his martyrdom. On the other side were the royal arms of Scotland awaiting their rightful claimant.

The national emblem of the thistle appears for the first time in 1318 on the seal of Robert Bruce.

The first Stewart king, Robert II (1370–1390) son of Walter, the High Steward, and Marjorie, daughter of Robert Bruce, had a very elaborate seal which continued the tradition of the martial leader and the sovereign in state. Falcons, or eagles, appear on his seal and the plate armour is similar to the contemporary armour on the English royal seals.

Mary, Queen of Scots, used her feminine privilege to constantly change the designs of her Great Seals. Her third seal in 1559 styled her husband Frances II of France and herself also as 'of Scotland, England, and Ireland, King and Queen'—a cause of great offence to Queen Elizabeth I of England.

James VI, before he took the royal road to the throne of England, had an equestrian seal rich with armorial bearing, badges of the thistle, plumes of ostrich feathers and arabesque foliage. On the reverse were the royal arms supported by the two unicorns each holding lance flags charged with the saltire and the repetition of the royal arms.

His accession in 1603 as James I of England gave rise to the need for a new Royal Seal which introduced the lion of England to share the honours with the unicorn of Scotland; behind the equestrian figure was a landscape, intended perhaps for the surroundings of Edinburgh.

Scotland continued to have a Great Seal of the Realm after the Union of 1707, despite suggestions that there should be one Great Seal for the United Kingdom. The Lord Lyon King of Arms, Sir Thomas Innes of Learney, wrote: 'Had the post-Union seals of Scotland not being designed in the Lyon Office, it being part of the Lord Lyon's function in relation to the Royal Arms to see that this was done, it seems unlikely that the Scottish quartering would have survived.'

A measure of economy has been used for the Scottish Seals— the reverse of the Great Seal, bearing the Royal Arms of Scotland, has not always been newly designed for each reign. The reverse of the present Great Seal was cut and engraved for King George V in 1911. A new obverse was however made for Queen Elizabeth II, showing the Queen in majesty, robed and holding sceptre and orb with the royal shield of Scotland on each side of the throne.

As in England, there are several royal seals in use in Scotland: there is the Cachet Seal, a facsimile of the Queen's signature, used for the admission of Notaries Public, and a Quarter Seal used to record any property reverting to the Crown. The Prince of Wales also has a seal to authenticate deeds granted by him as Prince of Scotland—the lands of his Scottish Principality are situated in the counties of Ayr and Renfrew, and any deeds executed in relation to these estates must be authenticated by the Prince's seal.

APPENDIX : GENEALOGY OF SCOTTISH KINGS

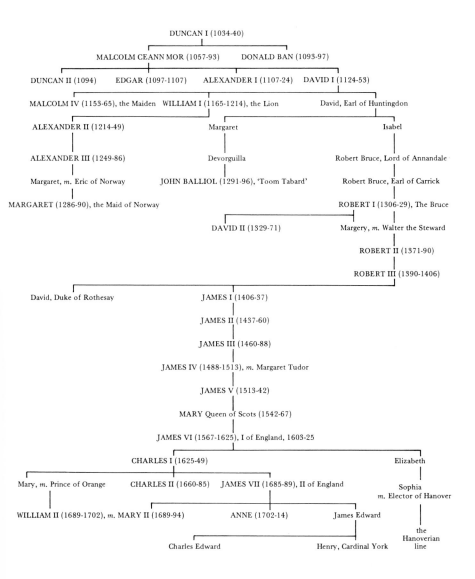

SELECT BIBLIOGRAPHY

ENGLAND

I have attempted to keep close to original sources. The information on the English regalia since 1660 is based mainly on the accounts of two successive Keepers of the Jewel House—Sir George Younghusband and Major-General H. W. D. Sitwell, supplemented by the researches of Martin Holmes on the crowns and regalia. I had access to material collected for the 1953 Guide to the Regalia and made notes on my official visits to the Tower of London.

The earlier history of the regalia has been derived from many sources: Rymer's *Foedera; Giraldi Cambrensis Opera;* Matthew Paris, *Chronica majora; Rotuli Parliamentorum; The Antient Kalenders and Inventories of the Treasury of His Majesty's Exchequer* (vols 1–11, ed. Sir Francis Palgrave); A. J. Taylor, *The Jewel Tower, Westminster* (Official Handbook 1975); *The Anglo-Saxon Chronicle* and contemporary chronicles by William of Malmsbury, Henry of Huntingdon, Roger Hovedon, Froissard and others. More recent references include the volumes of the *History of the King's Works*; A. J. Collins, *Jewels and Plate of Queen Elizabeth 1;* Lord Twining, *European Regalia* 1967; Martin Holmes, *The English Regalia, 1972;* P. E. Schramm, *Herrschaftszeichen und Statssymbolik*, 1955, as well as his *History of the English Coronation Ceremony*, 1937; other references on the coronation were L. G. Wickham Legg, *English Coronation Records;* E. C. Radcliff, *The English Coronation Service*, as well as my previous book *When the Queen was Crowned*, which has a full bibliography.

The account of Colonel Blood is derived from the *Calender of State Papers* (Domestic and Ireland 1660–75); the *Ormonde Papers* and Carte's *Life of Ormonde*; Sir Gilbert Talbot's account of the robbery appeared in Strype's *Continuation of Stowe's Survey of London*.

For the prehistoric period I am indebted to the reports of the excavations on Salisbury Plain by the Ancient Monument Inspectorate of the then Ministry of Works, including the accounts by Professors Stuart Piggot and Richard Atkinson of their excavations of the West Kennet Long Barrow in 1954–1955, also the 1977 *Guide to the Avebury Monuments* by Faith and Lance Vatcher. Other valuable sources were P. Asbee, *The Earthen Long Barrow in Britain*, 1970; G. E. Daniel, *Prehistoric Chamber Tombs of England and Wales* 1950; G. S. Hawkins, *Stonehenge Decoded;*

Stuart Piggot, *Neolithic Cultures of the British Isles*, 1954; as well as various guides to ancient monuments in the care of the Department of the Environment and numerous papers in the *Proceedings of the Society of Antiquaries*, on the Windmill, Beaker and Wessex cultures.

Bruce Mitford, *The Sutton Hoo Ship Burial*, 1972; R. Jessup, *Anglo-Saxon Jewellery*, 1974; F. M. Stenton, *Anglo-Saxon England*. Other references consulted included J. H. Bloom, *English Seals*, 1966; W. de G. Birch, *Seals*, 1907; M. Bond and D. Beamish, *The Lord Chancellor*, 1977; William Palmer's note on *The Coronation Chair* (MOW 1953); A. & H. Taylor, *The Stuart Papers at Windsor*, 1939. The new edition of Boutell's Heraldry, revised by J. P. Brooke-Little, Richmond Herald of Arms, was indispensible for the chapter on the Royal Arms.

SCOTLAND

Few public records from before 1286 have survived in Scotland. The depredations of Edward I were recorded in a rare document of 1298 concerning the destruction by the English of the chests holding the records and charters of the Abbey of Scone. The fires of the Scottish Reformation and the removal of the Scottish records by Cromwell to London has deprived Scotland of other authentic records.

Sir Walter Scott made the first attempt to write a history of the regalia in 1829 in *Papers Relative to the Scottish Regalia* (Bannatyne Club). The most detailed and accurate description and history of the regalia was published by J. Reid and H. S. Brooke in the *Proceedings of the Society of Antiquaries of Scotland*, 1889–1890. In 1951 W. D. Collier, the then King's and Lord Treasurer's Remembrancer, published additional material with the collaboration of Sir James Ferguson, Keeper of the Records of Scotland.

On these firm foundations I have added information drawn from other sources: The collection of chronicles in the Rolls series, including RS 82, which includes the work of Ailred of Rievaulx and the accounts of the reign of David I; the *Chronicle of John Fordun*, ed. W. F. Skene, 1878; *The Scotichronicon ed*, W. Goodall, 1959; *Scottish Annals from English Chronicles*, A. O. Anderson; *Chronicles of the Picts and Scots*, ed W. F. Skene; *The Annals of Ulster*, ed. W. M. Hennessy, 1887–1901, part of which are now thought to have been the annals kept on Iona from AD 563—*c* 740. *Regesta Regum Scottorum*, ed C. W. S. Barrow, 1960, and the *Annals of Scotland from the Accession of Malcolm III . . . to James I*, Lord Hailes, 1776.

Other references for early Scotland included: J. Bannerman, *Studies in the History of Dalriada*, 1974; *Report of the Excavation at Dunadd* (Proceedings of the Society of Antiquaries of Scotland vol xxiv pp 292–322) and the report on the Boar in the ceremonies at Dunadd (vol xiii 28—47); Stuart Piggot, *The Prehistoric Peoples of Scotland*, 1962; M. Dillon and N. Chadwick, *The Celtic Realms*, 1967; J. Bullock, ed. *The Life of the Celtic Church*, 1963; J. A. Duke, *The Columban Church*, 1958; Reeves ed. *Adamnan's Life of Columba*, 1857; F. T. Wainwright, *The Problem of the Picts*, 1955; I. Henderson, *The Picts*, 1967; M. O. Anderson, *Kings and Kingship in Early Scotland*, 1973; W. F. Skene, *Celtic Scotland*, vols I and II, 1886; *Chronicle of Andrew Wyntoun* (d 1420) Scottish Text Society; R. G. Ritchie, *The Normans in Scotland*, 1954.

Lord Bute, *Scottish Coronations*, 1867; F. Cooper, *Four Scottish Coronations*, 1902; H. Laing, *Descriptive Catalogue of Scottish Seals and Supp*, 1866; T. Astle, *Seals of the Kings of Scotland*, 1972; W. de G. Birch, *History of Scottish Seals*, 2 vols, 1905–7; G. Seton, *Law and Practice of Heraldry*, 1863; J. H. Stevenson, *Heraldry in Scotland*, 1914; Sir Thomas Innes of Learney (Lord Lyon), *Scots Heraldry*, 1956; G. S. Pryde, *Treaty of Union of Scotland and England*, 1950; D. Daiches, *Scotland and the Union*. 1977.

I have, where necessary, consulted the *Cambridge Medieval History* and the new Edinburgh *History of Scotland* vols i–iv, and the standard biographers of some English and Scottish kings and queens.

COLOUR PLATES
All are Crown copyright and reproduced by permission of the Controller of Her Majesty's Stationery Office with the following exceptions: The Sutton Hoo Burial helmet (*British Museum*) and The Royal Arms of Scotland (*The Trustees of the National Library of Scotland*).

BLACK AND WHITE ILLUSTRATIONS
Acknowledgments in the captions have been abbreviated as follows: *BM* – British Museum; COI – Central Office of Information; DOE – Department of the Environment; HMSO – Her Majesty's Stationery Office; RTH – Radio Times Hulton Picture Library.

INDEX